WARFARE IN THE
SEVENTEENTH CENTURY

WARFARE IN THE SEVENTEENTH CENTURY

John Childs

General Editor: John Keegan

CASSELL&CO

Cassell & Co
Wellington House, 125 Strand
London WC2R 0BB

First published 2001

British Library Cataloguing-in-Publication Data
A catalogue record for this book is available from the
British Library.
ISBN 0-304-35289-6

Cartography: Arcadia Editions
Picture research: Elaine Willis
Design: Martin Hendry

Typeset in Monotype Sabon

Acknowledgements

I would like to thank Penny Gardiner of Cassell & Co. for her help, kindness, patience and good humour. I have often wondered why authors thanked their editors; now I understand.

JOHN CHILDS
Leeds

The siege of Spanish-occupied Dunkirk, 1658, by Turenne's Franco-English forces, covered by ships of the Royal Navy.

CONTENTS

KEY TO MAPS

Military units–types

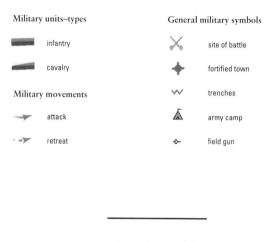

infantry

cavalry

Military movements

attack

retreat

General military symbols

site of battle

fortified town

trenches

army camp

field gun

Geographical symbols

urban area

urban area (3D maps)

river

seasonal river

canal

internal border

international border

MAP LIST

CHRONOLOGY OF THE WARS

1600	Charles IX of Sweden invades Livonia.		**1622** 27 April	Tilly defeated by Mansfeld and Baden at Wiesloch.
1605 27 September	Battle of Kirkholm; Sweden defeated by Poland.		6 May	Battle of Wimpfen; Baden beaten by Tilly.
			20 June	Battle of Höchst; Christian of Brunswick defeated by Tilly.
1609 28 February	Treaty of Viborg; Sweden intervenes in Russia.		**1623** 6 August	Battle of Stadtlohn; Christian of Brunswick defeated by Tilly.
April	Twelve Years Truce between Spain and the Dutch Republic.		**1624** 28 August	Spínola besieges Breda.
September	Poland invades Russia; siege of Smolensk (to 1611).		**1625** 5 June	The Spanish Army of Flanders captures Breda.
1610 12 March	Jakob de la Gardie leads Swedish forces into Moscow.		July	Wallenstein raises a new Imperial army.
4 July	Russo-Swedish army defeated by the Poles at Klushino.		**1626** January	The Swedes beat the Poles at the battle of Wallhof. The Swedes open a campaign in Prussia.
1611	Christian IV of Denmark declares war on Sweden, the War of Kalmar (until 1613).		April	Mansfeld checked at Dessau Bridge.
			26 August	Battle of Lutter-am-Barenberg; Christian IV of Denmark defeated by Tilly.
1613 21 January	Peace of Knäred between Denmark and Sweden.		**1628** May–July	Unsuccessful Imperial siege of Stralsund.
1617 27 February	Peace of Stolbova between Russia and Sweden.		September	Battle of Wolgast (eastern Pomerania); Christian IV defeated and Jutland conquered.
1618	Truce of Tolsburg between Sweden and Poland (for two years).		**1629** 22 May	Peace of Lübeck between Denmark and the emperor.
23 May	Defenestration of Prague. Outbreak of Thirty Years War.		28 March	Edict of Restitution.
			27 June	Swedish advance on Warsaw halted by the Poles at the battle of Stuhm (Honigfelde).
1620 8 November	Bohemian rebels beaten by Tilly at the White Mountain.		16 September	Gustav II Adolf concludes six-year Truce of Altmark with Poland.
1621 July	Swedish–Polish War resumed.		28 October	The Huguenots surrender La Rochelle to Louis XIII.
April	War between Spain and the Dutch Republic recommenced.			
12 September	The Swedes capture Riga.			

1630

6 July   Gustav II Adolf lands at Peenemünde in Pomerania.

1631

20 May   Tilly storms Magdeburg.

17 September   Gustav beats Tilly at the battle of Breitenfeld.

1632

5 April   Tilly mortally wounded at Rain, Bavaria.

24 August   The Swedes attack Wallenstein at the Alte Feste.

17 November   Battle of Lützen; Gustav II Adolf killed.

December   War of Smolensk (to June 1634).

1634

5–6 September   The Swedes defeated by the Imperialists at Nördlingen.

1635

19 May   France declares war on Spain.

30 May   Peace of Prague.

12 September   Truce of Stuhmsdorf between Poland and Sweden.

1636

4 October   Battle of Wittstock; the Imperialists beaten by the Swedes under Banér.

1637

October   Breda recaptured by the Dutch.

1638

10 March   Battle of Rheinfelden; Bernard of Saxe–Weimar victorious over an Imperial–Bavarian army.

1639

14 April   Battle of Chemnitz; the Saxons defeated by the Swedes.

1640

Dec   The Portuguese revolt against Spanish rule (until 1668).

1642

August   Outbreak of the English Civil War.

23 October   Battle of Edgehill; Parliament defeated by Charles I.

2 November   The Imperialists beaten by the Swedes at second battle of Breitenfeld.

1643

May   Sweden attacks Denmark.

19 May   Battle of Rocroi; Condé victorious over the Army of Flanders.

August   Peace negotiations begin in Münster and Osnabrück.

24–25 November   A French army beaten by the Bavarians at Tuttlingen.

1644

2 July   Parliament and the Scots beat the Royalists at the battle of Marston Moor.

August   Battle of Freiburg; Turenne defeated by the Bavarians under Franz von Mercy.

1645

6 March   Battle of Jankov; Swedish victory over the Imperialists.

May   Battle of Mergentheim; the French defeated by the Bavarians.

June   The Turks attack Crete.

14 June   Charles I beaten by Cromwell and Fairfax at the battle of Naseby.

August   Peace of Brömsebro between Sweden and Denmark.

3 August   Battle of Allerheim; the Bavarians and Imperialists beaten by the French and Hessians.

1648

Revolt of the Fronde in France (until 1653).

30 January   Peace of Münster between Spain and the Dutch Republic.

17 May   Battle of Zusmarshausen; Bavaria defeated by France.

20 August   Battle of Lens; Spain defeated by France.

24 October   Peace of Westphalia ends the Thirty Years War.

1650

26 June   The Congress of Nuremberg agrees on a demobilization schedule.

1654
July — Sweden invades Poland.
Russia invades Lithuania.

1656
May — Russia declares war on Sweden.

1657
1 June — Denmark declares war on Sweden.

1658
14 June — France defeats Spain at the battle of the Dunes, near Dunkirk.

1659
7 November — Treaty of the Pyrenees between France and Spain.

1660
3 May — Peace of Oliva between Sweden, Poland and Brandenburg–Prussia.
6 June — Peace of Copenhagen between Denmark and Sweden.

1661
21 June — Peace of Kardis between Poland and Russia.

1665
14 March — Anglo-Dutch Naval War (until 1667).

1667
9 February — Truce of Andrussovo between Poland and Russia.
24 May — France invades the Spanish Netherlands; beginning of the War of Devolution (until 1668).
8 July – 28 August — French siege of Lille.

1668
2 May — Treaty of Aix-la-Chapelle between France and Spain.

1672
17 March — England declares war on the Dutch Republic (until 1674).
6 April — France declares war on the Dutch Republic (until 1678).

1673
6–30 June — French siege of Maastricht.

1674
19 February — Treaty of Westminster between England and the Dutch Republic.
16 June — Battle of Sinzheim; Turenne defeats Caprara.
11 August — Battle of Seneffe between Condé and William of Orange.
4 October — Turenne beats Bournonville at Enzheim.
December — Sweden invades Brandenburg.

1675
5 January — Battle of Türkheim; Turenne defeats an Imperial army.
28 June — Swedes defeated by Brandenburg at Fehrbellin.

1676
11 September — The Imperialists capture Philippsburg.
14 December — Battle of Lund; Swedes defeat Danes.

1678
6 July — Battle of Rheinfeld. Starhemberg beaten by Créqui.
10 August — Treaty of Nijmegen between France and the Dutch Republic.
14 August — Battle of Saint-Denis between Luxembourg and William of Orange.
17 September — Treaty of Nijmegen between France and Spain.

1679
6 February — Treaty of Nijmegen between France and Austria.
June — Peace of Saint-Germain between Brandenburg, Denmark and Sweden.

1683
16 July – 12 Sept — Siege of Vienna by the Turks.
12 September — Duke of Lorraine and John III Sobieski of Poland defeat the Turks at the battle of the Kahlenberg.
26 October — Spain declares war on France (until 1684).

1684
17–28 May — French bombardment of Genoa.
29 April – 3 June — Siege of Luxembourg City by the French.

15 August	Truce of Ratisbon (Regensburg).

1685

22 October	Revocation of the Edict of Nantes.

1686

July	League of Augsburg formed in Germany.
3 September	Buda (Ofen) falls to an Imperial army.

1687

12 August	Battle of Mohács (Berg Harsan or Nagyharsány); the Turks defeated by the Imperialists.

1688

6 September	Belgrade falls to the Imperialists.
27 Sept – 30 Oct	Siege of Philippsburg by the French.
5 November	William III of Orange lands in England.
26 November	The Dutch Republic declares war on France.
Dec–June 1689	Devastation of the Palatinate.

1689

25 August	D'Humières defeated by Waldeck at the battle of Walcourt.

1690

1 July	Battle of Fleurus; Luxembourg beats Waldeck.
11 July	Battle of the Boyne; James II defeated by William III.
18 August	Battle of Staffarda; Catinat defeats the Duke of Savoy.
8 October	Belgrade retaken by the Turks.

1691

15 Mar – 10 Apr	Siege of Mons by France.
24 Mar – 2 Apr	Siege of Nice by Catinat.
10–11 July	Bombardment of Barcelona.
19 September	The Duke of Luxembourg engages Waldeck's rearguard at Leuse.

1692

25 May – 1 July	Siege of Namur by France.
3 August	Battle of Steenkirk; William III narrowly repulsed by the Duke of Luxembourg.

1693

21 April – 2 May	French siege of Heidelberg.

1–13 June	Siege of Rosas by France.
29 July	Battle of Landen/Neerwinden; William III defeated by the Duke of Luxembourg.
10 Sept – 10 Oct	Siege of Charleroi by France.
4 October	Battle of La Marsaglia; Catinat defeats the Duke of Savoy.

1694

27 May	Noailles forces a crossing of the River Ter and invades Catalonia.
29 May – 10 June	Siege of Palamós by Noailles.
17–29 June	Siege of Gerona by Noailles.
17–27 September	Siege of Huy by William III.

1695

25 June – 29 July	Siege of Casale by the Duke of Savoy.
1 July – 6 Sept	Siege of Namur by William III.
14–15 July	Action at Aarsele, Flanders.
13–16 August	Bombardment of Brussels by Villeroi.

1696

15–17 March	Raid on Givet by Coehoorn.
29 August	Treaty of Turin between France and the Duke of Savoy.

1697

2 May	French raid on Cartagena.
15 May – 5 June	Siege of Ath by France.
12 June – 10 Aug	Siege of Barcelona by Vendôme.
11 September	Battle of Zenta; the Imperialists under Prince Eugene defeat the Turks.
20 September	Treaty of Rijswijk between England, France, the Dutch Republic and Spain.
30 September	The Holy Roman Emperor signs the Peace of Rijswijk.

1699

26 January	Peace of Karlowitz.

1700

	Opening of the Great Northern War (until 1721).
30 November	Charles XII of Sweden defeats the Russians outside Narva.

INTRODUCTION

DEATH OF THE 'MILITARY REVOLUTION'

SEVENTEENTH-CENTURY BATTLES were crude slogging matches, fought at hideously close quarters amidst fogs of powder smoke. Victors usually lost as many men as the vanquished and were too disorganized, understrength and exhausted to pursue. Manoeuvres and sieges, both of which produced more predictable and tangible results, were much preferred to the hazard of battle. This detail from a rather fanciful engraving of the battle of Breitenfeld, 1631, illustrates the confusion which rendered battle such a risky enterprise. Note the leakage from the rear ranks; numerous men 'disappeared' during a battle only to rejoin after the event. Armies nearly always disintegrated from the rear to the front, rarely the other way round.

DEATH OF THE 'MILITARY REVOLUTION'

WITHIN A GENERAL HISTORY of only 40,000 words, attempting to cover every war and military change across the whole world during the seventeenth century would have produced vagueness and generality at the expense of detail and discussion. Instead the emphasis has been placed upon those conflicts and campaigns that best illustrate contemporary military techniques and the conduct of war. Warfare should not be studied in isolation, so, through a marriage of narrative and analysis, the key martial events and developments have been set within their social, political and economic contexts.

Over the past fifty years, military historians of sixteenth- and seventeenth-century Europe have been obsessed with defining the nature and chronological location of a 'Military Revolution'. Because of the length of wars, improvements in fortification design and advances in firearm technology, armies became larger, more permanent and better disciplined. The resultant financial costs obliged princes and rulers to control their resources more effectively through the reform and improvement of their administrative and fiscal apparatus and the reduction of local interests and franchises. Most governments, whether monarchical or republican, thus became more absolute and centralized. In 1954 Michael Roberts reviewed these trends and suggested that they occurred principally between 1550 and 1650, an era that he dubbed the 'Military Revolution'. Subsequently Geoffrey Parker extended the concept to include the years from 1450 to 1800, stressing the contribution of the new military methods to the European acquisition of overseas empire. In contrast, Jeremy Black has restricted it to the second half of the

Positions in rapier play, from Antonio Marcelli, Regole della Scherma *(Rome, 1686). Both in war and for personal defence, blade weapons retained their importance throughout the century. Swordplay was taught in all gentlemen's academies and military schools.*

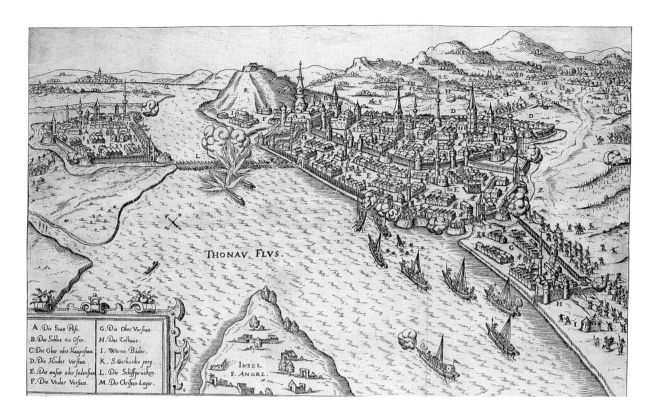

A .Die Staa Pesi.
B.Der Schlos zu Ofen.
C.Die Ober oder Hauptsan.
D.Die Hinder Vorstat.
E.Die wasser oder Judensta
F.Die Vnder Vorstat.
G.Die Ober Vorstatt.
H.Das Zolhaus.
I. Warme Bäder.
K. S.Gerhardis perg.
L.Die Schiffprucken.
M.Der Christen Leger.

THONAV FLVS.

INSEL
S.ANDRE.

seventeenth century, arguing that the adoption of the flintlock musket and socket bayonet by the new standing armies was the crucial, 'revolutionary' development.

Although it served successfully to focus scholarly attention upon the military history of early modern Europe, the notion of a Military Revolution does not find favour here. Advances in technology during the later Middle Ages resulted in new weapons that gradually modified all aspects of war between 1450 and 1700, but revolutions are sharp, sudden events: they do not occur across 350 years, or even a century. A revolution is often identified by its contrast with preceding and succeeding eras, yet the nineteenth century saw huge and rapid military mutations whilst stasis was hardly a feature of the fourteenth and fifteenth centuries.

Gradually and logically, by adopting best practice and rejecting less profitable innovations, practitioners altered the nature of seventeenth-century warfare: the flintlock musket replaced the matchlock; the pike gave way to the bayonet; infantry squares shrank into more linear formations; the standing army spread; the mercenary system altered; uniform became common; and cavalry regained some of its former importance. These cautious and unspectacular changes were evolutionary, not revolutionary. Designed specifically for fighting in Western Europe, the new techniques were adopted by neither Poland nor the Ottoman Turks whilst India and China, although partially receptive to firearms, did not embrace European organization and tactics. Even with their enhanced machinery and methods, European states made only slight inroads into North America and Asia during the seventeenth century.

All dates are according to the Gregorian calendar.

Turkish-occupied Buda (west bank of the Danube) and Pest (east bank) unsuccessfully besieged by Austrian forces, 1602, during the Thirteen Years War, 1593–1606. Friction between Christian and Turk in the Balkans and Eastern Mediterranean continued throughout the seventeenth century.

The Austrian siege of Buda, 1686, was complicated by the vigorous defence mounted by Abdurrahman Pasha and the presence in southern Hungary of a Turkish field army under Grand Vizier Suleiman. Arguments raged between the Duke of Lorraine and his senior officers. The decision to assault the city on 2 September was taken at an acrimonious council of war that lasted from 30 August to 1 September.

CHAPTER ONE

THE THIRTY YEARS WAR
1618–48

*FERDINAND II (1578–1637), Archduke of Austria (1617–19)
and Holy Roman Emperor (1619–37), painted before
an imaginary scene from the battle of Nördlingen,
5–6 September 1634, by Peter Paul Rubens. Nördlingen,
which the Swedes lost through over-confidence and poor
tactical co-ordination, finally persuaded France to enter the
Thirty Years War in order to confront Spain directly.
Ferdinand was not present at the battle; the Imperial army
was nominally commanded by his son.*

THE THIRTY YEARS WAR 1618–48

O N 23 MAY 1618 two of the Catholic regents of Bohemia and their secretary were 'defenestrated' from the Hradcin Castle in Prague by Count Mathias Thurn (1567–1640) and his Protestant acolytes. They survived: 'held aloft by angels', claimed the Catholics; 'landed on a dung heap', replied the Protestants – the moats of seventeenth-century forts were usually replete with rubbish and outpourings from latrines. Now in open revolt against the Holy Roman Emperor, Matthias, the Bohemian rebels invited Elector Frederick V of the Palatinate to become their king. He accepted, expecting assistance from the member states of the Protestant Union, of which he was director, but, alarmed at Frederick's impetuosity, most demurred. Isolated, Frederick paid Count Ernst von Mansfeld and Prince Christian of Anhalt–Bernburg (1568–1630) to raise an army in support of Thurn.

While the major Protestant countries – England, Sweden and the Netherlands – plus France, Catholic but anti-Habsburg, dithered, Catholic rulers acted. The Catholic League pledged Matthias its army of 30,000 men under the highly experienced Tilly. Together with the Frenchman Charles de Longueval, Count of

ABOVE: *Emperor Rudolf
II's guarantee of religious
liberty in Bohemia was
violated in 1617 when
Habsburg officials closed
Protestant chapels. The
resulting defenestration*
*of the Catholic regents
William Slavata and
Jaroslav Martinic
replicated a similar
incident that marked the
beginning of the Hussite
Revolt in 1418.*

The Thirty Years War
1618–29

Imperial campaigns, with dates

Tilly

Wallenstein

Spínola

other Spanish armies

Protestant campaigns, with dates

Christian IV of Denmark

Mansfeld

Bethlen Gábor

battle

towns captured by Habsburgs, with dates

border of Holy Roman Empire

Spanish Habsburg territories

Austrian Habsburg territories

100 km

100 miles

N

SWEDEN

Kristiansand

Gothenburg

North Sea

Arhus
1627

Copenhagen

Malmö

Baltic Sea

DENMARK

Stralsund

Wolgast
September 1628

Wismar
1627

Glückstadt

Hamburg

Emden

Bremen 1625

Verden

Elbe

Osnabrück

NETHERLANDS

Amsterdam

Oldenzaal

Groenlo

BRANDENBURG

Berlin

Oder

Magdeburg
1626

Warsaw

POLAND

Poznan

Lodz

Rotterdam

Bergen-op-Zoom

Breda
1625

Stadtlohn
6 Aug. 1623

1626

Lutter
26 Aug.
1626

Dessau
25 April 1626

Leipzig

Breslau
1626

Warta

Düsseldorf

Antwerp 1622

Cologne

1623

SAXONY

SPANISH NETH.

Jülich
1622

Brussels

Fleurus
26 Aug.
1622

Liège

Frankfurt

Höchst
20 June 1622

1626

White Mountain
8 Nov. 1620

1622

Prague

Pilsen

BOHEMIA

Olmütz

1627

Cracow

1626

1619

Luxembourg

1622

Rhine

1620

Heidelberg

Nuremberg

Wimpfen
6 May 1622

Záblati
10 June 1619

Brno

1626

MORAVIA

Putnok
1626

Mannheim

Wiesloch
27 April 1622

Donauwörth

Danube

1621

1620

Levice

Stuttgart

Strasbourg

Augsburg

BAVARIA

1620

Munich

Salzburg

AUSTRIA

Linz

Vienna

Bratislava

1620

Pest

Pápa

STYRIA

Kösseg

IMPERIAL HUNGARY

FRANCE

Dijon

FRANCHE
COMTÉ

Basel

Zürich

SWISS
CONFEDERATION

Berne

CARINTHIA

CARNIOLA

Ljubljana

Zagreb

OTTOMAN
EMPIRE

Geneva

Lyon

1620

Spanish Road

SAVOY

Milan
1628

1629

REPUBLIC OF VENICE

Venice

Mantua

Casale

Pinerolo

Modena

Bologna

Genoa

Adriatic Sea

Belgrade

Nice

Rhône

After missing some strategic opportunities in 1618 and 1619, the polyglot Bohemian Army was trapped by Tilly and Bucquoy on the White Mountain outside Prague on 8 November 1620. Despite adopting the new-fangled Dutch formations, the Bohemian forces were routed within sixty minutes.

Bucquoy (1571–1621), who directed the Austrian contingents, Tilly swept into Bohemia through Lusatia and Upper and Lower Austria, whilst the Spanish Army of the Netherlands, commanded by Spínola, invaded the territories of the Palatinate along the Rhine. In less than an hour on the morning of 8 November 1620, across the slopes of the White Mountain outside the walls of Prague, Tilly and Bucquoy smashed the Bohemian Army of Anhalt, Thurn and Mansfeld.

So began the Thirty Years War. Struggles between Protestant and Catholic had occupied much of the sixteenth century, reaching a temporary hiatus after the termination of the French Wars of Religion in 1598. In the German lands of

the Holy Roman Empire, the princes, dukes, counts, knights and Imperial
Free Cities, numbering over 330 separate polities all owing allegiance
to the Habsburg emperor in Vienna, used the pause to prepare for a
renewal of hostilities. Landgrave Maurice of Hesse-Kassel founded a
militia of 9,000 men in 1600 and a training school for officers in 1618. The
Prussian estates voted funds in 1601 to refortify the ports of Memel and
Pillau and maintain two warships to patrol the Baltic. Between 1553 and 1585 the
electors of Saxony founded a magnificent arsenal in Dresden. After 1600 the
Elector Palatine refortified Frankenthal and Heidelberg and, in 1606, created a

fortress-city at Mannheim. Calvinist Hanau, allied to the Palatinate, received a set of artillery fortifications between 1603 and 1618. The Catholic powers in the Rhineland reciprocated. Ehrenbreitstein, overlooking the confluence of the Rhine and the Mosel at Koblenz, was fortified by the Elector of Trier, whilst Christopher von Sötern, Bishop of Speyer, built the massive fortress of Philippsburg at Udenheim on the Rhine south of the Palatinate. Construction, begun in 1615, took eight years.

Tranquillity in the empire depended upon the Religious Peace of Augsburg of 1555, which had established the principle of *cuius regio, eius religio* – the religion of the ruler determined the religion of the state. Protestant princes, who had nationalized the church, thereby greatly increasing their territorial, financial and administrative power, sought to consolidate their gains. Catholic rulers were prepared to support the emperor's attempts to recover lands lost to the heretics in return for political rewards. Maximilian I, Duke of Bavaria, contravened the

Religious Peace of Augsburg in 1608 by seizing and catholicizing the Lutheran Imperial Free City of Donauwörth, which housed a vital bridge across the Danube on Bavaria's northern border. At the Imperial Diet in the following year, the Protestant members walked out in protest to found the Protestant Union, a ten-year defensive pact ultimately comprising nine princes and seventeen Free Cities. Directed by Elector Frederick IV of the Palatinate (r. 1583–1610), its leaders were Elector John Sigismund of Brandenburg (r. 1608–20), the Duke of Württemberg, and the Landgrave of Hesse-Kassel. France, weakened by three decades of civil war, supported the union as a cheap weapon in her contest with the Habsburgs. In response, on 10 July 1609 Maximilian of Bavaria formed the Catholic League. Although it eventually included fifteen archbishoprics and bishoprics, the principal member was Bavaria, but Philip III of Spain subsidized Tilly and the league's army. The states of the empire were ready to act as surrogates in the rivalry between Habsburg Spain and Valois France.

Most seventeenth-century campaigns were 'affairs of posts and ambuscades', involving small garrisons attempting to maintain or extend their control over an area in order to extract supplies. Convoys, either mercantile or military, were regular targets. Full-scale battles and sieges were infrequent.

After defeating Tilly at Wiesloch, Mansfeld and Margrave George of Baden separated their forces. Tilly, reinforced by a Spanish corps under Don Gonzalo Fernández de Córdoba, defeated Baden in detail at the battle of Wimpfen, 6 May 1622, before Mansfeld could rejoin him. Here, Tilly's cavalry has been successful on both flanks and is pressing upon the infantry of Baden's centre. Both sides deployed huge pike squares flanked by musketeers.

The Twelve Years Truce between Spain and the rebellious Dutch expired in 1621. In order to position herself for the resumption of hostilities, Spain became directly involved in Imperial affairs because of her concern for the 'Spanish Road', a military corridor linking Lombardy with the Spanish Netherlands via the Valtelline, the Tyrol, Upper Swabia and the Rhine valley. Because English and Dutch naval power blocked the sea route from Iberia to the Netherlands, Spain relied upon the Spanish Road to supply and reinforce her armies in the Low Countries. Control of the Valtelline was vital, and in 1623 Spain occupied the Canton of the Grey Leagues, the Grisons, through whose territory the Valtelline extended. Spínola's seizure of Jülich in 1622 had also improved communications along the road, and so too did the occupation of Alsace by the Austrian Habsburgs in the same year and the capture of Frankenthal in the Rhenish Palatinate in 1623.

Following the collapse of the Bohemian revolt at the White Mountain, the forces of the Austrian Habsburgs, now answerable to Emperor Ferdinand II, and the Catholic League attacked the lands of the Elector Palatine. Some Bohemian garrisons held out – Pilsen surrendered in 1621 and Wittingau in 1622 – but

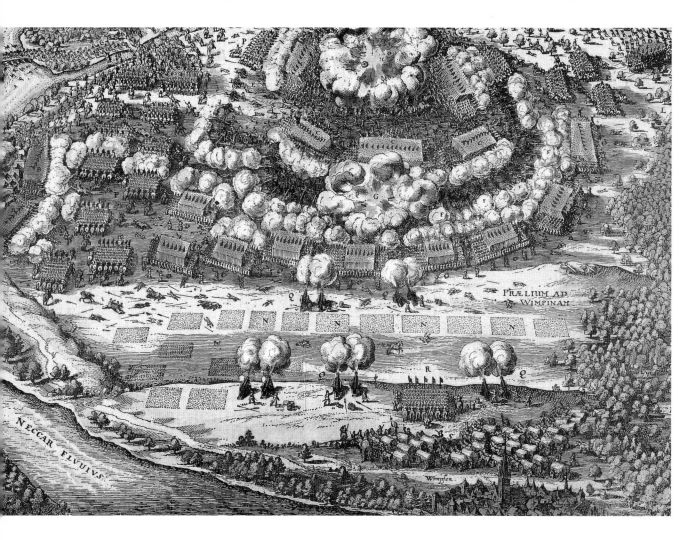

Frederick was without an army until Mansfeld, his pockets stuffed with Dutch and English money, took over the 21,000 troops of the dissolved Protestant Union. He promptly withdrew into Alsace to recruit his command up to 43,000 men, where the small corps of Margrave George Frederick of Baden (1573–1638) joined him. Mansfeld and Baden interrupted Tilly's campaign of conquest in the Rhenish Palatinate at Wiesloch, 12 kilometres south of Heidelberg, on 27 April 1622 but failed to continue their co-operation, and Baden was smashed by Tilly at Bad Wimpfen, on the Neckar to the north of Heilbronn, on 6 May. Tilly next marched to block the small army of Christian of Brunswick (1599–1626), a young adventurer of questionable judgement, whom he defeated at Höchst in the Odenwald on 20 June. Thoroughly beaten, Frederick dismissed Mansfeld and Baden and retired into exile in the Netherlands. Mansfeld and Baden sold their army to the Dutch but, while attempting to join them in East Friesland, Christian of Brunswick was intercepted by Tilly on 6 August 1623 at Stadtlohn, close to the Netherlands' eastern border.

Although the Dutch had attacked Spain indirectly by providing financial support to Frederick of the Palatinate, the termination of the Twelve Years Truce

The siege of Breda

Jacob Kemp fortified Breda, a key border fortress of the Dutch Republic, during the 1570s. Spínola laid siege using a ring of redoubts and small forts rather than a continuous entrenchment, a method perfected by his predecessors in the Netherlands, the Dukes of Alva and Parma. Breda was difficult to attack because of the extensive aquatic defences.

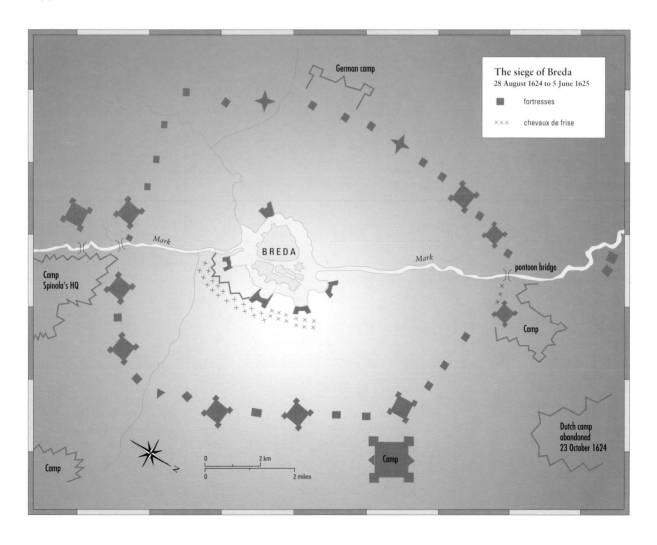

The siege of Breda
28 August 1624 to 5 June 1625

◼ fortresses

××× chevaux de frise

obliged them to confront their enemy openly. Spínola, his supply line via the Spanish Road secure, took the offensive, capturing Jülich in February 1622 and besieging Bergen-op-Zoom in the autumn. This siege was raised on 4 October when Mansfeld's army arrived in the Netherlands and defeated Fernández de Córdoba at Fleurus, 26 August. However, Spínola continued his offensive in 1624 culminating in the successful siege of Breda, 28 August 1624 – 5 June 1625. The Count-Duke of Olivares, who directed Spanish foreign and military policy for

Spínola's offensive into the Dutch Republic culminated in the successful siege of Breda, despite furious relief efforts by the Dutch under Princes Maurice and Frederick Henry. This vital border fortress had been captured by Spain in 1581 and recaptured by the Dutch in 1590. It finally returned to Dutch possession in 1637, confirmed at the Peace of Westphalia in 1648.

Philip IV until 1643, intended to attack the Dutch both militarily and economically, so he formed an anti-Dutch trading league called the *almirantazgo*, comprising Spain, the Spanish Netherlands, the Hanse towns and Poland, with co-operation from the Catholic League and the emperor. In response, during June 1624 the Dutch formed an alliance with England and France committed to the restoration of Frederick to the Palatinate. The marriage of Prince Charles, the future Charles I of England, to Louis XIII's sister, Henrietta Maria, sealed the agreement.

The Surrender of Breda,
1625, *by Velázquez. Spínola
receives the key to Breda
from the defeated Dutch
governor, Justinus of
Nassau (1559–1635).
Painted in Madrid ten years
after the event, the
background is probably
fanciful although Velázquez
may have met Spínola.
Despite the barbarity and
unrestrained conduct of
war, senior officers,
especially at sieges, carefully
observed ceremonial
niceties.*

MERCENARIES AND THE MILITARY ENTREPRENEUR

Although the wars of the sixteenth century had demonstrated the inefficiency of mercenaries, it was not until the second half of the seventeenth century that standing armies partially replaced the 'military entrepreneur' and his hirelings. The experiences of the Thirty Years War were instrumental in bringing this about; standing armies were exceptional in 1600 but commonplace within a century. The standing army was scarcely a novel concept. The Roman Army was the most notable amongst numerous predecessors, whilst many rulers during the Middle Ages retained permanent garrison troops in their strategic fortresses as well as small units of bodyguards. In addition to the Yeomen of the Guard (1485) and Gentlemen Pensioners (1539), Henry VIII of England had 3,000 regular troops garrisoning the permanent fortifications along the south coast and the Scottish border.

Charles VII of France (r. 1422–61) had founded a standing army in 1445 during the final stages of the Hundred Years War, the *compagnies d'ordonnance*, which Louis XI (r. 1461–83) reorganized into the Picardy Bands and trained according to the Swiss model. Under Francis I (r. 1515–47) this cadre matured into a standing army composed of volunteers recruited through a state agency. The Burgundian standing army of Duke Charles the Bold (r. 1467–77) imitated the French pattern. Between 1445 and 1624 the peacetime French military establishment ranged between 10,000 and 20,000 troops, who guarded the royal person and garrisoned the frontier strongholds. During wartime this cadre was expanded to a maximum of 55,000, the level reached under Henry IV during the final stages of the French Wars of Religion. Individual field armies did not normally exceed 20,000 men, the most that could be supplied and administered on campaign.

The Ordinance of Valladolid of 1496 prepared Spain to follow a similar course. Also adopting Swiss methods, Gonsalvo de Córdoba reorganized the Spanish foot in 1504 as the Ordinance Infantry. Half the men were armed with the long Swiss pike, one-third with a round shield and thrusting sword, and the remainder with the arquebus. In 1534 this system matured into the tercio, which, befitting the age of the Renaissance, pursued the example of the internal articulation of the Roman legion. The tercio, a combination of pikemen and arquebusiers, was initially organized into twelve companies of 250 men, each subdivided into ten *esquadras* of twenty-five. Pay was monthly, deductions being made for medical insurance, but the soldier could earn additional money via long-service and technical skill bonuses. Every tercio was equipped with a commissariat, legal section and health service consisting of a physician, surgeon, apothecary and ten barbers. In action the tercio was tactically flexible, capable of forming task forces – *escuadróns* – mixing varying numbers of troops and types of weapons. The sixteenth-century Spanish standing army operated principally beyond the Iberian Peninsula, garrisoning bases in northern Italy, countering the rebellious Dutch in the Netherlands and Protestants in Germany, and opposing the Muslims in North Africa.

In Germany the military systems that fought the Thirty Years War were in place by the 1590s. Militias provided a minimum level of defence and deterrence in nearly all states. Ancient feudal obligations, including mass mobilization (*Landsturm*) and personal cavalry service by members of the nobility, continued as mechanisms of last resort. Larger states – Bavaria, Saxony and the Palatinate – retained small bodyguard and garrison cadres capable of wartime augmentation through the recruitment of mercenaries and the pressing of militiamen. The first proper German standing army belonged to the Habsburg Holy Roman Emperors. Since 1535 the Habsburgs' borders with the Ottoman Empire in the northern Balkans had been protected by a permanent militia organization, the *Militärgrenze*, whilst garrison regiments were established in the Hungarian and Austrian fortresses during the 1580s. There were also some cavalry units, a naval flotilla on the Danube, and a military administration attached to the Court War Council (*Hofkriegsrat*). After the outbreak of war in 1618, contractors, most already closely associated with the royal house, raised new regiments. Gradually these mercenary leaders mutated into officers of the state army, to be joined by a host of minor nobility and imperial knights in pursuit of the new career opportunities and cash rewards.

There was rarely a shortage of mercenaries; wars peppered the continent, and accommodating their human requirements was a major international business. Rulers contracted with mercenary generals, who then subcontracted to colonels and captains. Most mercenary captains, over 1,500 of whom were active in Germany during the Thirty Years War, maintained their companies on a permanent basis. Many smaller Italian and German states paid an annual retainer to a military entrepreneur in the knowledge that he could exploit his contacts to raise troops quickly in an emergency. Periods of agricultural dearth – and there was at least one bad harvest every seven years – plus overpopulation in Ireland, Scotland, Poland, eastern Germany, Switzerland, Serbia and Croatia, produced fodder for the recruiting parties. A soldier's life was not unattractive. Battles were infrequent, there was the prospect of loot and plunder, whilst living conditions were no worse than those endured by civilians. The greatest danger was disease, particularly prevalent in crowded and insanitary camps.

Born in Luxembourg, Count Ernst von Mansfeld (1580–1626) was the leading Protestant military entrepreneur. He specialized in the swift production of large, poor-quality armies but lost them equally quickly. Should Mansfeld so miscalculate that he had to fight a battle, his ill-equipped armies invariably disintegrated. However, his prices were very low. He served the Habsburgs between 1594 and 1610 before transferring to the Protestant Union from 1610 to 1617. After a year with Savoy he was appointed general to Frederick V of the Palatinate. Sacked in 1622, he entered Dutch service, but his funding expired in 1623 so he disbanded his troops, most entering Dutch service, and looked around for a new employer.

On 14 April 1624 he arrived in England to raise 12,000 men with whom to

A camp of the Spanish Army of Flanders during the three-year siege of Ostend, 1601–4. During sieges and on campaign, seventeenth-century armies spent long periods in camp, normally moving only when local supplies of food and forage had been exhausted. Sanitation was primitive and a camp could usually be detected by its smell long before it came into view.

recover the Palatinate for Frederick. France and England had each agreed to meet half the costs of Mansfeld's expedition, whilst the former undertook to provide 3,000 cavalry to join the English infantry when they arrived in France prior to marching east into Germany. An international celebrity, Mansfeld was lodged in state apartments at Whitehall. Despite orders to every parish to conscript fit young men – the trained bands, the élite of the county militias, were sacrosanct – mostly the unemployed, social misfits and petty criminals were listed, ideal material for Mansfeld, who specialized in destruction and pillage. En route to Dover they deserted in droves, and those who remained were thoroughly disruptive. Mansfeld had been given £55,000 but was determined to spend as little as possible, refusing to take financial responsibility for his men until their arrival in Dover. Mansfeld then ignored his instructions and decided to march to the

Palatinate via the Netherlands rather than France. When he landed on the island of Walcheren in the estuary of the River Schelde, no preparations had been made and the army evaporated through starvation and disease.

Mansfeld's English contract illuminated the salient disadvantages of mercenaries. Although good-quality companies could be effective, the bargain-basement varieties were useless. Expecting their men to support themselves through pillage and requisition, entrepreneurs made scant supply arrangements. Mercenary armies were thus particularly unsuitable for siege operations. Whereas marching troops could usually find enough forage and sustenance, immobile troops were liable to starve. Finally, as Mansfeld demonstrated, once money had been handed over, the hirer surrendered control and the mercenary leader could conduct operations as he wished. The mercenary system offered few advantages

except that troops could be raised rapidly and the state avoided having to maintain an expensive military infrastructure. The latter point was persuasive at the start of the Thirty Years War but experience soon taught that the loss of political authority reinforced the case for maintaining a standing army.

DENMARK JOINS THE WAR

Christian IV, the alcoholic King of Denmark, volunteered to lead a new coalition against Emperor Ferdinand. Although Sweden was Denmark's main rival, the advance of the Imperial and Catholic League armies into northern Germany threatened both his southern border and his territorial ambitions. Christian had founded the port of Glückstadt on the Elbe in 1616 as a rival to Hamburg and was anxious to acquire the bishoprics of Verden, Bremen and Osnabrück, which controlled the lands between the Elbe and the Weser and thus the lucrative river traffic. Moreover, he was rich from the tolls that Denmark charged on every ship

Christian IV, King of Denmark from 1596 to 1648, was a drunkard, womanizer and gambler but also a capable domestic ruler who substantially developed and increased Danish economic resources. His ambition to lead the Protestants in north Germany led to defeat and the invasion of the Jutland peninsula in 1627–8. War with Sweden, 1643–5, resulted in a second occupation of Jutland followed by a humiliating peace settlement.

passing through the 'Sound', and there was no better way for a king to spend his money than by starting a war.

Lacking both support from his coalition partners and reliable knowledge of the political situation, in January 1625 Christian advanced across the Elbe with 17,000 men, a mixture of mercenaries and peasant conscripts, heading for Hameln on the Weser. Expecting to encounter only Tilly's army, billeted in Hesse and Westphalia, Christian ran into Wallenstein, whose 30,000 men had marched north to Halberstadt and Magdeburg. Luckily for Christian, Tilly and Wallenstein quarrelled and failed to combine, allowing the Danish army to run away. Christian promptly informed his partners that he would make peace if they did not come to his aid. Accordingly, the Hague Convention of 9 December 1625 initiated a loose alliance between England, Denmark, the Dutch Republic and Frederick of the Palatinate, supported by France, Bethlen Gábor, Prince of Transylvania (r. 1613–29), and his suzerain, the Sultan of the Ottoman Empire. Supplied with English and Dutch gold, King Christian undertook to attack Lower Saxony while Christian of Brunswick invaded the Wittelsbach bishoprics in Westphalia and the lower Rhineland. Mansfeld, the coalition's generalissimo, decided to advance along the Elbe into Silesia, ravaging the Habsburg lands, before joining Bethlen Gábor, who was to operate against Austria and Moravia. The scheme was too complicated – liaison between the various forces was bound to break down – and Emperor Ferdinand had reorganized his armies. Bavaria, whose Army of the Catholic League was bearing the brunt of the war thus allowing the emperor's troops to operate against Bethlen Gábor in Hungary, asked Ferdinand to contribute to the campaigns in Germany. Already chafing at the political restraints imposed by his reliance on Tilly and the league, Ferdinand turned to Wallenstein.

Arrogant, vain and ambitious, Albrecht Wenzel von Wallenstein (1583–1634) was amongst the minority of Bohemian noblemen who had supported the Habsburgs during the Bohemian Revolt. In 1609 he had married an elderly but rich Czech widow, Lucretia Neksova, owner of vast estates in Moravia. Her death enabled him to buy, at knock-down prices, lands confiscated from rebellious Protestants. Although blessed with some slight previous military experience – he had fought against the Hungarians in 1604, provided mercenaries for Ferdinand of Austria's war with Venice in 1617, and rejoiced in the title of Colonel of Prague – Wallenstein was more businessman than soldier. Placing his agent, the Antwerp banker Johan de Witte, in charge of logistics, Wallenstein answered the emperor's call by offering to raise 24,000 troops at his own expense, a proposal that Ferdinand found irresistible. A contract was finalized in April 1625, and when Wallenstein exceeded his target by recruiting nearer to 50,000, on 13 June a grateful Ferdinand created him Duke of Friedland. Wallenstein's quid pro quo was to be allowed to recover his expenses and appoint his own officers.

Wallenstein provided equipment, weaponry and foodstuffs for his troops from his personal estates but made his profit through the ruthless extortion of

OVERLEAF: *Wallenstein: a scene from the Thirty Years War, by Ernest Crofts (1847–1911), first exhibited in Leeds City Art Gallery in 1884. Although the scene is imaginary, the artist's anti-Catholic stance provides an unromantic verisimilitude. Albrecht von Wallenstein is indeed lord of all he surveys: mud, filth, destruction, death, fire, cruelty, lowering skies and an atmosphere of menace.*

'contributions'. When his troops occupied a region, every town and village was assessed and ordered to pay a sum in cash or kind. Failure to deliver by the deadline saw the houses put to the torch ('*brandschatzen*') and hostages executed. It was a slight improvement over random pillage *à la* Mansfeld, but in order to operate the system, sizeable tracts of land had to be occupied and contributions frequently exacted from friendly as well as hostile areas. Should a region become economically exhausted, then the army had to move whether or not this served a strategic purpose. Wallenstein's men were barely the superiors of Mansfeld's, but better equipment and cohesion gave them the advantage during the Danish War.

Opposed to Tilly and Wallenstein, Christian commanded neither such numbers nor organization. Probably imitating the Swedish model of 1544, in 1614 he founded a small territorial army composed of conscripted peasants from crown estates. Seven years later the system was rethought. On royal and church lands every nine peasant households formed a 'file', which was obliged to provide a soldier who served for three years and, if not mobilized, worked on one of the farms and drew a wage. 'Files' could rarely afford to hire a substitute, so one of their own had to be 'persuaded'. Conscripts drilled for just nine days a year and the highly unpopular scheme produced a low-calibre peasant army, hardly better than a militia. More significantly, in 1624 Christian formed a permanent corps of regular troops to garrison the three Danish fortresses on the Norwegian–Swedish peninsula and this became the cadre of the later Danish standing army.

Mansfeld's campaign began discouragingly when his attempt to cross the River Mulde, a left-bank tributary of the Elbe, was checked at Dessau Bridge in April 1626. After regrouping, in June Mansfeld advanced again, the Imperial forces having been weakened by the need to send troops to quell a peasant revolt in Upper Austria. Erroneous intelligence (two words that are closely associated in military history) led Christian to believe that Wallenstein had committed his entire army to the pursuit of Mansfeld when he had actually sent a considerable corps to reinforce Tilly in Lower Saxony. Assuming that he was opposed by weak forces under Tilly, Christian marched south from Wolfenbüttel in August 1626 along the valleys of the Innerste and the Neile between the Hainberg and the Oderwald. Rain poured down and Tilly slowly withdrew, skirmishing with Christian's vanguard, until he made a stand at the important road junction of Lutter-am-Barenberg. Christian blundered into Tilly's position on 26 August and the battle was lost when the Danish cavalry defected. As the Danes straggled northwards towards Wolfenbüttel, their retreat was harried by ambushes that Tilly had placed during the fighting withdrawal to Lutter.

Mansfeld, closely followed by Wallenstein, joined Gábor in Silesia on 30 September 1626 only to discover that the latter was about to withdraw from the conflict. Gábor had received news of the sultan's defeat by the Persians at Baghdad and, realizing that he could not fight without the sultan's support, made peace with Ferdinand at Bratislava in December 1626. Abandoning his army, which now numbered no more than 5,000 men, Mansfeld rode south, heading for

Ragusa (Dubrovnik) in Croatia to take up a pre-arranged contract with Venice, but died en route at Rakovica near Sarajevo on 29 November. His men subsisted in Silesia over the winter but surrendered to the Imperialists in July 1627.

Tilly and Wallenstein joined forces in 1627 to sweep through Saxony, defeat Christian at Eutin, and occupy the whole of the Jutland peninsula. Lacking a navy, Wallenstein could not capture the Danish islands, but by 1628 he and Tilly were established on the Baltic coast and had reconquered Germany for the Catholic faith. At the Peace of Lübeck on 22 May 1629, Christian was restored to his possessions on condition that he supported the Spanish and Imperial ambitions to control the waters of the Baltic by the creation of a navy at Wismar. To complete the zenith of Imperial power, Wallenstein was created Duke of Mecklenburg and a prince of the Holy Roman Empire.

GUSTAVUS ADOLPHUS

Warfare in the Baltic was dominated by the rivalry between Sweden and Denmark. Populations were sparse, resulting in both conscription and the widespread employment of mercenaries. Whereas campaigns in Central and Western Europe were conducted between late spring and mid autumn, in the Baltic lands the summer season was shortened by spring mud, caused by the melting snows, and autumn rains. Usable roads were scarce everywhere in Europe

An improbable nineteenth-century depiction of the death of Mansfeld, painted by Robert Forelle in 1886: the reality was probably a great deal more squalid. His death may have been regretted by his men but only because they had been abandoned in Silesia without pay. Note the window, opened to assist the departure of the soul.

but even more so in the North: armies often campaigned in the depths of winter when frost had hardened the ground. Ski-troops were regularly used in the wars between Sweden and Muscovy along the Finnish–Karelian border and between Sweden and Poland in Livonia. Four hundred reindeer pulled the supply sledges of the Swedish army that attacked the fortress of Kola on the White Sea in 1611.

Despite its remoteness, the Baltic was increasingly important to the European economy: Swedish copper and iron; Norwegian cod; Russian hemp, tar and timber; and, particularly, grain from Poland and German lands east of the Elbe. Much of the trade rested with Dutch and English merchants but every ship had to pass through the Sound, controlled by the Danes.

Gustav II Adolf, better known as Gustavus Adolphus, ascended the Swedish throne at the age of 16 during the Kalmar War with Denmark (1611–13). The Treaty of Knäred brought peace at the price of Sweden's surrendering in perpetuity Gothenburg and Älvsborg, possession of which had allowed the Swedes to outflank the Danish Sound tolls, unless she could redeem them by a

GERMANY DURING THE
THIRTY YEARS WAR,
1630–39

The Swedish campaigns in Germany, 1630–32, were determined by logistics. Following the conquests in 1631, Gustavus Adolphus fought to maintain his lines of communication with the Baltic, through Erfurt.

Gustavus Adolphus inspected German military organizations and fortifications during 1620. He was not the first to adopt Dutch tactics: advisers from the United Provinces also worked in Brandenburg, Baden, Württemberg, Hesse, Brunswick, Saxony and Holstein. Even the Berne militia was 'Nassaued' in 1628. Neither should the efficacy of Gustavus's military reforms be exaggerated. At Honigfelde-Stuhm in Ducal Prussia, 27 June 1629, Polish hussaria and German reiters under Stanislaw Koniecpolski and von Arnim heavily defeated Gustav's corps. Also, his success in Germany was short-lived. After Breitenfeld, his methods were widely imitated whilst heavy casualties eroded Sweden's trained manpower.

payment of 6 million riksdaler within six years. Much to Danish annoyance, with the help of heavy taxation and Dutch loans, the money was paid in 1619 and the region reclaimed. At Stolbova in 1616, in return for renouncing her claims to Novgorod, Sweden received Ingria and Keksholm from Muscovy, completing a land bridge between Estonia and Finland and bringing the whole coast of the Gulf of Finland under Swedish occupation. Having achieved peace with both Denmark and Russia, Gustav turned his attention to Poland, his position strengthened by a fifteen-year defensive alliance with the Dutch, signed in 1614. A premature attempt to seize Pernau from Poland in 1617 misfired and Sweden agreed a two-year truce in 1618.

The failure at Pernau convinced Gustav that the Swedish Army needed radical reform. Accordingly, during the 1620s he improved the conscription machinery. The 1620 'Ordinance of Military Personnel' registered all males over 15 years of age in every parish and grouped them into 'files' of ten men; as many as required could then be drafted from each file. Sweden–Finland was split into eight recruiting districts, subdivided into two or three provinces each raising one 'provincial' infantry regiment consisting of three field regiments comprising two 408-man squadrons apiece. Recruiting districts were allocated to the cavalry in 1623, each field regiment consisting of two 175-man squadrons, and, later, to the artillery. Light cavalry was recruited by offering tax exemptions to any farmer willing to provide a fully equipped trooper. A War Board, an embryonic ministry of war, supervised military administration – a much-improved system that produced the largely national army with which Gustav Adolf invaded Germany in 1630. The human implications, however, were considerable. The village of Bygdeå in northern Sweden sent 230 young men to fight in Poland and Germany between 1621 and 1639; 215 died overseas and only five returned home, crippled.

Equally important were the tactical innovations devised by Gustav. Many links existed between the Dutch Republic and Sweden – economic, military, naval and diplomatic. When reforming the Dutch Army during the 1590s, Captain-General Prince Maurice of Orange and his cousin, Louis-William of Nassau, had drawn upon the writings of Vegetius, Aelian, Frontinus and Emperor Leo VI of Byzantium as well as the ideas of mathematician Simon Stevin and the philosopher Justus Lipsius. Previously the Dutch Army had assumed the tactical organization of the Spanish, French and Swiss whose pike-and-halberd squares, or tercios, initially of 3,000 men, later reduced to about 1,500, were fringed with arquebusiers. They were essentially defensive formations against which enemies hurled themselves until spent, at which point the tercio counter-attacked. Such formations, although preferred by under-motivated mercenaries, were ill-suited to Dutch bogs and deployed firepower inefficiently, only the arquebusiers facing the enemy being able to use their weapons, whilst most of the pikemen could not participate directly in combat.

Learning from the articulation within the Roman legion, Maurice split the tercios into five-company battalions of 675 men, each combining the pike with the arquebus, later superseded by the matchlock musket. Battalions were arrayed in ten ranks, pikemen in the centre and 'shot' to either flank. In theory the arquebusiers could maintain continuous fire, each rank successively discharging its weapons before 'counter-marching' to the rear to reload. The pikemen protected the arquebusiers from attack by cavalry: the 16-foot pike out-ranged the cavalry lance, and formed the offensive arm of the battalion in an advance or charge – the 'push of pike'. In the cauldron of the war with Spain, Maurice forged a system of drill and discipline, reduced his artillery to four basic calibres, reorganized logistics, and, in 1599, equipped the troops with firearms of the same size and calibre. Stevin and the engraver Jacob de Gheyn translated Maurice's infantry drill into a series of pictorial representations, *Wapenhandlingen van roers, musquetten ende spiessen*, published in Amsterdam in 1607 and quickly followed by English, German, French and Danish editions. Reinforced by the conquest of Geertruidenberg in 1593 and victory at Nieuport in 1600, the reputation of the 'Dutch method' spread rapidly.

Polish armies were rich in cavalry, both heavy horse recruited from the aristocracy and light horsemen from Volhynia and Podolia, their skills honed by constant raiding across the Turkish and Muscovite borders. Polish and Turkish horsemen charged at a fast trot with the lance or sabre. Unable to penetrate tercios bristling with pikes, most West European cavalries, the Swedes included, practised the *caracole*, in which several ranks of horsemen trotted towards the enemy, discharged their pistols, and retired to the rear to reload while another rank moved forward. Only when the pistol fire had 'disordered' the enemy foot did the horsemen close in with the sword. Charles IX of Sweden, who was well informed about Dutch innovations by Jacob

FIRING MECHANISMS

Muzzle-loading, black powder, smooth-bore firearms were discharged by igniting a small amount of powder in the flash pan, which vented through a hole to fire the propellant. In the matchlock, a glowing slow match was lowered into the pan; in the wheel-lock, a piece of iron pyrites (iron sulphide) *in the cock was held against a revolving serrated wheel to produce a shower of sparks; whilst the flintlock, also known as the snaphance or firelock, relied upon a flint in the cock striking a downward blow against the steel. The wheel-lock mechanism was insufficiently robust for widespread military use.*

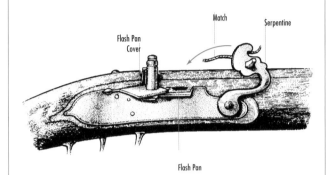

A BRITISH MATCHLOCK MUSKET, *c.* 1690

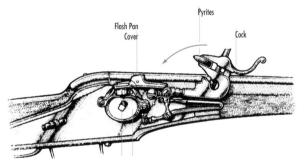

A GERMAN WHEEL-LOCK, *c.* 1600

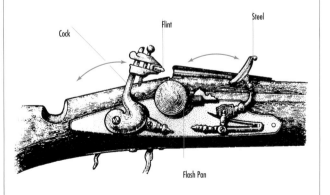

A SNAPHANCE, OR FIRELOCK, *c.* 1620

de la Gardie, unwisely introduced them into an army of mercenaries and reluctant conscripts when already fighting Poland during the early stages of a sixty-year conflict. In 1605, at Kirkholm outside Riga, Charles met a small Polish corps commanded by Karl Chodkiewicz, but was uncertain whether to employ the new-fangled tactics or accustomed formations. The Swedish cavalry was initially positioned between the infantry squares but, in response to enemy attacks, was switched to the flanks, where it was charged and broken by lancers. Outflanked and split into three separate bodies, the Swedish infantry suffered 9,000 casualties (82 per cent) as the Polish *hussaria* and Cossacks penetrated their pike squares: the Poles lost just 100 men. On 4 July 1610 a Russo-Swedish army under Jacob de la Gardie was smashed by the Poles at Klushino while attempting to relieve the siege of Smolensk, only 400 survivors straggling back into Estonia; the remainder of Gardie's mercenaries joined the victors.

War against the Poles and Prussia (1620–29) was the laboratory for tactical experiment. Gustav Adolf abandoned the caracole and imitated the Poles, training his cavalry to charge at the trot with the sabre. In addition, sections of musketeers accompanied the horse to disrupt enemy formations by fire prior to the charge. The introduction of the pike and the musket increased the shock and firepower of the infantry. Battalions were thinned from ten ranks to six, with pike in the centre and 'shot' on either wing, increasing both the frontage and the volume of fire sufficiently to break up enemy formations and allow the pikemen to attack. The counter-march was employed only when the battalion was engaged at extended range, typically about 100 metres. At close range of 30 to 40 metres, where battles were decided, he introduced 'volley firing' by advancing the three rear ranks of musketeers into the intervals between the front three. Volleys were usually delivered as the prelude to a 'push of pike'. At Breitenfeld in 1631 the Scots Brigade in the Swedish army

> ordered themselves in several small battalions, about 6 or 700 in a body, presently now double their ranks, making their files then but 3 deep, the discipline of the King of Sweden being never to march above 6 deep. This done, the foremost rank falling on their knees; the second stooping forward; and the third rank standing right up, and all giving fire together; they powered so much lead at one instant in amongst the enemy's horse that their ranks were much broken with it. (Robert Monro, *Monro his expedition with the worthy Scots regiment call'd Mackays*, London 1637)

Alternatively, when within pistol-shot, the first three ranks of musketeers gave a volley, followed by the remainder, before the battalion charged home with pike, sword and musket stock. The emphasis on volley firing, rather than the Dutch rolling fire, rendered musketeers vulnerable while reloading, and dependent upon the pikemen for protection. However, battles were won and lost by furious close-quarter combat and Gustav's tactics ensured that his men enjoyed maximum advantage when they closed with the enemy.

Further to augment infantry firepower, in 1629 two or three light, 3-pounder cannon – infantry guns – were attached to each battalion: over eighty accompanied the army to Germany in 1630. Pre-packed cartridges increased the rate of fire. Gustav deployed his heavier field guns in mobile batteries. Although Maurice's and Gustav's reforms enhanced the efficacy of infantry, the shallow, linear battalions were more vulnerable than the older pike squares to attacks on their rear and flanks. Consequently, battlefield deployment assumed a chequer-board appearance with the spaces between the battalions in the first line covered in echelon by the battalions of the second and, if present, third lines. Cavalry, supported by parties of musketeers, was customarily positioned on the wings where it had the space and freedom to charge before turning against the enemy's flank or rear.

Gustav, with 18,000 men, renewed the campaign in Livonia in 1621, culminating in the capture of Riga. Employing modern siege techniques acquired from the Dutch – an ability and willingness to dig was another characteristic of the new military discipline – 15,000 Swedes overcame the garrison of 300 regulars and 3,700 militia after a six-day bombardment. With only 3,000 field troops available, the Poles were unable to intervene. Mitau in Kurland was the next target but that was the extent of Swedish achievement; the men were weary, their ranks emaciated by sickness and the constant harrying of the Cossacks. Gustav had also run out of funds. Mitau was lost in November 1622 but Sigismund III Vasa of Poland was in an equally parlous condition, defeated by the Turks in 1621 and no longer in receipt of Danish support, Christian IV being more interested in northern Germany. Sigismund and Gustav were content to sign a truce until 1625.

When hostilities resumed, Gustav quickly overran Livonia north of the Dvina, capturing Mitau and Dorpat, but an expedition into Kurland stalled before Windau and Libau. In January 1626, at the battle of Wallhof, south of Riga, Gustav employed his new tactics to smash the Polish army. The Swedes next invaded and occupied Royal Prussia, a rich province where 'war could be made to pay for war'. This was imperative because the Livonian campaigns had been financed from Sweden's own scarce resources. Prussian ports exported Polish grain, and their annual customs income averaged 600,000 riksdaler. In addition, Sweden levied tolls on all ships visiting the southern Baltic ports between Danzig and Narva, the 'licence system', which yielded a further 500,000 riksdaler. Taken together, these dues realized more money for Sweden than later French subsidies.

Having subdued Prussia, Gustav struck inland to force Sigismund to make peace. The famous Polish cavalry was overcome by the remodelled Swedish horse at Dirschau on the Vistula in August 1627, but an advance on Warsaw in 1629 was halted at Stuhm (Honigfelde) on 27 June by the Poles, reinforced with 12,000 men from Wallenstein. After failed efforts to negotiate peace in 1627 and 1628, the French, anxious to deploy the Swedish army in Germany to counter the emperor and the Catholic League, brokered a deal in 1629. By the terms of the six-year

THE BALTIC STATES,
1600–99

*Campaigning in the
forested, underpopulated
Baltic States was largely
restricted to the coastal
fringes of Prussia,
Lithuania, Livonia, and
Estonia. Only Poland was
sufficiently developed to
permit commanders to
operate further inland
although, even here, armies
clung to the major rivers.*

Truce of Altmark of September 1629, Gustav abandoned most of his Prussian gains but retained the 3½ per cent tolls from the Prussian ports and direct control over Elbing, Braunsberg and Pillau. In 1630 the Duke of Kurland surrendered the customs from his ports of Windau and Libau. In total, Gustav gained 600,000 riksdaler per annum, one-third of Swedish military expenditure.

On 12 January 1628 the Secret Committee of the Riksdag had given Gustav permission to intervene in Germany if necessary. It was invoked on 9 January 1629 because, with the Imperialists on the Baltic coast and Wallenstein constructing a navy at Wismar, there was a possibility that Sweden herself might be invaded. Gustav aimed to drive the Imperialists from the Baltic, restore the pre-1618 political situation in Germany, and establish bases at Stralsund and Wismar through which troops could rapidly deploy should Swedish territory again be endangered. Gustav entered Germany without assurances of foreign aid and uncertain that Denmark would not attack while his back was turned. He did, however, take with him a reformed and battle-hardened army.

Sailing from Stockholm on 27 June 1630 with 13,000 men packed aboard thirteen transports, escorted by twenty-seven warships, Gustav landed on 6 July at Peenemünde on the northern tip of the island of Usedom in the estuary of the River Oder, whence he probably intended to attack down the line of the Oder into Imperial Silesia, threatening Austria and Vienna. His sole ally was the port of Stralsund, which had withstood an Imperial siege from May to July 1628. Usedom and Stettin were quickly subdued, obliging the Duke of Pomerania to sign an agreement providing the invaders with a larger base area. Only the dispossessed rallied to the Swedish cause, principally the Duke of Mecklenburg and Duke Christian William of Brandenburg (1587–1665), the Protestant ex-administrator of the archbishopric of Magdeburg, who sought to regain the office he had lost following the Edict of Restitution. Magdeburg was a vital post commanding the passage of the Elbe and the routes from Pomerania into Lower Saxony and Thuringia. On 1 August 1630 Magdeburg and Sweden signed an alliance that restored Christian William and inserted a Swedish governor.

Even better was an alliance with Landgrave William V of Hesse-Kassel (r. 1627–37) that gave Gustav a potential opening into Westphalia and the valleys of the Main and Rhine, but for the remainder of 1630 the Swedish army was penned into Pomerania. The major north German princes sat on their hands, especially Electors John George of Saxony and George William of Brandenburg, who were as wary of Gustav as they were of the emperor and Wallenstein.

Another problem was supply. Through Stettin and Stralsund Gustav could receive supplies directly from Sweden, but that negated a prime objective. Gustav intended to support his army from German resources, so he needed to expand his beachhead southwards along both banks of the Oder. Eastern Pomerania was cleared, and by Christmas 1630 the ejection of the Imperial garrisons from Gartz and Greifenhagen (Gryfino) opened the lower Oder, but it was not until February 1631 that Gustav succeeded in seizing most of Mecklenburg.

The Baltic States
1600–99

- Swedish territory *c.* 1600
- by 1617
- by 1629
- by 1645
- by 1648
- by 1658
- border of Holy Roman Empire
- battle

0   100 km
0   100 miles

ARCTIC OCEAN

Norwegian Sea

Kola Peninsula

Kola

White Sea

Kabelvåg

RUSSIAN EMPIRE

Lapland

Alstahaug

Tornea

Lulea

Uleaborg

SWEDISH EMPIRE

Trondheim

Jämtland

Gulf of Bothnia

Umea

Karelia

Finland

Björneborg

Lake Ladoga

Härjedalen

Viborg

Bergen

Dalarna

Aland

Helsingfors

Gulf of Finland

Ingria

Reval

Narva

Estonia

Novgorod

Oslo

Uppland

Uppsala

Stockholm

Oesel

Livonia

Pskov

Kristiansand

Gothenburg

Bohusland

Väster-götland

Östergötland

Jönköping

Norrköping

Gotland

Windau

Riga

Kirkholm
27 Sept. 1605

Velikiye Luki

Kurland

Dünaburg

Dvina

Halland

Varberg

Småland

Kalmar

Oland

Libau

Wallhof
17 January 1626

Vitebsk

The Sound

Blekinge

Scania

Karlskrona

Baltic Sea

Memel

Samogitia

DENMARK

Copenhagen

Malmö

Bornholm

Vilna

Lithuania

Fredericia

Funen

Zeeland

North Sea

Königsberg

Minsk

Kiel

Rügen

Stralsund

Rostock

Wolgast

Usedom

Wismar

Stettin

Danzig

PRUSSIA

Fehrbellin
28 June 1675

Elbe

Weser

Berlin

Oder

GERMAN STATES

Poznan

KINGDOM OF POLAND

Vistula

Bug

Warsaw

Vistula

Pripyet

28–30 July 1656

NORWAY

72°

68°

Arctic Circle

64°

60°

56°

52°

0° 8° 16° 24° 32° 40° 48°

On 23 January 1631 Gustav and his chancellor, Oxenstierna, signed the Treaty of Bärwalde with the envoys of France. In return for a subsidy of 400,000 taler per annum over five years, they agreed to field an army of 30,000 infantry and 6,000 cavalry but retained freedom of action, Richelieu calculating that any Swedish success would disadvantage the Habsburgs.

Gustav had been able to land unopposed because much of the Imperial Army had been redeployed to northern Italy, where a dispute over the succession to the Duchy of Mantua, ultimately settled in favour of the French candidate, the Duke of Nevers, gave France control of the Grisons and access to northern Italy via Pinerolo. Gustav was also greatly aided by the dismissal of Wallenstein.

At the height of his territorial power, on 28 March 1629 Emperor Ferdinand issued the Edict of Restitution, which restored all Roman Catholic Church property sequestered by the Protestant princes and cities since 1552. In political terms the edict established Imperial–Wittelsbach control over north-western Germany, displeasing Lutheran, Calvinist and Catholic princes. Associated with this was disquiet at the cavalier manner in which the emperor had transferred the Palatinate electorate to Bavaria in 1625 whilst supporters of Denmark – the Dukes of Calenberg, Wolfenbüttel and Mecklenburg – had been dispossessed and their titles and lands given to Imperial generals. Wallenstein rashly accepted the Duchy of Mecklenburg, and Gottfried Pappenheim wanted the dukedom of Wolfenbüttel but was thwarted by Maximilian of Bavaria and had to be content with becoming an Imperial count. Tilly, older and wiser, accepted a gratuity of 400,000 guilders instead of the Duchy of Calenberg.

Aware that Ferdinand's dominance rested entirely upon Wallenstein's army and organization, the anti-Imperial princes undermined the generalissimo. His contribution system, which affected friend and enemy alike, was a major grievance, as was his employment of numerous Bohemian Protestants. At the Diet of Regensburg (June to August 1630) the electors made it clear to Ferdinand that they would elect his son, Ferdinand of Hungary, as king of the Romans (i.e. Ferdinand's successor) only if he sacked Wallenstein, promoted Tilly to command of the Imperial Army, and revoked the Edict of Restitution. Ferdinand had no option but to concede his entire position.

CAMPAIGNING IN GERMANY: GUSTAV VERSUS TILLY

Scattered in winter quarters across Mecklenburg and northern Brandenburg, Tilly's combined Imperial and Catholic League army was in poor condition, still dependent upon supply, at inflated prices, via the Elbe and Oder from Wallenstein's Bohemian magazines. In addition, von Arnim, Tilly's outstanding subordinate, transferred from Imperial to Saxon employment to raise an army for Elector John George. At the end of January 1631 Tilly concentrated his forces before manoeuvring to contain Gustav within his Pomeranian beachhead. During February Gustav seized Mecklenburg. Tilly responded in March by pouncing upon and massacring the Swedish garrison in Neu-Brandenburg. Gustav rapidly

FRANCOFVRTVM AD VIADRVM·

assembled his army and marched towards Tilly at Neu-Brandenburg but, although superior in numbers, he hesitated, sought the wisdom of a cautious council of war, and a chance was missed.

This mistake sealed the fate of Magdeburg. Taking the advice of his second-in-command, Pappenheim, at the end of March Tilly upgraded the blockade of Magdeburg into a formal siege, safe in the knowledge that the city was effectively isolated because Gustav could not reach it without violating neutral Electoral Saxony, which he was unlikely to attempt as he could ill afford to antagonize potential allies. Contrary to Swedish expectations, the Imperial siege proceeded quickly and most of Magdeburg's outworks had fallen by early April. Gustav tried to draw Tilly away from Magdeburg, simultaneously improving his supply and strategic position, by operating against George William of Brandenburg. He struck southwards along the Oder, brushing aside weak garrisons before storming Frankfurt-an-der-Oder on 13 April. Although Gustav's cause was damaged when unpaid troops vented their frustration upon the Protestant population, the navigation of the Oder had been secured and the Swedes' eastern flank protected against attack from Poland.

Frankfurt fell too rapidly to distract Tilly from Magdeburg. Gustav now had no choice but to infringe both Saxon and Brandenburg neutrality by taking the direct route over the Elbe bridges at Wittenberg or Dessau. He advanced towards

When Frankfurt-an-der-Oder was stormed and sacked, the Swedes lost 800 men but the Imperial garrison of 3,000 was massacred along with many of the inhabitants. It took six days to bury all the dead and 'in the end they were cast by heaps in great ditches, above a hundred in every grave' (Robert Monro, Monro his expedition with the worthy Scots regiment call'd Mackays, London 1637*).*

Berlin, but George William would only accept Swedish garrisons in Spandau and Küstrin. Thwarted, Gustav moved to Potsdam and started to bully Elector John George into allowing him to march across Saxony; but it was too late. On 20 May Magdeburg was stormed, looted and burned: out of 20,000 inhabitants, only 5,000 survived. Gustav was in an awkward situation. He had lost his principal ally whilst Saxony and Brandenburg had resisted Swedish pressure. The sole comfort was negative: had Gustav succeeded in marching to Magdeburg he would have encountered superior Imperial forces and probable defeat.

On 11 June 1631 Gustav finally browbeat George

The siege of Magdeburg
1631

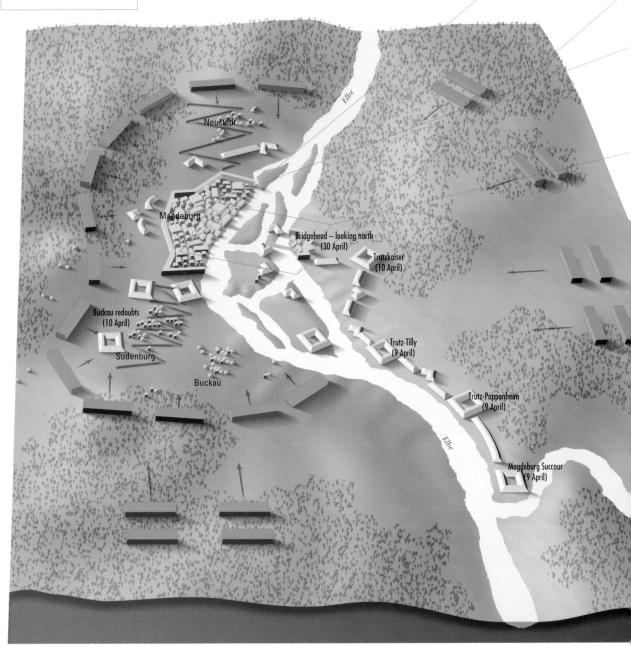

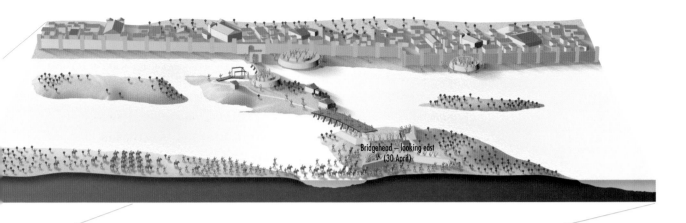

Bridgehead – looking east
(30 April)

THE SIEGE OF MAGDEBURG
SEPT 1630 – 20 MAY 1631

Magdeburg, showing the positions of Tilly's besieging forces and the defences east of the Elbe constructed by the defenders in the hope of maintaining communications with the Swedish army in Brandenburg.

Released from months of deprivation in the siege lines, Tilly's soldiers poured into Magdeburg. Most towns that resisted capture were sacked but Magdeburg was exceptional. Across Europe, the sack of Magdeburg was represented as a deliberate slaughter of Protestants by the Catholic forces of the Holy Roman Emperor.

THE FIRST BATTLE OF BREITENFELD
17 SEPTEMBER 1631

The defeat of Tilly's all-conquering army at Breitenfeld shocked rulers and generals in Western Europe, Gustav's earlier campaigns in Poland having been little regarded. The effectiveness of the Swedish Army presented the German Protestants with the powerful military tool they had previously lacked.

William into dividing Brandenburg into ten quartering districts each contributing 30,000 riksdaler per month to the Swedes. Having entered Germany without allies, invitation, or any clear idea of what he was going to do, Gustav was forced by strategic defeat to devise a policy. On the advice of Dr Jakob Steinberg, his adviser on German affairs, Gustav decided to seek victory on the battlefield and then form a league of Protestant states militarily bound to Sweden. Only then could military costs be met from German resources. Tilly, who had intended to use Magdeburg as a base and pivot for his campaign against Gustav, was the proud possessor of a heap of insanitary rubble. Unable to feed his men, he had to move, but his options were limited. Protestant principalities in southern Germany, especially Württemberg and Baden, were arming, and threatened to block the return of Imperial troops from the Mantuan war in northern Italy. William V of Hesse-Kassel was also preparing to take the field. Hoping to force Tilly to battle before he was reinforced from Italy, Gustav marched west from Brandenburg to cross the Elbe at Tangermünde, bringing him within reach of a new supply area. He then turned north to Werben, south of Wittenberge, where he excavated a fortified camp within a bend in the Elbe. Tilly advanced northwards from Magdeburg but could make no impression on the Swedish field fortifications and lost a cavalry engagement at Burgstall, to the west of Tangermünde. He withdrew on 29 July.

Tilly demanded that John George of Saxony disband his new

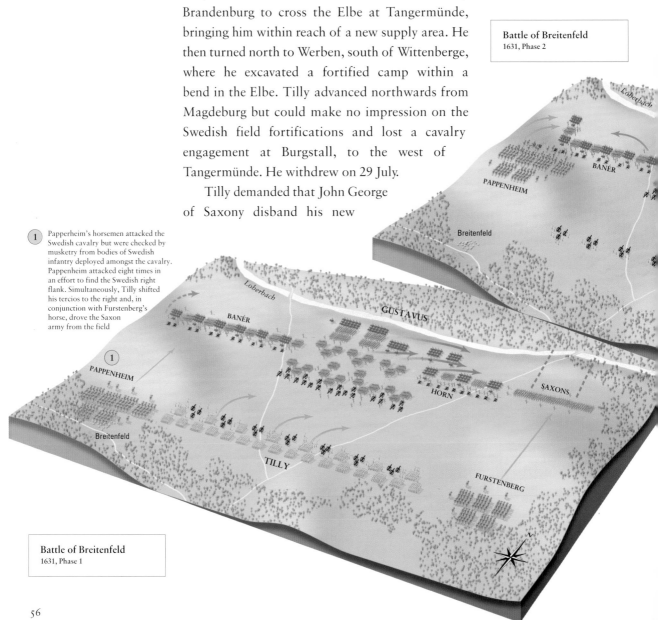

Battle of Breitenfeld
1631, Phase 2

1 Papperheim's horsemen attacked the Swedish cavalry but were checked by musketry from bodies of Swedish infantry deployed amongst the cavalry. Pappenheim attacked eight times in an effort to find the Swedish right flank. Simultaneously, Tilly shifted his tercios to the right and, in conjunction with Furstenberg's horse, drove the Saxon army from the field

Battle of Breitenfeld
1631, Phase 1

army, but he refused and opened negotiations with Sweden. Short of supplies, possibly through Wallenstein's continued awkwardness, on 25 August Tilly invaded Saxony, storming Merseburg and Leipzig. Gustav concluded an agreement with John George on 2 September that added 18,000 Saxons to his 24,000 Swedes. Gustav pushed down the Elbe from his camp at Werben and encountered Tilly's twenty-seven field guns and 31,000 men on 17 September at Breitenfeld, a village on the northern edge of modern Leipzig. The Imperial

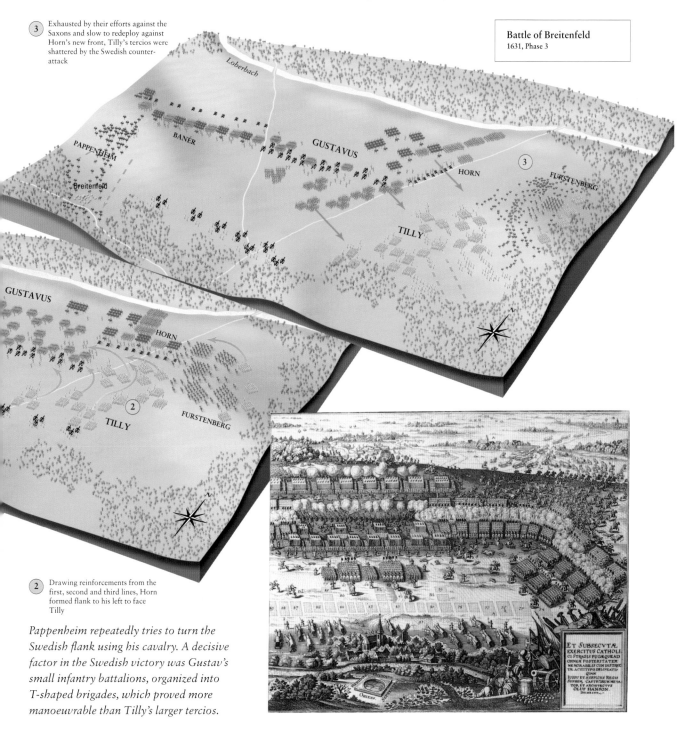

3 Exhausted by their efforts against the Saxons and slow to redeploy against Horn's new front, Tilly's tercios were shattered by the Swedish counter-attack

Battle of Breitenfeld
1631, Phase 3

2 Drawing reinforcements from the first, second and third lines, Horn formed flank to his left to face Tilly

Pappenheim repeatedly tries to turn the Swedish flank using his cavalry. A decisive factor in the Swedish victory was Gustav's small infantry battalions, organized into T-shaped brigades, which proved more manoeuvrable than Tilly's larger tercios.

infantry were arrayed across Tilly's centre in seventeen tercios, each fifty files wide and thirty ranks deep, whilst cavalry covered the flanks. The Swedish–Saxon force comprised two separate armies: von Arnim's 18,000 raw, untried Saxons took the left and the Swedes the centre and right. Both commanders deployed infantry in the centre flanked by cavalry. Unlike the Imperialists and Saxons, the Swedish infantry fought in six-rank, 500-man battalions each supported by a battery of four 3-pounder cannon. In addition, Gustav had fifty-one heavy field guns.

At dawn, amidst artillery salvoes, Pappenheim led forward the Imperial cavalry of the left, but the Swedish horsemen, supported by musketeers from the reserve, held them. In the meantime the Swedish infantry slowly advanced, firing. Tilly then attacked the Saxons and drove them from the field, exposing the Swedish left. General Gustav Horn, exploiting the flexibility and articulation of the battalion organization, formed front to his left flank, ordered reserves from the third line, and launched a vigorous assault on the closely packed tercios before they had time to recover from their exertions against the Saxons. After the Swedish cavalry had finally checked and defeated Pappenheim, who had made seven charges, the infantry, directed by Horn and Banér, advanced to crush the Imperial foot in a mêlée of musketry, cannon fire and hand-to-hand combat: 7,600 Imperialists were killed, 9,000 wounded or taken prisoner, and 4,000 deserted. Most of the prisoners 'accepted' immediate service in the Swedish Army.

Tilly, wounded, withdrew north-west, covered by Pappenheim. Three strategic choices opened before Gustav. He could advance on Vienna through Silesia; pursue Tilly into the Lower Saxon Circle (see p. 91); or march to the fertile lands of the Rhine and the Main in search of supplies and contributions. From necessity he selected the latter, leaving von Arnim and the Saxon army to campaign into Silesia and Bohemia, capturing Prague on 15 November 1631. Gustav reached Erfurt on 22 September, a major road junction in Thuringia whence he commanded extensive supply areas for an army already engorged as mercenaries flocked to a successful leader, and threatened Tilly's communications with his principal bases in Bavaria. By early October Gustav had reached the upper Main, seizing Würzburg on 4 October and its citadel, the Marienburg fortress, three days later. Meanwhile, Tilly had scraped together the Imperial garrisons in north Germany, collected stragglers, and effected a junction with the corps of Charles IV of Lorraine, a member of the Catholic League. Tilly marched south, feinted towards Gustav at Würzburg, then continued into winter quarters around Ingolstadt, the Danube fortress guarding the northern frontier of Bavaria. With Tilly removed, Gustav resumed his march, entering Frankfurt-am-Main on 17 November, Worms on 7 December, and Mainz on 12 December. The Elector-Archbishop of Mainz fled, along with the Bishop of Würzburg, whilst the Elector-Archbishops of Trier and Cologne appealed to France for protection. Richelieu was happy to oblige and placed French garrisons in the Trier fortresses of Ehrenbreitstein and Philippsburg, thus denying the line of the Moselle to Sweden and establishing a French military presence on the Rhine. In one campaign Gustav had marched from the estuary of the Oder to the Middle Rhine, defeated the fearsome Tilly, expanded his army, and placed his logistics on an improved footing. Extreme good fortune plus astute operations had made Gustav the dominant force in Germany.

Any opportunity to make trouble for Poland was impossible to resist, but Gustav was content merely to assist Tsar Mikhail Romanov of Muscovy (r. 1613–45). Gustav gave him permission to recruit troops in the Swedish-controlled portions of Germany, the Scottish mercenary Alexander Leslie raising 5,000 men in 1632. The Russian attack on Smolensk was unsuccessful and peace between Poland and Russia was signed at Polyanovka in June 1634. In 1635 French agents brokered a truce at Stuhmsdorf that kept the Poles and the Swedes from each other's throats for twenty years: Poland ceded Livonia to Sweden whilst the latter evacuated the Prussian ports, their tolls having been replaced by German revenues.

By Christmas 1631 Sweden ruled half Germany. Early in 1632 Oxenstierna arrived at Mainz from Prussia, where he had been governor, to administer the conquered territories. Over the winter Gustav recruited another 108,000 men to bring his total forces in Germany to 210,000. Such extravagance could not be long supported so a rapid end to hostilities was imperative.

Sweden's German 'empire' was a tenuous affair. Pomerania and Mecklenburg were connected to the main base at Mainz via a corridor through Thuringia controlled by the fortress of Erfurt, garrisoned by one of eight field armies. Another four armies, numbering 30,000 men, faced Pappenheim, who was operating from Hameln on the Weser against the western edges of Thuringia. Should Pappenheim sever the Erfurt corridor, Gustav's communications with the Baltic ports and Stockholm, plus the flow of supplies and money from north Germany, would be interrupted. However, the cause of the Imperialists and the Catholic League had collapsed: Sweden threatened Bavaria and occupied Würzburg, Mainz and Bamberg; France controlled Lorraine, Trier and Cologne; the Dutch had captured the Spanish treasure fleet off Cuba in 1628 and attacked Brazil in 1624–5 and 1630; and the fortresses of 's-Hertogenbosch and Wesel had been lost to Prince Frederick Henry of Orange.

THE RETURN OF WALLENSTEIN

In extremis, on 5 December 1631 Emperor Ferdinand reinstated Wallenstein. From his bases in Bohemia he rapidly raised 70,000 men and stood ready to advance against Electoral Saxony, Silesia and Thuringia but was restrained by von Arnim's army in and around Prague.

Returning to the field in March 1632, Gustav marched with 37,000 men from Nuremberg to Donauwörth, where he crossed the Danube intent upon crushing

Reverse of a silver medal struck in 1634 by Sebastian Dadler (1586–1657) to commemorate the successful defence of Smolensk by King Ladislas IV of Poland (r. 1632–48) against the Russians in 1633. By the Treaty of Polyanovka, June 1634, Russia renounced her claims to the city.

Tilly before moving on Vienna via Bavaria and Austria. Maximilian of Bavaria joined Tilly at Ingolstadt, but their combined army numbered only 22,000 men. Gustav could not afford to waste time and so, on 5 April, under cover of smokescreens, diversionary attacks and an artillery barrage, he threw a pontoon bridge over the Lech and forced a crossing. Carrying the mortally wounded Tilly, the Imperial–Bavarian army withdrew to the modern fortress of Ingolstadt whilst Gustav marched south down the Lech to Augsburg, which was forced to pay a monthly contribution of 20,000 riksdaler. While Maximilian was penned into Ingolstadt on the north bank of the Danube, Gustav devastated Bavaria, thereby augmenting his own supplies whilst denying them to Maximilian.

Having raped the country, Gustav intended to march east to Regensburg but Maximilian, leaving a strong garrison in Ingolstadt, slipped away and occupied the city. Gustav had anticipated that Wallenstein would march into Bavaria to relieve the pressure on Maximilian, but Wallenstein showed no sign of leaving Bohemia and thus maintained the threat to Saxony and Thuringia. A fleeting possibility of help for the Catholic League and the emperor occurred when the Spanish Army of the Netherlands took Speyer and a few places along the Lower Rhine in order to reopen the Spanish Road and protect it against Swedish depredations. However, in June the Dutch Army captured Venlo, Roermond, Straelen and Sittard, obliging Spain to recall her troops from the Palatinate.

Even worse, the Dutch then laid siege to the vital fortress of Maastricht, which commanded communications between the Spanish Netherlands and Westphalia. Despite an attack on the Dutch siege works by an Imperial relief army under Pappenheim, Maastricht fell on 23 August 1632. No assistance could be expected from Italy, where an epidemic of plague ravaged the northern provinces.

Gustav decided to secure Swabia as a forward base and supply area. Accordingly, having captured and thoroughly plundered Maximilian's capital of Munich, he marched west to Memmingen as a preliminary to turning towards Lake Constance. On 25 May 1632, while at Memmingen, he received intelligence that von Arnim had evacuated Prague on 15 May and was retreating from Bohemia, leaving Wallenstein free to manoeuvre against Saxony and the Erfurt corridor. On 4 June 1632 Gustav marched for Nuremberg, a rich city untouched by war, with 18,500 men, leaving the rest of his army to guard the Bavarian conquests and Swabian base. Gustav built a fortified camp abutting the modern fortifications, the 'Nuremberg Leaguer', flanking any advance by Wallenstein into Saxony. In reply, Wallenstein joined with Maximilian's army, bringing his total forces to 48,000 men, before marching north to build his own fortified camp at Zirndorf, just west of Nuremberg, to interfere with Swedish supplies from Bavaria and Swabia. Gustav and Oxenstierna summoned to Nuremberg all troops that could be spared from other sectors, enabling the Swedes to interdict Wallenstein's supply lines from Bohemia.

Gustav's supply situation was more critical, and he sought to solve the tactical conundrum by battle. The Imperial position stretched north–south along a ridge parallel to the River Rednitz. It could not be attacked from the east as Wallenstein's artillery covered all crossing-points. From the south and west the country was more hospitable but entirely lacked roads capable of supporting artillery. To the north the ridge rose to a hill, the Alte Feste, which lay just outside the perimeter of Wallenstein's camp, before tumbling in rocky slopes and thick woodland towards the town of Fürth. On the night of 22/23 August Gustav moved his command to Fürth, but Wallenstein anticipated his move and drew up his whole army in line of battle on the northern edge of his leaguer. Thinking that Wallenstein was withdrawing westwards and that he faced only a rearguard, early on 24 August 1632 Gustav sent his cavalry to interfere with Wallenstein's supposed retreat and launched his infantry against the Alte Feste. All day the Swedish infantry sweated up the steep slopes, but they were unable to develop their full firepower because the infantry guns could not be deployed. Despite sacrificing 2,400 men, the Swedes failed to take the Alte Feste; Wallenstein lost only 600. The myth of Swedish invincibility was severely dented.

Back at Fürth, supplies ran low, disease broke out, and within two weeks one-third of Gustav's fickle mercenaries had deserted. Leaving Oxenstierna to hold Nuremberg, he marched on 8 September uncertain of the next move. Wallenstein had won the war of position.

Gustav crossed the Danube into Swabia on 26 September and then threatened Ingolstadt, but neither operation was sufficient to deflect Wallenstein, who was preparing to unite with Pappenheim, crush the Swedes in the Lower Saxon Circle, and then overwhelm John George of Saxony. On 10 October at Nördlingen Gustav received intelligence that Pappenheim and Wallenstein were still separated, Maximilian was returning to Ingolstadt, and the corps of Generals Holck and Gallas had been detached from Wallenstein's main army. There was a chance for Gustav to exploit Wallenstein's imbalance. A week later, after learning that Wallenstein had invaded Saxony – Leipzig fell on 1 November – he covered 630 kilometres in seventeen days to secure the Thuringian passes before Pappenheim.

Despite his speed, Gustav would have been too late had not Bernard of Saxe-Weimar moved his army into the area and stood firm until Gustav joined him at Arnstadt, south of Erfurt. Another dash to the north-east by the combined armies of Gustav and Bernard guaranteed the crossing of the Saale at Naumburg, where Gustav built a fortified camp within a bend of the river. Wallenstein approached, but after hovering for a fortnight decided that the Swedes had taken winter quarters. Accordingly, on 14 November he dispersed his forces into seasonal billets suitably located to enable his men to cut Gustav's communications and ruin his supply areas. Pappenheim's corps of nine regiments was dispatched to Halle, 30 kilometres to the north.

Wallenstein had misread Swedish intentions. Gustav marched from Naumburg on 16 November to attack Wallenstein's headquarters at Lützen,

The battle of Lützen, 16 November 1632. This engraving by Mattheus Merian, Theatrum Europaeum *(1637), is an example of the unreliability of contemporary illustration: the topography is inaccurate and Wallenstein's infantry deployed in Swedish-style battalions rather than tercios. In this scene, after the death of Gustav, Pappenheim's cavalry has arrived on Wallenstein's left whilst the Swedish left towards Lützen village is coming under severe pressure from Piccolomini's horsemen.*

27 kilometres distant to the north-east and 9 kilometres south-west of Leipzig. When crossing the River Rippach he skirmished with an Imperial detachment, which both delayed his advance and gave Wallenstein sufficient notice to summon his dispersing forces to march on Lützen.

Wallenstein could recover only about 19,000 men to face a similar number of Swedes. Pappenheim received Wallenstein's recall order at Halle around midnight on 16 November, and although he marched immediately with his cavalry, leaving the infantry to follow six hours later, he was not expected on the battlefield before midday. Fixing his right on a line of windmills near Lützen Castle and village, Wallenstein extended his centre along the foot of a valley behind a sunken road and ditch which he lined with musketeers, but his left was unanchored, awaiting the arrival of Pappenheim. To his rear, Wallenstein formed his baggage and supply train into a 'wagon-laager', a line of heavy wagons linked by iron chains, a tactical device perfected by the Hussites and much used on the Polish and Ukrainian steppes. Not only did this constitute a final line of defence for his infantry, but it caused uncertain mercenaries to think twice before quitting the

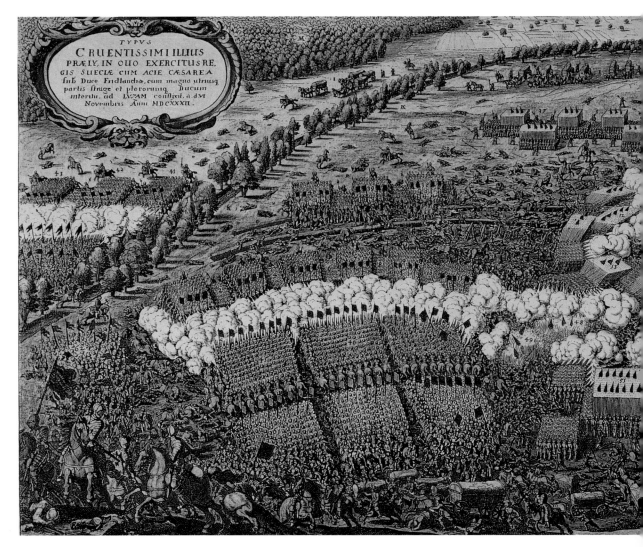

field. Wallenstein learned quickly: no longer was his infantry arrayed in tercios but in Swedish-style battalions.

Appreciating the weakness in the Imperial position, the Swedish army was ready to attack at 7 a.m. but fog was slow to clear and operations did not begin until 11 a.m. Although he had been denied four vital hours, it was still possible for Gustav to snatch a rapid victory. His foot advanced across the sunken road and ditch to fix the Imperial infantry while Gustav's right began to envelop Wallenstein's unsupported left. Progress was encouraging until, about noon, Pappenheim appeared with his cavalry and immediately launched an attack to restore the situation on Wallenstein's left. Pappenheim fell, struck by a cannon ball early in the attack, and an Imperial regiment deserted: signs of panic were evident in the disintegrating Imperial left, and the Swedish centre pressed forward and captured seven of Wallenstein's cannon.

The battle was virtually over when fog descended, hiding the chaos on the Imperial left, leaving Gustav unaware of the propinquity of complete victory. The Swedish attack on Lützen village on the Imperial right, the strongest section of

OVERLEAF: *An episode from the battle of Lützen, 16 November 1632, by Palamedes Palamedesz (1607–38). The figure in the centre is presumed to be Gustav II Adolf riding his white charger, Streiff, at the head of the Småland cavalry regiment.*

their line, stalled, and Gustav led forward the Småland cavalry regiment to inject momentum. Gustav was shot three times, fatally, and command of the army passed to Bernard of Saxe-Weimar. Ottavio Piccolomini led his cuirassiers against the Swedish right in a series of vigorous charges that threatened to become overwhelming but the Swedish centre held on the far side of the road and ditch, assisted by a battery of heavy field guns in the middle of the line, while the left worked forward to capture the Lützen windmills.

By dusk at 5 p.m. the keys to Wallenstein's position had fallen, all his cannon were lost, and only hard fighting by the Imperial infantry prevented a Swedish breakthrough. Pappenheim's infantry arrived around midnight but Wallenstein had already decided to abandon the field. He had lost over half his army; the Swedes about one-third.

Even in 1630, mercenaries had comprised half the Swedish Army, although they were mostly deployed in Livonia, leaving the native conscripts to sail for Germany. By 1631 three-quarters of the Swedish army in Germany was mercenary, and in 1632, when Gustav's total forces in Germany had reached 150,000, nine-tenths. Lützen and the Alte Feste ruined the native army. The domestic conscription system functioned erratically, whilst the German replacements and mercenaries could not deliver the high standards of drill and discipline required to implement Gustav's tactics. After 1632 Sweden's military edge was blunted.

Money was also a persistent problem. In peacetime, native Swedish levies drew their wages from the farms where they were based, the farmer deducting that sum from his taxes. In wartime, the king paid his native soldiers only a small monetary wage, the balance coming from contributions levied upon occupied territories. Mercenaries had to be paid either directly from the Swedish treasury or, preferably, also out of contributions. From the landing at Peenemünde, this issue, plus its close relative, supply, dominated Swedish policy and decision-making. Gustav's death made possible a political settlement in Germany, but the cost of demobilizing the Swedish Army and its numerous contractors was too high for the princes, both Catholic and Protestant, to accept.

Although he forced 8,000 Swedish troops under the Bohemian Count Thurn to surrender at Steinau in Silesia on 10 October 1633, Wallenstein had outstayed his rehabilitation. Mistrusted by Emperor Ferdinand, who strongly suspected that he was using the Imperial Army to pursue his own, private agenda in Germany, Wallenstein was murdered by Scottish, Irish and English mercenary officers in the Bohemian frontier fortress of Eger on 25 February 1634.

Ferdinand then summoned his son, Ferdinand of Hungary, the future Emperor Ferdinand III, to command the Imperial armies, but actual control rested with Gallas, who was rewarded with Wallenstein's duchy of Friedland. In 1634 Sweden and Saxony launched a double-pronged offensive. Von Arnim and the Saxons invaded Silesia and Bohemia, arriving again beneath the walls of Prague. In the meantime, the army of Sweden and the League of Heilbronn, principally

Brandenburg plus the Swabian, Franconian, Upper Rhenish and Electoral Rhenish Circles, commanded by Gustav Horn and Bernard of Saxe-Weimar, attacked Bavaria. The fortress of Landshut, north-east of Munich, was captured and Johann von Aldringen (1588–1634), a Luxembourger who succeeded Tilly in command of the Catholic League–Bavarian army, killed. However, Ferdinand of Hungary recaptured Donauwörth and Regensburg during July, thus re-establishing communications between Bavaria and the Habsburg lands in Austria. Von Arnim withdrew from before Prague, and on 30 July Ferdinand besieged the Protestant city of Nördlingen and awaited the arrival of the Cardinal-Infante Ferdinand of Austria (1609–41), governor of the Spanish Netherlands, who was marching with 15,000 Spanish troops from northern Italy. The two Ferdinands united on 2 September, before the arrival of the Swedes under Horn and Bernard, and constructed a fortified camp in the hills south of Nördlingen. They had 35,000 men, whereas the Swedes, who had been obliged to send substantial reinforcements into Poland following Russia's withdrawal from the War of Smolensk, had 10,000 fewer.

In the two-day battle of Nördlingen (5–6 September 1634) the Swedes were badly beaten, losing 12,000 casualties, of which 4,000 were prisoners including Horn. Bernard led the remnants into Alsace. The Swedish position in Germany collapsed – all garrisons south of the Main were abandoned, the Heilbronn League disintegrated – but the most important outcome was that France could no longer hide behind Sweden. A Spanish attack on French-garrisoned Trier spurred Richelieu to declare war on Spain on 19 May 1635. Anxious for reconciliation, Bavaria, Saxony, Brandenburg, Mainz, Cologne, Hesse-Darmstadt, Mecklenburg, Trier, Lübeck, Frankfurt-am-Main and Ulm signed the Peace of Prague with the emperor. Under the terms of the peace, all the princely armed forces were gathered into a single Imperial Army – the electors would continue to command

THE FIRST BATTLE OF NÖRDLINGEN
5–6 SEPTEMBER 1634

Defeat at Nördlingen finally shattered the illusion of Swedish invincibility and ended the territorial conquests begun in 1630. Not until the early 1640s, after France had weakened the Imperial armies, was Sweden able to reassert her military power in central Germany and Bohemia.

their own contingents but only as Imperial generals – the Edict of Restitution was suspended for forty years, alliances between princes of the empire were forbidden, and the supremacy of the emperor was recognized. In August 1635 unpaid mutinous soldiers in Swedish service held Oxenstierna hostage in Magdeburg and released him only when promised that arrears would be met from Sweden herself if money could not be prised out of Germany. France's war against Spain diverted Habsburg resources from northern Germany and allowed Sweden to recover.

Richelieu allied with the Dutch Republic, Savoy, Mantua and Parma. Between 1634 and 1636 the French Army contained about 9,500 horse and 115,000 foot, divided amongst field armies in the Spanish Netherlands, northern Italy, Lorraine and Franche-Comté, but there were insufficient troops to meet commitments in Germany. This hole was plugged by Bernard of Saxe-Weimar, who agreed to leave Swedish service and maintain an army of 18,000 men for France in Germany at an annual cost of 1,600,000 taler. Wastage was considerable. Of the 26,000 French soldiers consigned to the Spanish Netherlands in 1635, only 8,000 remained at the end of the campaign.

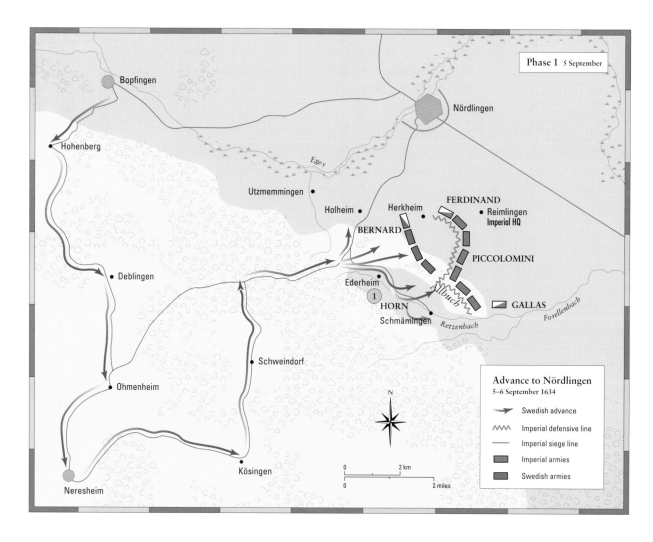

Between November and December 1635, Banér, commander of the Swedish army in Germany, and Lennart Torstensson, the artillery commander, beat the Saxons in a series of actions preparatory to striking down the Elbe and Saale towards Naumburg in the spring. Spain replied with an offensive against France in the summer of 1636 during which Gallas invaded Lorraine and Franche-Comté. Piccolomini, with troops from the Spanish Netherlands, was halted only at Corbie on the Somme, a mere 130 kilometres from Paris.

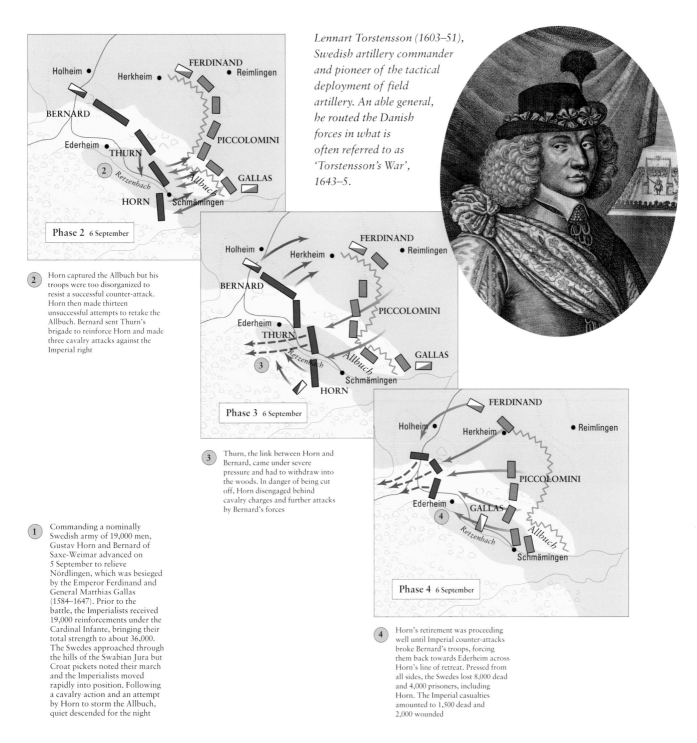

Lennart Torstensson (1603–51), Swedish artillery commander and pioneer of the tactical deployment of field artillery. An able general, he routed the Danish forces in what is often referred to as 'Torstensson's War', 1643–5.

Phase 2 6 September

② Horn captured the Allbuch but his troops were too disorganized to resist a successful counter-attack. Horn then made thirteen unsuccessful attempts to retake the Allbuch. Bernard sent Thurn's brigade to reinforce Horn and made three cavalry attacks against the Imperial right

Phase 3 6 September

③ Thurn, the link between Horn and Bernard, came under severe pressure and had to withdraw into the woods. In danger of being cut off, Horn disengaged behind cavalry charges and further attacks by Bernard's forces

① Commanding a nominally Swedish army of 19,000 men, Gustav Horn and Bernard of Saxe-Weimar advanced on 5 September to relieve Nördlingen, which was besieged by the Emperor Ferdinand and General Matthias Gallas (1584–1647). Prior to the battle, the Imperialists received 19,000 reinforcements under the Cardinal Infante, bringing their total strength to about 36,000. The Swedes approached through the hills of the Swabian Jura but Croat pickets noted their march and the Imperialists moved rapidly into position. Following a cavalry action and an attempt by Horn to storm the Allbuch, quiet descended for the night

Phase 4 6 September

④ Horn's retirement was proceeding well until Imperial counter-attacks broke Bernard's troops, forcing them back towards Ederheim across Horn's line of retreat. Pressed from all sides, the Swedes lost 8,000 dead and 4,000 prisoners, including Horn. The Imperial casualties amounted to 1,500 dead and 2,000 wounded

Ottavio Piccolomini (1599–1656), Duke of Amalfi and Imperial field marshal. He served several masters during the Thirty Years War, including Wallenstein, before directing the embryonic Austrian standing army 1651–6.

On 4 October 1636 a combined Imperial–Saxon army of 25,000 men under Hatzfeld intercepted Banér and Torstensson, with about 18,000 soldiers, in wooded hills south of Wittstock in Brandenburg, 93 kilometres north-west of Berlin. Banér dispatched half his force on an 11-kilometre flank march against the enemy's rear, while with the remainder he seized and held a hill before the enemy's line in order to pin them in position. Although outnumbered by fifty squadrons to seventeen, the Swedish cavalry resisted the Imperialists from mid afternoon until sunset, at which point the pressure was relieved when the flanking corps struck the Imperial–Saxon army in its rear and flank. Assaulted from three sides, the Imperial–Saxon troops collapsed and fled. In a vigorous pursuit on the following day the

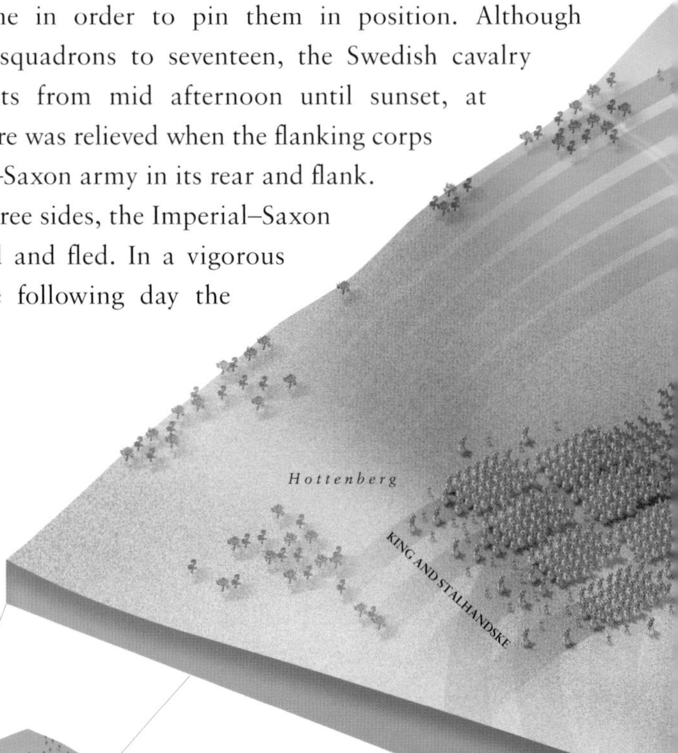

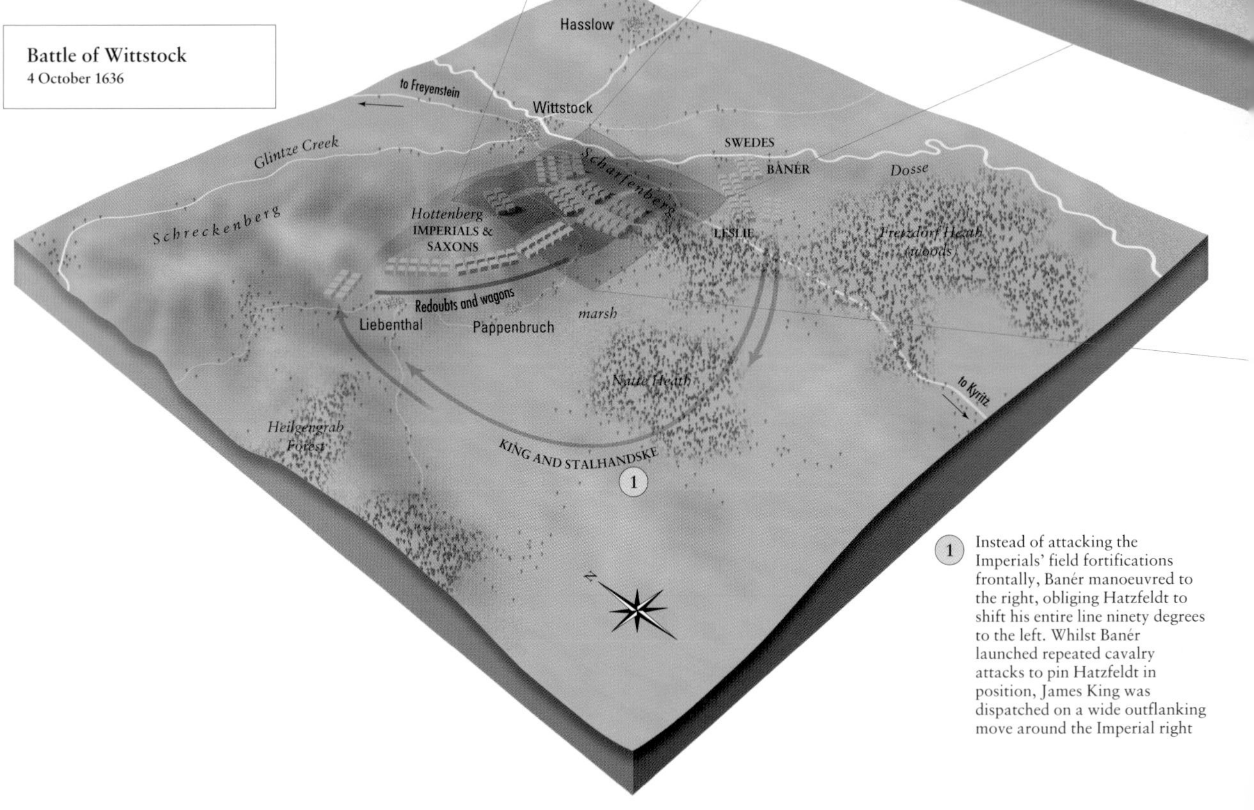

Battle of Wittstock
4 October 1636

Hotttenberg

KING AND STALHANDSKE

Hasslow

to Freyenstein

Wittstock

SWEDES

BANÉR

Dosse

Glintze Creek

Scharfenberg

LESLIE

Freudorf Heath (woods)

Schreckenberg

Hottenberg
IMPERIALS &
SAXONS

Redoubts and wagons

marsh

Liebenthal   Pappenbruch

Naute Heath

to Kyritz

Heiligengrab
Forest

KING AND STALHANDSKE

(1)

N

(1) Instead of attacking the Imperials' field fortifications frontally, Banér manoeuvred to the right, obliging Hatzfeldt to shift his entire line ninety degrees to the left. Whilst Banér launched repeated cavalry attacks to pin Hatzfeldt in position, James King was dispatched on a wide outflanking move around the Imperial right

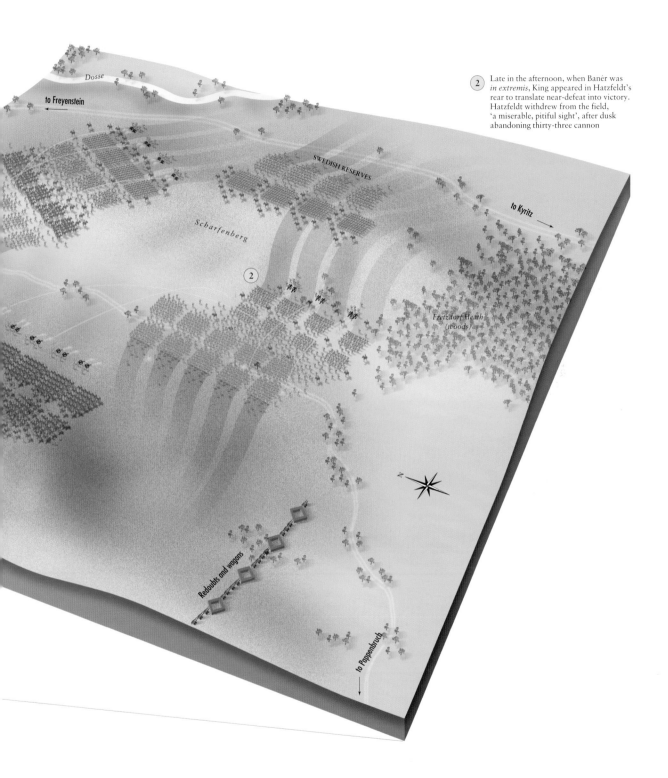

(2) Late in the afternoon, when Banér was *in extremis*, King appeared in Hatzfeldt's rear to translate near-defeat into victory. Hatzfeldt withdrew from the field, 'a miserable, pitiful sight', after dusk abandoning thirty-three cannon

Dosse

to Freyenstein ←

Scharfenberg

SWEDISH RESERVES

to Kyritz →

(2)

Fretzdorf Heath (woods)

Redoubts and wagons

to Poppenbruch

BATTLE OF WITTSTOCK, 4 OCTOBER 1636

Johan Banér, his subordinates claimed, was a better soldier drunk than sober. Skilled at extracting the maximum from under-strength and poor quality forces, his decision at Wittstock to risk dividing his forces was the only means by which his moth-eaten troops could have achieved victory.

Soldiers plundering a farmhouse, by Sebastian Vrancx (1573–1647), painted c. 1600. This scene from the Eighty Years War between Spain and the Dutch Republic could have applied to any contemporary conflict. Unpaid and poorly disciplined soldiers regularly looted civilians, making no distinction between friend and foe. The opportunity to plunder was one of the sinews that held mercenary armies together. Improved logistics during the final quarter of the century brought some alleviation.

Imperial–Saxon army was destroyed and Sweden regained control of Pomerania, Brandenburg, Saxony and Thuringia. In January 1637 Banér advanced to besiege Leipzig but was repulsed, and Imperial and Saxon forces under Gallas drove him back to Pomerania where, short of both money and supplies, the Swedish army then cowered for over twelve months.

Gallas's pursuit of Banér gave Bernard of Saxe-Weimar an opportunity in south-west Germany. Marching east along the Rhine from his winter quarters around Basel, Bernard attacked a Bavarian–Imperial army at Rheinfelden in Swabia and exploited his victory by taking the fortresses of Rheinfelden, Neuenburg and Freiburg-im-Breisgau, before besieging Breisach, a key post on the Spanish Road (June to December 1638). Master of Alsace, Bernard then sought to consolidate his gains into a personal duchy but he died of smallpox on 18 July 1639 before reaching agreement with Richelieu. His Bernese lieutenant general, Hans Ludwig von Erlach (1595–1650), promptly sold Bernard's Alsatian possessions to France, thereby improving Richelieu's strategic position. Like Bernard, Banér probably dreamed of acquiring a German principality but died in 1641 before realizing this ambition.

CONTINUING DEVASTATION

The war in Germany was losing political direction. Armies campaigned simply to conquer territory and levy contributions sufficient to support themselves and aggrandize their commanders. The adage of Gustav and Richelieu that 'war must pay for war' had mutated to 'war is the purpose of war'. Desperately searching for money and food for their largely mercenary forces, Swedish commanders often acted on their own initiative, ignoring the instructions of Oxenstierna, whose authority diminished substantially after Queen Christina achieved her majority in 1644. During this period the most extensive destruction and depredation occurred. The ravagings by Tilly, Wallenstein and Gustav had stripped large stretches of Bavaria, north Germany and the Rhine valley of supplies and population, but at least the contribution system imposed some kind of order on military demands. After the mid 1630s depredation became an end in itself, with all soldiers struggling for a share of what remained of German resources. Garrisons, some Brobdingnagian, many Lilliputian, dotted across the country did most of the damage because each depended for supplies upon dominating its local hinterland; incursions by large armies were relatively

The graphic artist Jacques Callot (1592/3–1635) published two sets of drawings: Les Misères et Malheurs de la Guerre *(Paris, 1633 and 1639). There was a tradition, dating from the early sixteenth century, of governments and religious denominations commissioning and publishing accounts and illustrations of atrocities as propaganda. Callot was unusual in that his drawings appear to have been motivated by no special interest other than social commentary.*

infrequent and were possible only through less ravaged regions. To add to these burdens, all states demanded greatly increased taxation to meet escalating military costs.

Historians have long debated the actual extent of the destruction visited upon Germany by the war: by any criteria, it was enormous. Perhaps one-quarter of the pre-war population of around 20 million people was lost, most to epidemics spread by armies and malnutrition, although numbers emigrated into Poland, Denmark, France, Switzerland and Italy. Bohemia had 3,000 fewer villages in 1648 than in 1618; Mecklenburg's 3,000 cultivated farms had been reduced to just 360 by 1640; Württemberg, occupied by Imperial and Bavarian troops between 1634 and 1638, had 450,000 inhabitants in 1620 but just 100,000 in 1639.

*Princes of the blood
assumed heavy military
responsibilities when very
young. The Prince de Condé
(1621–86) first commanded
in battle at Rocroi, 1643, at
the age of 22 and fought
his last at Seneffe in 1674,
when 53 and in poor health.
Victory at Rocroi gained
Condé a high reputation
that was belied by his
subsequent career.*

Not everyone suffered. Hamburg enjoyed a good war, benefiting from trade redirected from other ports, whilst Amsterdam grew rich on the Baltic grain trade and arms manufacture.

Torstensson led the Swedish army out of Pomerania to campaign deep in the Habsburg heartlands of Bohemia, Silesia and Moravia. During the spring of 1642 he marched through Saxony into Silesia, defeating John George's army at Schweidnitz, before entering Moravia, capturing the capital, Olmütz, in June. Vienna was threatened but Torstensson retired to besiege Leipzig: Emperor Ferdinand III's brother, the Archduke Leopold, and Piccolomini hurried to its relief. Torstensson withdrew a little to the north and offered battle at Breitenfeld where he repeated Gustav's earlier success. The Imperialists lost 10,000 men, forty-six cannon and their supply train, plus the archduke's treasury and chancery. Leipzig fell in December, remaining in Swedish possession until 1650. Breitenfeld was the last in a series of Habsburg disasters: Breda had fallen to the Dutch in 1637, who also destroyed two Spanish fleets during 1639, one in the Downs and the other off Recife; in 1640 Catalonia rebelled, aided by the French, and Portugal declared its independence from Spain, beginning a war that was to run until 1668. Arras and Artois were lost to France in 1640; Salces and Perpignan in 1642.

France was principally concerned with Spain. In the spring of 1643 Don Francisco de Melo, governor-general of the Spanish Netherlands from 1641 to 1644, encouraged by news of Richelieu's demise, invaded France. Crossing the border with 19,000 infantry and 8,000 cavalry, he besieged the small fortress of Rocroi, which commanded the confluence of two routes to Paris, one through Reims, the other via Soissons. The French government sent a relief force of 17,000 foot and 6,000 horse under the 22-year-old Condé. The approach on the Reims road ran through a wooded defile, but Condé's passage on 18 May was uncontested and the armies drew up in line of battle on the plateau to the south of the town, Melo's army depleted by the forces he was obliged to leave in the siege works around Rocroi. Both armies deployed their infantry in two lines, staggered so that the tercios in the second line covered the spaces in the first, with cavalry on the flanks, but Condé had sufficient troops to enable him to form a third, reserve line comprising horse and foot. Probably this was intended to cover the anticipated arrival of 6,000 Spanish reinforcements.

At dawn on 19 May Condé launched cavalry attacks to either flank. On the right the French swept away the Duke of Albuquerque's horse and turned to attack the Spanish infantry in the flank, but the reverse occurred on the left, where the Spaniards proceeded to drive in the exposed wing of the French foot. Intervention by Condé's reserve prevented collapse but the situation was not stabilized until Condé brought his successful cavalry around the rear of the Spanish army and assaulted the attacking forces from behind.

BATTLE OF ROCROI, 19 MAY 1643

Following successful cavalry charges by Isembourg on the Spanish right and Condé on the French right, the latter won the battle by keeping his horsemen in check, riding across the rear of the Spanish infantry, and attacking Isembourg's cavalry from behind. Once the Spanish horse had been defeated, Condé's artillery opened gaps in the Spanish tercios that were exploited by his horsemen.

Battle of Rocroi
19 May 1643

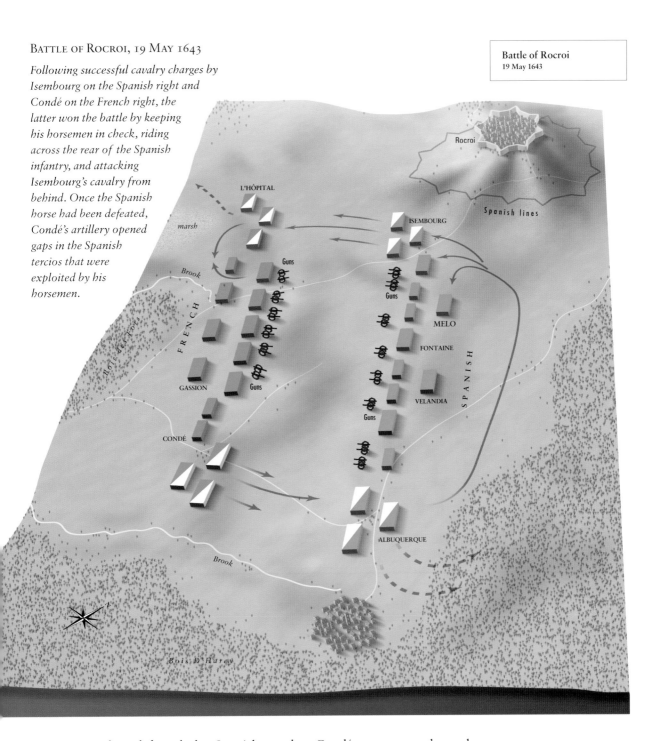

Having thus defeated the Spanish cavalry, Condé concentrated on the infantry. Musketeers and artillery opened gaps in the tercios that were then exploited by the horsemen. After three assaults the Spaniards surrendered. Condé lost 4,000 men: Melo suffered 7,000 casualties, whilst 8,000 of his men were taken prisoner.

As the Habsburg cause declined, Sweden turned from Germany to deal with Christian IV of Denmark. Early in 1643 the Swedish royal council decided to end Denmark's intrigues and machinations by depriving her of control over the Sound

The Thirty Years War
1640–48

Swedish campaigns, with dates

- Banér
- Torstensson
- Wrangel
- other Swedish campaigns

other campaigns, with dates

- Austrian
- French
- Dutch
- George Rákóczy, Prince of Transylvania
- Swedish victory
- Swedish defeat
- towns captured by Swedes, with date
- towns captured by French, with date
- towns captured by Dutch, with date
- siege
- border of Holy Roman Empire
- Spanish Habsburg territories
- Austrian Habsburg territories

0   100 km
0   100 miles

N

North Sea

SWEDEN

Kristiansand

Gothenburg

Baltic Sea

Arhus

Copenhagen • Malmö

DENMARK

Stralsund
1644
Wismar POMERANIA
Stettin

Hamburg
1643
Emden

Bremen
Verden 1643

NETHERLANDS
Amsterdam
Hanover
Magdeburg
1644
BRANDENBURG
Berlin
1648
Jüterbok
Nov. 1644
1647
1644

Ghent
1644
Rotterdam Venlo
1646
Hulst Breda
1645 1644–5 1637
Dunkirk 1646
1646

Düsseldorf
Cologne

Wolfenbüttel
29 June 1641
Breitenfeld
2 Nov. 1642
Leipzig
SAXONY
1642
Breslau
POLAND

Antwerp

Brussels
1645
SPANISH
Arras NETHERLANDS
1640

Rhine

Giessen
1646
Erfurt
1640
1640
1646
Frankfurt
1642
1646
Triebel
25 Aug.
1647
Prague
1645
1642
Schweidnitz
9 June 1642
Cracow

Rocroi
19 May 1643
Luxembourg
1645
Herbshausen
4 May 1645
Heidelberg
1643
Allerheim
3 Aug. 1645
1645
Nuremberg
Pilsen
BOHEMIA
Jankov
6 March 1645
1645
Olmütz
1642
Brno
1645
1642

F
R
A
N
C
E

Mannheim
Strasbourg
Stuttgart
1641
1647
Danube
1645
MORAVIA
1645
HUNGARY
Banska
Bystrica
Kosice
Szerencs
1644

Freiburg
3–4 Aug. 1644
Freiburg-im-
Breisgau
Tuttlingen
24–5 Nov. 1643
Zusmarshausen
17 May 1648
1645
BAVARIA
Munich
AUSTRIA
Krems
1645
Vienna
Bratislava
Levice
1644
Pest

Bregenz
1647
Salzburg
1648
Linz
STYRIA
Kösseg
Papa
1644

Dijon
FRANCHE-
COMTÉ
Basel
Zürich
SWISS
Berne
CONFEDERATION
CARINTHIA

Geneva

Lyon

SAVOY
Milan
CARNIOLA
Ljubljana
Zagreb
OTTOMAN

Casale
Pinerolo
1646
Genoa
Finale
Nice
Mantua
Modena
Bologna
REPUBLIC
OF
VENICE
Venice
Adriatic Sea
EMPIRE
Belgrade

IMPERIAL

Elbe

Rhône

and the provinces of Scania, Halland and Blekinge. In December Torstensson and the Brandenburg general Hans Christoff Königsmarck (1605–63) marched the Swedish army from Bohemia to the southern border of Jutland, from where Königsmarck overran the secularized bishoprics of Bremen and Verden while Torstensson invaded Holstein.

Early in 1644 Torstensson commenced the conquest of Jutland, a process that took only two months. Operating on the Scandinavian peninsula during February 1644, a second army under Horn occupied all of Scania except for Malmö and Kristianstad. Fifteen out of seventeen men-of-war in the Danish Navy were lost to the Swedes off the island of Femern in October 1644 and, although Torstensson temporarily abandoned Jutland because of supply problems, his lieutenant, Karl Wrangel, later reoccupied it and, in conjunction with a landing on the Danish islands, forced Christian to make peace. By the Treaty of Brömsebro of 1645, Sweden retained Halland for thirty years and took outright possession of Gotland and Oesel plus the Norwegian provinces of Jämtland and Härjedalen.

Ferdinand III had expected the Danes to resist the Swedes and sent 18,000 men under Gallas to help, but Sweden had formed an alliance with George Rákóczy, ruler of Transylvania from 1630 to 1648. Supported by his overlord, the Sultan of Turkey, and French money, he invaded Hungary in February 1644. Without an army, Ferdinand recalled Gallas, but Torstensson obliged him to retreat through ruined countryside and only 1,000 of the original corps of 18,000 troops returned to Bohemia, the remainder having deserted or died from starvation.

PEACE

Governments by this time had exhausted their resources, whilst populations were increasingly restless because of high taxation, depredations and conscription. Numerous peasant revolts had already broken out – Brandenburg–Kulmbach in 1632, France between 1636 and 1643, Lower Austria in 1635–6, Upper Austria in 1626 and 1632, and Styria in 1635 – whilst miniature wars between peasants and marauding soldiers were commonplace. There was a danger that law and order, indeed the entire deferential social hierarchy upon which political authority depended, might collapse. In 1642 a civil war broke out in England between the Parliament and King Charles I (r. 1625–49) which, although a contest amongst the governing classes about the location and limits of royal power, involved, prima facie, elements of social war.

Peace in Germany was difficult and complicated to arrange. By the Treaty of Hamburg of 1638, France and Sweden had agreed to make peace jointly, not separately. The initial sites for preliminary peace talks, Hamburg and Cologne, were replaced in 1643 by Protestant Osnabrück and Catholic Münster: the surrounding area was declared a 'demilitarized zone'. Invitations to all parties were sent in 1643 but serious negotiations did not commence until 1645.

Following the defeat of Denmark and the wrecking of Gallas's army, the

THE THIRD PHASE OF THE THIRTY YEARS WAR 1640–48

By 1640 marauding armies and garrisons had destroyed much of rural Germany, obliging the principal participants to support their troops by occupying new areas. Operating from Pomerania, the Swedes extended their conquests into Bohemia and Austria whilst France exported military costs by campaigning into Württemberg and the Palatinate.

OVERLEAF: The siege of Freiberg-im-Meissen, 1643. Freiberg, situated in the Erzgebirge south-west of Dresden, had grown rich and prosperous from its silver mines. The mint of Electoral Saxony until 1536, it suffered severely during the Thirty Years War because of its wealth and the fact that it lacked modern fortifications.

Habsburg heartlands were vulnerable. Early in the spring of 1645 Torstensson led 15,000 men equipped with sixty cannon into Bohemia and attacked a similar-sized body of Imperialists, commanded by Count Hatzfeld, on 6 March at Jankov, south-east of Prague. In a day-long battle, characterized by the speed and frequency with which the Swedish field guns were able to redeploy to give maximum fire support, Hatzfeld lost all his artillery and half his men; the Imperial Army was finished. After Jankov, said Oxenstierna, 'the enemy begins to talk more politely and pleasantly'. Ferdinand fled to Graz whilst Torstensson occupied Bohemia before moving to within gunshot of Vienna, threatening a siege. However, Transylvania defected from the alliance because the sultan had declared war on Venice over the possession of Crete. The 'Great Elector' of Brandenburg, Frederick William, had already signed a truce with Sweden, and John George of Saxony followed suit at the Truce of Kötzschenbroda on 6 September 1645.

The Bavarian–Imperial army was now the only field force left to the Habsburgs. Under Franz von Mercy this force had thrashed the French under Turenne at Tuttlingen on the Danube in November 1643. During the winter retreat Turenne lost almost two-thirds of his 16,000 men. Near Freiburg-im-

Breisgau in August 1644, as he attempted to break out of the Rhine valley through the Black Forest, Turenne was again defeated by Mercy. Turenne's invasion of Swabia in 1645 was blocked by Mercy at Bad Mergentheim in May. However, in the wake of Jankov, Swedish reinforcements reached Turenne, who then proceeded to attack Mercy at Allerheim on 3 August 1645. Mercy was killed and his army destroyed.

As operations diminished, attention was focused on the negotiators in Osnabrück and Münster. Spain and the Netherlands agreed the Treaty of Münster on 30 January 1648, ending the Eighty Years War and granting independence to the Dutch Republic. The Peace of Westphalia was signed at the lodgings of the Imperial ambassador in Münster on 24 October 1648 and ratified on 8 February 1649, France and Sweden acting as guarantors.

The peace gave Sweden Western Pomerania: the islands of Usedom, Rügen and Wollin; the port of Wismar in Mecklenburg; and the bishoprics of Bremen and Verden. (Eastern Pomerania went to Brandenburg.) By thus controlling the lower Weser, Elbe and Oder, Sweden was secured against invasion from Germany and able to dominate trade in the Baltic. Further, the acquisition of the ports of Stettin, Wismar, Stralsund and Greifswald established firm communications

The Dutch envoy, Adriaan Pauw, arriving at Münster, January 1646. In 1947 the German poets and writers of 'Group 47' discussed how culture could contribute to the rebuilding of Germany. In his novel The Meeting at Telgte, *Günther Grass has an earlier gathering of German literary figures meet in 1647 at Telgte, in the demilitarized zone between Catholic Münster and Protestant Osnabrück, to discuss how art might heal and transcend political and religious divisions.*

between Sweden and her new German possessions, as well as beachheads for future attacks upon Brandenburg and Poland. France took Upper and Lower Alsace, plus the bishoprics of Toul, Metz and Verdun, and acquired the right to garrison Breisach and Philippsburg. Maximilian of Bavaria gained both the Upper Palatinate and the dignity of becoming the eighth elector of the empire. Brandenburg, through the acquisition of the bishoprics of Halberstadt and Minden, two counties in the Harz Mountains, and the reversion of the bishopric of Magdeburg, built land bridges between her easterly territories and the Hohenzollern lands around Wesel and Jülich on the lower Rhine. Saxony received Lusatia.

Apart from the territorial issues, the peace also settled religious and constitutional questions. The Peace of Prague and the Edict of Restitution were repealed and the states of the empire were granted full sovereignty, including the right to maintain their own armed forces and to conclude alliances both with each other and with foreign powers. *Cuius regio, eius religio* was abandoned.

The most difficult question was the financial 'satisfaction' of the Swedish Army, whose generals put forward their own personal claims regardless of the positions taken by Oxenstierna and his diplomats. The Swedes demanded 20 million taler but the estates of the empire offered only 1.6 million. Eventually a compromise of 5 million taler was reached.

Seventeenth-century peace treaties were paper exercises. Once the ink was dry, a treaty had to be realized by commissioners working on the ground to establish and mark new frontiers and settle details. Under the direction of

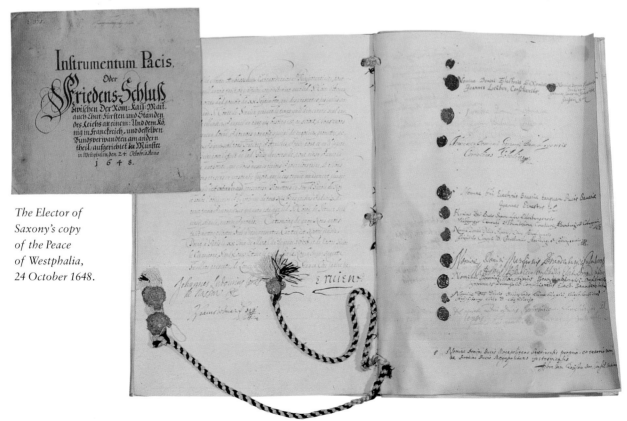

The Elector of Saxony's copy of the Peace of Westphalia, 24 October 1648.

Piccolomini the Congress of Nuremberg, which sat until July 1651, implemented the Peace of Westphalia by arranging the demobilization of the armies. Commencing later in 1648, small Catholic forces, such as those of the Archbishops of Cologne, Trier and Mainz, were disbanded on the issue of three months' pay. The Bavarian Circle was instructed to fund the arrears of the Bavarian Army, and in January 1649 all Imperial garrisons were withdrawn from Bavaria.

Real problems occurred in dealing with the big armies. The outbreak of aristocratic rebellion and civil war in France, the Frondes (1648–53), interrupted the flow of supplies and money to French troops in Alsace, resulting in the evaporation of discipline. In August 1649, 500 Imperial troops mutinied when ordered to evacuate Lindau on Lake Constance. Still occupying 127 garrisons in central and northern Germany, Swedish troops devoured 1,000,000 taler per month.

On 26 June 1650 Prince Charles Gustav of Zweibrücken, commander-in-chief of the Swedish Army and heir to the throne, and the Imperial representative, Ernest von Traun, agreed a timetable for the phased withdrawal of all Swedish troops in Germany. Complete demobilization took a long time. A Spanish garrison did not leave Frankenthal in the Palatinate until 1653 and the last Swedish soldiers were not withdrawn from the Baltic provinces until the following year.

The Congress of Nuremberg, 1649–51, implemented the Peace of Westphalia by arranging for the payment and demobilization of the armies. Piccolomini (centre at end of table) and Ernest von Traun (1608–68), for the Imperialists, and Prince Charles Gustav of Zweibrücken, the future Charles X of Sweden (on Piccolomini's left), played leading roles.

CHAPTER TWO

THE RISE OF THE STANDING ARMY 1648–1700

A CHILD'S ARMOUR (Italian, c. 1645). Similar sets can be seen in the Landeszeughaus, Graz. Child officers, sometimes as young as 10 or 11, normally served as cadets in a relative's company. However, it was rare to find children under the age of 16 or 17 serving in the rank and file, probably because the pike and musket were so heavy that only adults could handle them.

THE RISE OF THE STANDING ARMY 1648–1700

'WAR PAYING FOR WAR' implied depredation, contribution, and the despoliation of agriculture. Not only was the economy impaired, but a marauding soldiery forfeited the discipline vital for the implementation of the Dutch–Swedish combat drills. A partial answer was the adoption of the standing army, but it was not a panacea. Rhinelanders experiencing the two French 'Devastations of the Palatinate' (1672–4 and 1688–9) or the Piedmontese during the Nine Years War (see Chapter 5) would not have realized that a new era of 'civilized' warfare had arrived. When soldiers were unpaid, the supply system broke down, or 'scorched earth' was deemed a useful operational device, armies became voracious predators. In the spring of 1694 the peasants of Brabant, certain that the French and Confederate armies would devour their crops, decided not to sow their fields.

Although France, Sweden and Spain had founded standing armies during the later sixteenth and early seventeenth centuries, after 1648 the trend intensified. Wars remained frequent and protracted, rendering reliance upon mercenaries expensive, but garrisoning sophisticated fortifications and defending frontiers – the concept of a linear border emerged during the seventeenth century – presented rulers with the new problem of meeting extensive peacetime commitments. The solution was to raise permanent troops and pay the bill from taxation.

Reciprocity, fashion and necessity also accounted for the spread of the standing army. After 1648 France became the dominant political, military and cultural force in Europe, and because Louis XIV expressed his power partly through the medium of a standing army, so others followed suit. Petty German rulers built Lilliputian Versailles in their capitals, and even Charles II of England constructed his own version near Winchester, close to the fortress, garrison and naval base at Portsmouth. Through his pursuit of personal glory, hatred of the Dutch, and rivalry with the Habsburgs, Louis XIV was perceived by the United Provinces, Spain and the Rhenish principalities as an enemy intent on forcibly amending the Peace of Westphalia. France, attacking with ever-larger armies in 1667–8, 1672–8 and 1688–97, was opposed by states obliged to augment their own forces. Smaller German states, which could raise only limited numbers of troops, sheltered within anti-French coalitions whose pillars – England, the Dutch Republic and Austria – recruited, or hired, large agglomerations of troops to counter French military establishments that climbed above 400,000 men during the 1690s.

Within a few years of the Peace of Westphalia, states began to organize permanent defence forces, often recruited from amongst urban militias, which remained serviceable as local police forces, and old feudal levies. Mercenaries continued to be employed but upon altered contractual bases. The Congress of Nuremberg reduced Bavaria's 20,000-strong army to a handful of household

Louis XIV, King of France (r. 1643–1715). During his reign, through the administrative skill of the Le Telliers, father and son, the French Army became the largest, strongest and most modern in Europe. Many West European armies imitated its organization and methods, although Sweden and Brandenburg were also influential.

troops and fortress garrisons, but by 1664 Elector Ferdinand Maria had accumulated a small standing army of 1,750 soldiers which gained experience fighting in the Imperial Army against the Turks between 1663 and 1664. Gradually, as the wars of Louis XIV exacerbated insecurities within Germany, the Bavarian Army grew, until by 1675, 8,000 men cost the state 1,200,000 guilders per annum.

Similarly, by the mid 1660s Saxony and Hanover could each boast small armies comprising about 5,000 troops. The forces of Hesse-Kassel were mostly disbanded in 1648, leaving just 600 infantry and forty horse guards, but Landgraves Wilhelm VI and Karl steadily augmented the army until in 1688 it stood at over 10,000 men. Unable to support so many, Karl rented detachments to Venice, the United Provinces and England.

Another tiny state insistent upon the new status symbol was Jülich–Berg, which possessed just 900 soldiers in 1648. Despite opposition from the Estates, the representative assembly, the army grew to 2,600 in 1672. Between 1672 and 1678 the Rhenish principalities were engulfed in the Franco-Dutch War and Jülich–Berg's little army was powerless to prevent French incursions that cost 500,000 talers in contributions. Following this débâcle, confidence in an army temporarily declined but soon recovered. By 1684 Jülich–Berg had an army of nearly 5,000 troops, all of whom were obliterated during the French invasion of 1688. However, between 1690 and 1715 Duke Johann Wilhelm reconstructed an army of 14,000 soldiers, 4,000 of whom were paid directly by the Dutch.

Electoral Saxony, a much larger entity, had acquired an army of 8,260 by 1675, reaching 20,000 in 1700, the second largest establishment in the empire. Württemberg developed a standing army of 2,000 men in the thirty years following the Peace of Westphalia. However, the largest of the new German standing armies belonged to Brandenburg–Prussia. The Brandenburg field forces had been reorganized in 1644 but most had been demobilized in 1649. Surrounded by enemies – Saxony, Austria, Russia and Sweden – and chastened by the ease with which his territories had been violated during the Thirty Years War, Elector Frederick William set about building a strong army. Between 1660 and 1672 he maintained a core of 12,000 troops, supplemented by a territorial reserve of discharged soldiers settled on royal lands. Participation in the Franco-Dutch War allowed the army to expand again, and by 1688 Frederick William had 30,000 men. At the death of King Frederick I in 1713 the strength of the Brandenburg–Prussian Army stood at 40,000 soldiers.

Between 1663 and 1679, Denmark relied upon a mixture of peasant conscripts and mercenaries. However, by 1700 Frederick IV possessed a standing army of 33,500, mostly German volunteers: 23,000 were stationed in Denmark and 10,500 in Norway.

After 1648, Holy Roman Emperor Ferdinand III sent some troops to fight for Spain against France in the Spanish Netherlands and northern Italy, but the majority of the Austrian Army was retained and dispatched into the crown lands and the Hungarian frontier. Commanded by the Italian veterans Montecuccoli and Piccolomini, this formed the embryo of the Austrian standing army.

Two major powers not directly involved in the Thirty Years War, England and Russia, also created standing armies along Franco-German lines. Established during the winter of 1644–5 to bring efficiency and professionalism to Parliament's war effort, England's New Model Army initially consisted of 7,600 cavalry, including one regiment of dragoons, and 14,400 infantry. The execution of Charles I in 1649 ushered in eleven years of republican rule during which the New Model, a standing force, was the fount of political authority. By July 1652 the Commonwealth government had over 70,000 men in arms in England, Scotland and Ireland, reducing to 53,000 in 1654, 42,000 in 1658, and 28,342 in 1660.

Frederick William, the Great Elector of Brandenburg from 1640 to 1688, began the reorganization of the Brandenburg Army in 1644, when governing from distant Königsberg. It passed its first test, in alliance with Sweden, at the battle of Warsaw in 1656. At his death, the army of 30,000, supported by an absolute monarchy and state bureaucracy, had enhanced Brandenburg's international prestige and defined the state by welding together the electorate's widely separated lands.

The restored monarch, Charles II, disbanded the New Model during 1660 and 1661 but, to secure his regime, re-raised a standing army of two foot and two cavalry regiments, plus a smattering of garrison companies: it had reached 8,865 by 1685, 19,778 in 1686, and 22,364 in 1688. To counter William of Orange's invasion in November 1688, the English Army was increased to 34,320 whilst during the Nine Years War (1688–97) it reached a peak of 93,635, of whom 27,000 were mercenaries. After the Peace of Rijswijk in 1697 the English standing army was reduced to cadre strength of 7,000 men. Separate standing armies existed in Ireland and Scotland, although these became effectively combined with the English establishment after 1688. The Irish Army numbered 8,644 in 1685: the minute Scottish standing army achieved a maximum strength of 2,754 in 1679.

Ivan the Terrible (r. 1547–84) founded a standing army in 1556 but the social institutions on which it was based had stagnated by the mid seventeenth century. Subsequent expansion into the Ukraine and towards the Baltic demanded a larger and more proficient force. In preparation for the Smolensk War (1632–4), 'new formation' regiments were established, recruited mainly from North-West Europe, trained in Western methods and commanded by foreign mercenaries: half the Russian army at Smolensk was of the 'new formation'. Beginning in 1647, some 'new formation' regiments were raised through conscription based on the census returns and officered by foreigners. These 'new formation' regiments, plus numerous mercenaries, served in the Thirteen Years War (1654–67), annexing Kiev and much of the Ukraine. By the 1670s Russia could field huge numbers, but of poor quality and low motivation. In alliance with the Holy League against the Turks, in 1687 and 1689 Russian armies of over 100,000 men marched south against the Crimea under Vasily Golitsyn but were unable to force the Isthmus of Perekop against only 15,000 Tatars. Around 1689 Peter I, 'the Great', formed two modern, Westernized regiments, the Preobrazhenski and the Semionovski Guards, organizational exemplars for the Westernization of the Russian Army. In 1695 Peter sent 30,000 'new foundation' troops and 120,000 'old troops' to attack Azov and open a route to the Black Sea. Two wild assaults failed, but in 1697 Peter returned with German and Austrian gunners and engineers and successfully

Peter I, 'the Great', Tsar of Russia (r. 1682–1725), set out to modernize his country's government and institutions. He toured Europe from 1696 to 1698, incognito, to absorb Dutch and English techniques of shipbuilding and military administration. Reorganized Russian armed forces secured victory over Sweden in the Great Northern War, 1700–21.

subjected Azov to a regular siege. Between 1699 and 1700 a new Russian standing army was born, a mixture of volunteers and conscripts, but the débâcle at Narva in 1700 meant that the exercise had to be restarted.

There was a clear distinction between garrison armies, defensive formations that manned permanent fortifications, and field armies consisting of marching regiments capable of active campaigning. Most of the smaller German and Italian establishments were of the former type. Francesco Farnese, Duke of Parma, raised 3,500 regulars in 1694, supplemented by a militia of 38,000, to garrison the city-fortresses of Parma and Piacenza to dissuade foreign armies, principally the Austrians, from marching through his territories and devouring their resources. Although the garrisons successfully defended the cities during the War of the Spanish Succession, they could not prevent French and Austrian forces fighting across the duchy for five years after 1702 and the Austrians from regularly taking up winter quarters until 1713. During the first decades of the eighteenth century the Papal States maintained a garrison army of 5,000 men, whilst Tuscany and Genoa each possessed 2,500 garrison troops. Status symbols of this size were of limited utility, although they provided the ruler with a police force and a reservoir of patronage.

In Italy only Piedmont developed a significant field army. Controlling the Alpine passes from France and Switzerland into the Po valley, Piedmont required means of self-defence as she was perpetually involved in disputes between France and the Habsburg holdings in northern Italy. Using funds from the *taille*, a tax paid in lieu of compulsory military service, Duke Emanuel Philibert (r. 1553–80) initiated a programme of modern fortification, manned by 3,000 troops, and created a small military household plus a militia of 24,000 men, one-third of which would fight beyond the frontiers. To supplement the militia and provide an effective field army, Duke Emanuel depended upon military enterprisers who were paid annual refreshers and admitted to the ducal court in return for supplying troops at short notice.

Going to war with Genoa in 1625, Duke Charles Emanuel I (r. 1580–1630) fielded 25,381 infantry (comprising mercenaries from France, Lorraine, Lombardy, the Papal States, Naples and Switzerland), 1,213 cavalry (mostly Piedmontese and Italian noblemen with their retainers), plus garrisons of 8,000 militiamen and 2,000 regulars. Thereafter, the strength of the army's professional core fluctuated: 12,250 when Piedmont entered the Thirty Years War in 1635 on the side of France; 15,710 in 1637; 18,000 in 1649; but a mere 5,400 on the return of peace in 1660. During the 1660s Duke Charles Emanuel II (r. 1637–75) created the first Piedmontese standing field army, consisting of eight battalions. To attack Genoa in 1672, mercenaries augmented this cadre to 26,178 men, including 2,000 hired from Bavaria. Although heavily defeated, Charles Emanuel did not disband his army at the termination of the war but leased his troops to Louis XIV, thus retaining his army but avoiding the cost. Charles Emanuel rotated officers through these regiments to gain combat experience in readiness for senior

Victor Amadeus II, Duke of Savoy, whose combination of velvet force and iron diplomacy preserved his duchy during the Nine Years War, in which Piedmont–Savoy was the decisive theatre. The duke's defection from the Grand Alliance in 1696 allowed France to pressurize Britain and the Dutch Republic in the theatre of the Spanish Netherlands and force them to make peace.

wartime commands. Duke Victor Amadeus II (r. 1675–1730) expanded the standing army to 8,000 during the 1680s and 23,000 in 1695.

Amidst these new armies, those of the Holy Roman Empire and Poland were anachronisms. Between 1500 and 1512 the empire was divided into ten military districts or circles, *kreise* – the Franconian, Swabian, Bavarian, Upper Rhenish, Electoral Rhenish, Westphalian, Lower Saxon, Upper Saxon, Austrian and Burgundian. When the emperor required a German army he summoned the

In southern Slavic languages, husar was a mounted knight. Polish hussaria ('winged horsemen') dominated Central and Eastern Europe battlefields throughout the century and were central to the relief of Vienna, 1683.

Army of the Circles, which, according to an edict of the Diet of Worms in 1521, was fixed at a minimum of 4,000 cavalry and 20,000 infantry, each circle making pro rata contributions in troops, money and equipment. This basic establishment of 24,000, known as the *simplum*, was revised upwards to 12,000 horse and 28,000 foot in 1681; when more troops were required, the *simplum* was doubled (*duplum*) or, more rarely, tripled (*triplum*). The *duplum* was invoked in 1683 when the Turks besieged Vienna and again in the winter of 1688–9 during the Devastation of the Palatinate. Some small states commuted their obligations into a money payment that was used to raise additional men from the larger polities.

Being impermanent, the Army of the Circles was normally ill-trained, badly disciplined and indifferently commanded. Larger states donated their worst regular units because they were usually under some political obligation or mercenary treaty opposed to Imperial interests.

Poland's vast territories stretched from the Baltic in the north to the borders of Hungary in the south and from Muscovy in the east to Austria and Brandenburg–Prussia in the west. Paradoxically, Polish society was substantially militarized, yet the state was unable to defend itself adequately against a ring of predatory neighbours. The principal difficulty was the size and political independence of the Polish nobility: by 1773, 12 per cent of Poles claimed noble status, and in the provinces of Podlasia and Mazovia there were more aristocrats than peasants. Not that there was much to distinguish one from the other: most nobles were as poor as peasants and sought protection by joining the private armies of the few rich magnates. The king could not compete, hence in Poland the 'monopoly of violence' remained with the nobility and did not migrate to the sovereign. Although royal rents financed a standing force, founded in 1564, the Sejm (the noble diet), fearful that the elected monarch would institute military rule, ensured that he was starved of additional funds. Thus this 'Crown Army', rarely larger than 30,000 men and formally established at 24,000 in 1717, was confined to frontier defence and never grew sufficiently to enhance royal authority. When John III Sobieski (1674–96) raised an army to help raise the Turkish siege of Vienna in 1683, his 25,000 troops were accumulated very slowly from amongst the feudal noble cavalry, foreign mercenaries, and the infantry of the Crown Army. A feature of Polish armies was their preponderance of cavalry, recruited from the ubiquitous nobility, instead of cheaper and more flexible infantry. By the early eighteenth century the ratio was as high as four horsemen to each foot soldier, when most European armies enjoyed an inverse proportion.

MANPOWER AND RECRUITMENT

Manpower consumed the greater part of national military budgets. Although a soldier's life was nasty, brutish, ill-rewarded and short, it was no worse than the world he had left behind, where toiling peasants and landless serfs starved in bad times, eked a bare living in better, and died young from epidemic diseases. Joining up, with the prospect of wages, food and plunder, might even have represented an improvement. Pay was so beggarly, and frequently months in arrears, that a soldier could not have supported himself from the basic daily remuneration of between 2½p and 4½p, but it was augmented by an array of ex gratia payments. There were supplements for labouring on fortifications; soldiers worked as servants for their officers; recruiting parties received extra money; the dangerous task of excavating siege trenches was richly rewarded; men moonlighted during their spare time; and troops collected the harvest, cleared snow from mountain passes, dug canals and built roads. Officers were expected to support their men financially during times of hardship. Although a soldier's remittance was eaten into by deductions to his officers to pay for clothes, basic equipment and medicine, the average infantryman could accumulate sufficient money to buy

Soldiers at Cards in a Guardroom, by Gerard Terborch (1617–81). In any age, soldiers spend most of their time fighting boredom rather than the enemy.

food and drink from the sutler's wagon, gamble, and own a suit of civilian clothes. A cavalryman earned about 12½p a day, from which he paid 2½p in deductions and had to maintain both himself and his horse from the remainder.

A soldier was more likely to die from disease than enemy action; infantrymen often served throughout a war without fighting in a pitched battle, although it was more difficult to avoid a siege. Within societies characterized by high levels of violence, soldiering was not especially dangerous.

Some armies relied upon conscription. In Poland, from 1578 every peasant community on royal land was obliged to send one of their number, fully armed, to serve in the infantry of the Crown Army; if he became a casualty, the village had to find a replacement.

Lacking sufficient economic and human resources, Scandinavian states were the first to regularize conscription in both peace and war. Gustav I Vasa of Sweden (1523–60) introduced limited conscription, *utskrivning*, in 1544. Every ten peasant farms on royal lands, or twenty on estates belonging to the aristocracy, were arranged into a 'file' (*rota*). Each *rota* had to provide one infantryman, aged between 18 and 40, and contribute towards the cost of his equipment. Commissioners supervised an annual conscription assembly, which had to be attended by all inhabitants: absentees were automatically drafted. Men who could be spared from agriculture were preferred, such as younger sons of farmers, although there were numerous exempt categories including miners, armaments workers, and only sons of widows.

Contrary to later practice, every effort was made to conscript undesirables. Conscripts were paid a small wage by the crown and given a plot of land by the *rota*. Results were disappointing: conscripts were reluctant to serve; peasants refused to give up their land; whilst the alienation of royal estates to the aristocracy undermined the scheme. The result was that Sweden continued to rely upon mercenaries. However, the *rota* system, which actually created a territorial rather than a standing army, probably inspired later schemes in Denmark, Brandenburg–Prussia, Hesse-Kassel and Austria.

During the reign of Charles XI, Swedish conscription was revised to solve a fundamental problem: how best to sustain a standing army in a poor, sparsely populated country from a public revenue, much of which was paid locally in kind rather than cash. Enduring for two hundred years into the mid nineteenth century, Charles XI's military reforms, which took eighteen years from 1679, created an army of fifteen infantry regiments each of 1,200 men, ten cavalry and dragoons regiments, plus the Royal Life Guards, fortress garrisons and artillery, a total of 37,000 men. Twenty-four thousand mercenaries manned the Baltic colonies. Underpinning the military reorganization was the *indelningsverk*, whereby a permanent source of revenue was allocated to every item of public expenditure. Another essential precondition was the *reduktion*, a process of restoring to the crown the numerous royal estates that had previously been alienated to the nobility in lieu of debt and political obligations. Because the

Swedish Army was to be territorially based, sufficient crown properties in the appropriate geographical areas had to be earmarked in perpetuity in order to furnish adequate revenue from rents.

Commissioners were appointed to 'stabilize' first the cavalry and then the infantry. Some cavalry was provided by the more substantial crown tenant farmers, who each undertook to supply a trooper, horse and equipment for the duration of their occupancy in return for exemption from taxation. The trooper lived on the farm and, when off duty, worked for his employer. At the Diet of 1686, Charles XI revived the obligation on the nobility to provide cavalry: for every 500 marks of rental income, a nobleman had to produce an experienced cavalryman complete with horse and approved equipment, yielding a regiment of 636 horsemen in 1684 and 672 in 1689.

Although foot soldiers continued to be raised through conscription, there was an alternative: the *knektehåll*, or recruitment by contract, which had been practised by the independent and rebellious copper miners of Dalarna in central Sweden since 1611. In exchange for the abandonment of conscription, local peasants banded together to recruit and maintain a quota of infantrymen at their own expense. Noblemen hated the *knektehåll* because it removed an instrument of control over their peasantry, especially in Finland, where conscription was regarded as vital in maintaining aristocratic dominance. At the Diet in 1682, Charles initiated debate about how territorially based infantry regiments of 1,200 men could best be raised and supported. The Peasant Estate voted in favour of *knektehåll* whilst the nobility wanted to retain conscription for their own tenants: *knektehåll* was formally adopted and royal agents set out to negotiate contracts with the peasantry, province by province. Peasants formed a *rota*, usually consisting of two farms, and agreed to pay the enlistment money and wages of one soldier, his civilian clothing, and lodging complete with an allotment, either on one of the farms or in an adjacent cottage. On active service the king paid the soldier's wage and provided his clothing and equipment; off-duty, the soldier worked for a wage on one of the farms. Should he die or desert, the *rota* had to replace him at its own expense.

Charles XI, King of Sweden from 1660 to 1697. After securing peace with Denmark in 1679 Charles reformed the recruitment, organization, training and administration of the Swedish Army, creating the military instrument with which his successor, Charles XII, achieved numerous victories between 1700 and 1706.

Initially, the provinces of Småland, Västergötland and Österbotten opted to retain conscription, but eventually *knektehåll* was almost universally adopted. Charles acquired guaranteed manpower at minimal cost whilst the peasants were freed from the dreaded lottery of conscription.

The *rota* had no difficulty in finding infantrymen from amongst masterless men, landless labourers and surplus sons. The wealthiest farm managed the *rota*, paid the soldier and provided accommodation in return for first call upon his labour. Once a *knektehåll* contract had been finalized, officers and NCOs were allocated farms on crown lands within their unit's district, according to rank and status and funded through the *indelningsverk*. Because it was a principle of the reforms that officers and NCOs reside amongst their men to supervise welfare and training, as long as they remained in the service they lived on and drew their income from that farm. Higher-ranking officers were granted additional income from neighbouring crown farms. Should no suitable dwellings be available, special 'officer houses' were erected according to a standard design sealed in 1687, many of which still dot the Swedish countryside. Both the *indelningsverk* and the *knektehåll* were applied to Finland, except for the province of Österbotten, but not to the Baltic colonies. By increasing the number of farms in a *rota* from two to four and the king paying the recruit's civilian wage, 6,000 infantry – in regiments of 1,000 rather than 1,200 – were raised from Finland's meagre resources.

A seventeenth-century conscript usually forfeited any social status: in Russia he was regarded as dead the moment that he was marched away from his village. It took the French Revolution to devise the spurious concept of conscription as a quid pro quo for citizenship. However, by 1697 the Swedish soldier was neither conscript nor mercenary but a native volunteer, imbued with some notion of honour and patriotism and enjoying both legal and moral rights. Commanded by Swedish Protestants – only in the mercenary, colonial garrisons did Charles accept Germans and Balts as officers – he lived at home with his family, assured of pay, housing, subsistence and employment; if he retired or was invalided out, insurance schemes provided some security in his remaining years.

Other states also made provision for their old soldiers. Henry IV of France founded a hostel for retired and invalided soldiers in 1604, but it lapsed on his death in 1610. By an *ordonnance* of 26 February 1670, Louis XIV founded L'Hôtel Royal des Invalides. Construction was entrusted to Libéral Bruant and decoration to leading artists from Versailles. Those admitted were veterans who either were aged, disabled and infirm or had completed ten, later twenty, years with the colours. Charles II of England imitated Les Invalides in creating Kilmainham Hospital in Dublin in 1681 and Chelsea Hospital in 1682. A similar establishment, the Armenhaus, was opened in 1697 in Vienna for German veterans from the Austrian Army.

England, Piedmont–Savoy, Spain and France filled their ranks through voluntary enlistment and the press gang. The enthusiasm of Scottish and English volunteers was so intense that they had to be detained in gaol until embarkation for Flanders. Native soldiers were preferred but anyone was accepted; there were as many foreigners in the Duke of Savoy's 'native' regiments as in those officially designated 'foreign'. England and Savoy swept the prisons – English courts offered enlistment instead of custodial sentences – and vagrants were automatically enlisted. On campaign, deserters and prisoners of war, always an expensive embarrassment, were 'persuaded' to change sides.

Desertion was endemic. Men ran from their colours to escape punishment or debt and because they had originally been pressed into service and felt no loyalty towards their employer. Much desertion occurred when recruits or conscripts were marched to regimental depots. Nearly every edition of the *London Gazette* during the 1690s contained advertisements from recruiting officers anxious to recover their deserters, each of whom represented a financial loss. Much desertion occurred within armies. Soldiers left one battalion for another in order to collect enlistment bounties: the more egregious offenders, *billardeurs*, bounced from regiment to regiment. Battalions were perpetually short of men and readily absorbed deserters.

MERCENARIES

Governments continued to employ mercenaries, but there was a major change in the system during the second half of the seventeenth century. Instead of states contracting with private enterprisers, arrangements were made with other governments. The shift was gradual but had substantially occurred by 1700. Until 1670 the French government contracted with individual Irish military

Irish kerne (mercenaries) in Stettin during the Thirty Years War, probably serving as auxiliaries to the Swedish Army. The original German legend around this picture by G. Köler translates as 'In such bizarre costumes, the 800 Irishmen (or madmen) walk around Stettin … They are resilient and resourceful people who, if they don't have bread to eat, dig. When necessity demands, they can walk twenty miles a day. In addition to their muskets, they are armed with bows and arrows and long knives.'

enterprisers, such as Sir George Hamilton and the Earl of Roscommon, but in 1680 Whitehall directed that no Irishman could serve abroad without government permission and no contract was valid unless vetted by ministers. Mercenary service had to promote national policy.

Mercenary troops were incorporated within the standing army and did not form separate armies. Switzerland provided large numbers of soldiers, principally for France and the Netherlands. They came already grouped into battalions, the *régiments avoués*, and were placed at the disposal of foreign rulers through treaties struck with the cantons. The Dutch Army contained an Anglo-Scottish Brigade of six regiments until 1688 and a Scottish Brigade of three regiments until 1782, as well as numerous formations of Germans. Unable to afford their new standing armies, many German princelings hired them out. Louis XIV's army contained 20,000 foreign mercenaries during peacetime and up to 50,000 in war. They were formed into national regiments and commanded in their own language, but that was the limit of their separate identity: discipline and internal administration were identical with those in native French units. When, during the War of the Grand Alliance, Duke Frederick Karl of Württemberg was embarrassed by the rising cost of his army, he rented it to William III of England, who was already employing battalions and squadrons from Denmark, Sweden, Brandenburg, Brunswick-Lüneburg, Brunswick-Wolfenbüttel, Hesse-Kassel, Saxe-Gotha, the Palatinate, Liège and Münster.

In the aftermath of the Thirty Years War the emergent standing armies were mainly officered by former mercenaries taken into the pay of the state. During the next fifty years the officer corps came to be dominated either by the landed aristocracy or, in England and the Dutch Republic, elements of the landed and urban gentry. No longer able to challenge royal authority, in Russia, France, Spain, Brandenburg–Prussia, Austria and most German states the aristocracies were anaesthetized and emasculated, and their martial energies redirected towards the new armies. By appeals to their martial traditions and chivalric pretensions, the nobles were deployed in support of absolute monarchy, which, in return, subjected them to a code of discipline and tables of rank and precedence. Once the grandees had come to appreciate that armies represented channels to power, privilege and wealth, the system became entrenched. The change in attitude that transformed a mercenary captain into an officer of the royal army occurred in France between 1650 and 1680. So effective was the new system that in 1702 Louis XIV had to create 7,000 additional commissions to meet demand.

Improved recruitment was an important by-product. Most noble officers were landowners and recruited amongst their own tenantry, particularly east of the Elbe, where the peasant was contractually bound to his master's estates. Legal and social deference was thus transferred into the army to become the basis of discipline. Not every officer was born aristocratic. Successful soldiers in Austria and Brandenburg–Prussia were often ennobled. In Sweden, commoners promoted to captain were elevated and a ranker could become commander-in-chief; Erik

Dahlberg (1625–1703), director of Swedish fortifications, began as an NCO and was ennobled early in the 1660s. Malcolm Hamilton (1635–99), a Scot who enlisted as a pikeman in Queen Christina's Life Guards in 1654, rose to colonel in 1678, became a baron in 1693, and was made a major general in 1698. In 1682 over half the Swedish subalterns were commoners. A young Swedish noble would be promoted via one of three fast tracks: by enlistment as a ranker in the Life Guard, before moving rapidly to a line commission; by becoming a page at the royal court; or by securing a commission on graduation from a university. Noble ensigns were promoted directly to captaincies, skipping the rank of lieutenant.

Aristocratic officers expected rewards. No government possessed sufficient resources to manage all aspects of finance, personnel and logistics. Instead, the concept of the military entrepreneur was continued, although under state control, and officers played the same role as capacitors in an electrical circuit. Colonels partially owned their regiments and, in England and France, were allowed to sell commissions. In turn, captains sold subalterns' places until all regimental commissions became marketable properties. Prices ranged from several thousand pounds for field officers' commissions in prestigious peacetime formations to a few hundred for junior positions in wartime regiments. Numerous perquisites were offered in return for these capital investments. From their own pockets colonels and captains uniformed their men as cheaply as possible and were reimbursed, at an official rate, by deductions from daily pay. Naturally, the balance lay substantially in the officers' favour. 'False musters' were universal. Troops and companies were maintained below establishment for most of the year, officers collecting the pay of the non-existent men, whilst temporary 'faggots' were hired for the periodic 'musters', parades at which the soldiers were counted and inspected, and the payroll approved. Captains sold furloughs, exacted commission on foreign currency exchanges, and charged premium rates for discharges and marriages. Net profits were most encouraging, so much so that general officers augmented their salaries by always retaining both a regiment and a company. Periodic regulations temporarily calmed the worst abuses but there was an unwritten contract allowing peculation and sharp practice in return for officers assuming the detailed administration of the armed forces on the state's behalf.

Military training

Although permanent standing armies did not initiate military professionalism – officers of the Spanish tercios and Dutch battalions, as well as the mercenary captains of the Thirty Years War, were highly professional – they fostered its formal development. In France, England and Sweden the Life Guards and household regiments were officer seminaries, a model copied by Peter the Great of Russia in creating the Preobrazhenski and Semionovski Guards. The culture of militarism fomented by the Wars of Religion and the Thirty Years War spawned the military college. The Duc de Bouillon's military training academy at Sedan in 1606 was probably the forerunner. It was followed by the *Kriegs-und-Ritterschule*

François Michel le Tellier, Marquis de Louvois (1641–91), French Secretary of State for War, 1677–91, continued the work of his father, Michel Le Tellier, in creating the standing army of Louis XIV. He drew up regulations, appointed inspectors, organized a corps of artillery, supervised the administration, established the Hôtel des Invalides and controlled operations. In strategy, he supported Vauban and Chamlay in pressing for rational, defensible frontiers. He was one of the great creative administrators.

of John VII of Nassau in 1616 and Maurice of Hesse's military college at Kassel in 1618. Wallenstein founded his own military institutes at Friedland and Gilschin in Bohemia. Richelieu opened a college in Paris, whilst Mazarin's attempt to provide a military curriculum at the College of the Four Nations was obstructed by a jealous University of Paris.

Most of these experiments ended with the Thirty Years War, to be replaced by the cadet corps. In 1653 the Great Elector of Brandenburg gathered all the cadets serving with regiments into a single company attached to the Knight's College at Kolberg. Louvois copied the Brandenburg scheme, establishing in 1682 nine cadet companies each containing between 400 and 500 young men, but the scheme was abandoned after his death. Cadet companies were expensive, and no one could decide whether to risk the flowers of the nation's martial youth in battle or keep them safely out of action.

Like their predecessors in the sixteenth century and the Thirty Years War, most line officers learned on the job. The technical branches – the artillery and engineers – required men knowledgeable in mathematics, geometry, civil engineering and science, and consequently were open to the talents of the bourgeoisie. Aristocratic infantry and cavalry officers looked down upon their technical colleagues; gunners and sappers were tradesmen, not proper soldiers. A college for the French Royal Corps of Artillery was opened in 1679 and Vauban advocated the foundation of a similar college to instruct engineers.

For most regimental officers the concept of long-term attachment to a particular army made significant progress between 1648 and 1700, even amongst mercenaries. However, some general officers followed a code more akin to the old mercenary tradition. As members of an international brotherhood, they switched allegiance in pursuit of the highest retainer, although religion and their employers' alliances were partial restraints. Those who excelled – and successfully directing 25,000 men in battle was a rare talent – moved from employment to employment. A graduate of Bouillon's college at Sedan, the Calvinist Herman von Schomberg, born in Heidelberg in 1615, fought for the Dutch, Swedish, French, Portuguese, Brandenburg and English armies, eventually meeting his end in Ireland at the Boyne in 1690. Peter the Great's commander at Narva in 1700 was a Walloon, the Duc de Croy. On the Kahlenberg outside Vienna in 1683, the army of Emperor Leopold was directed by Duke Charles V of Lorraine. The Russian Army depended almost entirely on foreigners both to command its armies and to direct the 'new

formation' regiments. Scots gravitated towards the Russian and Brandenburg service, whilst Irishmen were attracted to the French and Austrian Armies.

Training, comprising mock battles, practices in unit evolutions, and use of weapons, occurred in camps, garrisons and winter quarters. In the territorial Swedish Army, companies held monthly training sessions whilst regiments attended summer camps to rehearse manoeuvres. Every third year Charles XI reviewed each regiment. The English Army introduced formal inspections during the 1690s. Although Dutch and Swedish tactics required superior levels of drill and discipline, a winter's instruction was sufficient to create proficient soldiers. Some authorities maintain that towards the end of the seventeenth century it took years of meticulous drill and ferocious discipline to hone effective soldiers, but this applied only to the parade-ground mannequins in household and guards formations, who, on the outbreak of war, soon became casualties and were replaced by hastily drilled replacements. These losses of highly trained manpower had little apparent impact on combat efficiency, demonstrating that competent soldiers could be produced rapidly.

The regiment was the building-block of armies and, usually, the largest permanent unit. Although some infantry regiments contained two or more battalions, the battalion and the regiment were usually synonymous. Battalions contained between 700 and 1,000 men divided into eight or ten companies, each commanded by a captain assisted by a lieutenant and an ensign, the latter carrying the colours. The three field officers – colonel, lieutenant colonel and major – were also company captains. A small staff comprising a chaplain, surgeon and mate, quartermaster, adjutant and provost marshal completed the battalion.

Infantry from c. 1620. The pikeman wears semi-armour: helmet, breastplate and tasset. The musketeer (right) fires his matchlock musket from a rest. His colleague on the left is blowing on his match, prior to giving fire. Cheap, iron infantry armour could not resist fire from heavy muskets so it was gradually abandoned, first in favour of leather coats, then textile uniforms.

Cavalry regiments were similarly organized although much smaller, normally containing between 300 and 400 troopers split into six or eight squadrons each officered by a captain, lieutenant, cornet (who bore the flag or guidon) and quartermaster. The field and staff officers were similar to those of the infantry.

Apart from the distinction between field and siege cannon (the former marched with the army whilst the latter was held at predetermined locations ready to move, usually by water, to a siege), the artillery lacked permanent organization. Trains of artillery were composed on an ad hoc basis according to the needs of each campaign. Engineering stores, such as digging equipment and bridging pontoons, travelled with the field artillery train.

On campaign, between three and five infantry battalions or cavalry regiments were grouped into a brigade under a brigadier general, a formation that first made its appearance in Germany during the 1630s. The brigade was thus an army's largest tactical sub-grouping: there were no divisions or corps, although commanders made 'detachments' as and when required. Prior to a campaign, an army was divided into two 'lines' corresponding to the first and second lines of battle into which it would formate in action. A 'line', directed by a lieutenant general, was split into a left and right 'wing' of cavalry plus the infantry of the centre, each constituting a major general's command. Brigades were allocated permanent positions in a 'line' corresponding to their battle stations. Armies camped in 'lines', one behind the other, so that they were always ready for battle, a precaution that saved the French army at Steenkirk in 1692. Usually the army marched 'by lines' – that is, in two columns – although it occasionally marched 'by wings', each of the six columns taking separate roads.

UNIFORMS, WEAPONS AND EQUIPMENT

In 1600, except for royal bodyguards and élite units, soldiers wore their own clothes, although the ubiquity of martial equipment and accoutrements gave a homogeneous appearance to any body of troops. The Duke of Neuburg's militia, created in 1605, assumed a common livery, as did the Duke of Brunswick-Wolfenbüttel's two regiments, raised in 1619, and the city guards of Nuremberg. Wallenstein's, Gustav II Adolf's and Tilly's men probably did not wear uniform but distinguished themselves by special favours. Gustav Adolf's soldiers sported blue hatbands with yellow edging, the national colours of Sweden. When they fought in concert with the Saxons at Breitenfeld, both armies wore sprigs of greenery in their hats. Habsburg troops usually assumed a red plume or sash, and in May 1632 Wallenstein ordered all his men to wear red tokens.

Between 1640 and 1680 most armies adopted uniform. In 1645 Gallas clothed his own regiment in pearl-grey coats, the colour that became standard in the Austrian Army. At the battle of Edgehill, fought in 1642, two regiments in the army of Parliament wore red, one purple, one blue, one grey and another green. So great was the diversity of colour that Parliament's men wore orange sashes and the king's troops red. At Marston Moor in 1644 the Duke of Newcastle's large

infantry regiment was dressed in white coats, probably undyed cloth, whilst Prince Rupert's had blue and Colonel Tillier's green. It was around this time that single colours began to predominate within national armies. By March 1644 red was the principal colour of the Parliamentary Eastern Association, and this was adopted by the New Model Army, which dressed in scarlet coats and grey breeches, the regiments being distinguished by different-coloured coat linings.

Uniform was a feature of Charles XI's reforms in Sweden. From 1686 all uniforms had to be made from domestic cloth, and quotas were allocated to different manufacturing centres, boosting Sweden's modest textile industry. The Danish cloth industry too relied on the market created by 20,000 soldiers. However, battles involving troops from many states remained multicoloured affairs, especially as uniforms wore out quickly on campaign and most soldiers were scruffy, ragged and filthy. At the battle of Almanza in Spain in 1707, the French and Spanish identified themselves with 'white papers', whereas the British, Dutch and Portuguese tucked green sprigs into their hatbands.

Contemporary with the adoption of uniform was the standardization of weaponry and equipment. From the mid sixteenth century the principal theatres of war shifted from Italy and the Mediterranean to Northern and Central

Uniforms of the army of Brandenburg–Prussia, 1676. Musketeer and officer of the Kurfürstin Infantry Regiment (left); dragoon (centre mounted); musketeer from the Derflinger Infantry Regiment (centre standing); and trumpeter of dragoons (right).

French cannon from c. 1660–70. The three swivel-mounted breech-loaders on the left are petraras. Powder and ball were packed into a removable chamber, which was fitted into the open breech-end and secured by wooden wedges. Pre-loaded spare chambers enabled a relatively rapid rate of fire. Although it had some limited value in coastal defence, the gun had gone out of use by 1700 because of the difficulty in achieving an effective seal between the chamber and the barrel.

Europe. Thus by 1700 large-scale weapons production had moved from Italy and Spain to Germany, Scandinavia, England, France and the Netherlands. Much of the European arms business passed through Amsterdam and the Dutch Republic. Based around its copper mines at Falun, the Swedish armaments industry was able to equip the entire army that Gustav II Adolf took to Germany in 1630. In the 1690s Swedish weaponry continued to be manufactured locally: sword blades in Vira; cannon at the Jönköping ironworks; harness and armour in Arboga; cavalry weapons by Lars Fleming in Uppland. Starting from a restricted manufacturing base in 1700, within twenty-five years Russia created forty new installations and became self-sufficient in armaments. Liège, neutral since 1492, was a long-established centre for weapons manufacture, its economy expanding substantially during the wars of Louis XIV. The Thirty Years War gave huge impetus to the German defence industries. Existing production in Nuremberg, Suhl, Aachen, Cologne, Augsburg and Essen was stimulated, and new centres opened in Thuringia and outside the main combat zones in Graz and Vienna. France exercised considerable state control over munitions production. Colbert upgraded facilities at Strasbourg and Lyon, organized a new installation in Douai in 1669, and created naval arsenals at Toulon and Rochefort in 1666. In 1689 English musket manufacture and assembly first extended beyond London to Birmingham.

Agriculture in the Low Countries, Germany, France, Eastern Europe, northern Italy and England prospered during wartime, profits outweighing incidental damage and destruction, as naval and military victualling contractors searched for the cheapest and most abundant sources of supply. The huge demand for horses – an army normally contained one horse for every two men – promoted the livestock industry and encouraged selective breeding. Peter I of Russia set up stud farms in 1712 to improve the quality and supply of cavalry mounts.

THE COSTS OF WAR

The costs of war reduced Spain to technical bankruptcy in 1607, 1627 and 1647 – 'rescheduling of debts' in modern parlance – whilst her army in the Netherlands mutinied for want of pay on over fifty occasions between 1570 and 1607. The lesson was clear: the maintenance of large and expensive standing armies required more efficient administrative institutions, heavier taxation and more reliable money markets. The bureaucracies with which governments managed war were initiated in Spain during the sixteenth century, refined in France by Le Tellier and his son, Louvois, and independently developed in Sweden. By the mid 1660s there was a war ministry in Paris dealing with recruitment, supply, pay, discipline, fortifications and soldiers' health. Sweden created a College of War in 1634, England established an embryonic war office in 1683, a war ministry existed in Piedmont–Savoy by 1692, whilst Russia under Peter the Great constantly experimented with administrative institutions. There were few salaried government employees beyond Westminster in 1688; by 1720 there were 5,000, nearly all involved in the assessment and collection of taxes, which the armed forces rapidly devoured. Between 1679 and 1725 the Russian Army and Navy consumed 60 per cent of total revenues in peacetime and 95 per cent when at war. Charles II of England, whose army amounted to only 8,000 men, spent a quarter of his peacetime revenues on the military. In the Nine Years War of 1688–97 the English Army accounted for 40 per cent of government expenditure and the Navy 35 per cent. France, in the same conflict, spent 65 per cent of revenue on the army and 9 per cent on the navy; between 1711 and 1715, 25 per cent went on feeding soldiers. Some states were better able to afford these commitments. From colonies in America, India and the West and East Indies, wealth entered England and the Dutch Republic, to be taxed by increasingly effective governments. Public finance and banking were modernized, enabling the English and Dutch governments to borrow through institutionalized national debts. As far as possible, war still paid for war but it also benefited investors in government stock.

Centralization of government functions was often achieved at the expense of local franchises and privileges, a process that frequently provoked serious opposition. France endured armed revolt during the Frondes (1648–1653) and then in the Boulonnais (1662), Guyenne (1664), Brittany (1675) and the Cevennes (1703). The English Civil Wars resulted from a rebellion against a monarch seemingly intent upon enhancing personal rule. Although armies were at the root of absolutism and thus revolt, they were also the instruments with which rebellion was crushed. The military patrolled highways, fought fires, suppressed internal discontent and rebellion, and, in Germany, France, England and Scotland, collected the taxes that maintained them. Towns or regions slow to pay discovered that the troops lingered, taking 'free quarter' until the oversight had been corrected. Whereas sixteenth-century French and Spanish peacetime standing armies had been employed to guard frontiers and occupy conquered territories, their seventeenth-century successors were additionally expected to garrison the homeland, overawe the potentially rebellious, and preserve law and order. Standing armies concentrated monarchical power.

The cost of fortification was a further factor in the extension of the power of the monarchy. Gunpowder had transformed the science of fortification and

The Paris Arsenal as it appeared in the mid seventeenth century. The first state arsenal in France, it had been established early in the sixteenth century by Francis I on a site near the Bastille and rebuilt in 1594. Additional, provincial arsenals were created between 1547 and 1559 at La Fère, Douai, Metz, Strasbourg, Auxerre and Grenoble. The state arsenal was a symbol of the increasing centralization of government.

sieges. The new 'artillery fortifications' were expensive, often beyond the means of cities and small states, yet without them they fell victim to greedy neighbours and predatory princes. Each of Amsterdam's twenty-two bastions cost half a million florins. Vauban took six years and 5 million livres to fortify Ath, the huge cost partly accounted for by the need to level a hill, whilst his construction of the brand new fortress of Neuf Breisach extracted 4 million livres from Louis XIV's treasury. Siena's independence was fatally compromised during the mid sixteenth century by the huge cost of building artillery fortifications. Even Rome's scheme of fortification was abandoned half-finished because of the enormous outlay. Between 1682 and 1691 Louis XIV spent 8.5 million livres per annum on fortification, although this was insignificant compared with the expense of besieging a fortress. The siege of the Huguenot stronghold of La Rochelle (1627–8) by the army of Louis XIII cost a reputed 40 million livres.

Here lay the kernel of the concept. In the long term, although the initial investment was much higher, fortifications were cheaper than standing armies. They economized on troops to such an extent that a defended town garrisoned by 5,000 men required an army at least ten times as large to reduce it. Fortifications thus enabled small field and garrison armies to punch above their weight. A well-designed defensive system, such as Vauban's 'iron frontier' between north-east France and the Spanish Netherlands, could delay and obstruct an invader at relatively little cost to the defender. Although fortifications did not win wars, they enabled weaker states to prolong contests, thus increasing the rate of attrition suffered by more powerful opponents. Attrition created war weariness and increased the chances of securing a neutral or compromise peace. With the exception of the War of Devolution, all Louis XIV's wars followed such a pattern; it was Vauban's fortifications, rather than the genius of Marlborough, which produced the Peace of Utrecht in 1714.

OVERLEAF: *The siege of the Huguenot stronghold of La Rochelle by the forces of Louis XIII, 1627–9, was a huge operation that lasted for fifteen months. The king's forces had to devise massive seaward barriers to prevent the English, who had occupied the Île de Ré, from assisting their Huguenot allies. Three-quarters of the population died from starvation. Richelieu is amongst the group of mounted officers in the foreground.*

VAUBAN'S FORTIFICATIONS AT LILLE

Vauban refortified Lille between 1667 and 1672, adding a regular pentagonal citadel with a double wet ditch, considered one of the strongest in Europe, separated from the town by an open space, the esplanade, *to provide a field of fire in the event of a two-stage siege. It was the first fortress in which he employed the* tenaille, *a* low infantry work in the ditch positioned to the rear of a ravelin. Extensive use was made of waterways and inundation to reinforce the northern fronts.

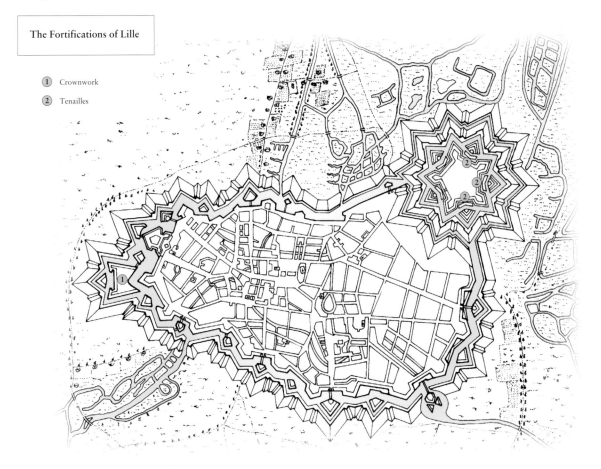

The Fortifications of Lille

① Crownwork

② Tenailles

CHAPTER THREE

THE WARS OF THE MID CENTURY

THE SIEGE OF VIENNA *by the Turks, 16 July – 12 September 1683. The Turks were able to open their trenches under cover of the Viennese suburbs, which approached dangerously close to the main enceinte and, in the panic induced by the Turkish advance, had not been destroyed. The siege of Vienna was the zenith of Turkish encroachments into Europe during the seventeenth century. In the ensuing war, 1683–99, Austrian forces recaptured most of Hungary.*

THE WARS OF THE MID CENTURY

THE PEACE OF WESTPHALIA addressed problems within the Holy Roman Empire. It solved neither tensions in the Baltic nor the dispute between France and Spain. Nevertheless, the peacemakers' achievements were considerable: a second civil war within the empire was prevented and a series of frontiers established that were to remain essentially unchanged until the French Revolution.

The Spanish and Dutch had agreed a compromise peace on 30 January 1648 because they both feared the emerging power of France. In 1652, at the height of the Frondes, Condé, commanding a mercenary army funded by Spanish silver, invaded France and temporarily seized Paris, whilst the Spaniards took advantage of the chaos to capture Gravelines, Dunkirk, Noyon and Casale. Condé's decision to invite Spain to enter France consolidated support behind the infant Louis XIV and his leading minister, Mazarin. Paris returned to its proper allegiance in October 1652, followed by Bordeaux in August 1653, whilst the French Army rejected Condé and rallied behind the loyal Turenne. Count d'Harcourt, governor of Alsace and Lorraine, attempted to become a latter-day Bernard of Saxe-Weimar by negotiating directly with Spain and the emperor but, his troops proving unreliable, he submitted to Mazarin. Gradually, during 1654 and 1655, Turenne expelled the invaders and advanced into the Spanish Netherlands, whilst Mazarin exploited a revolt in Catalonia to capture Roussillon. Cromwell revealed an anti-Spanish stance by capturing Jamaica in 1654. Spain declared war in 1656 and English troops co-operated with France during 1657–8, defeating the army of Flanders at the battle of the Dunes (1658) and capturing Dunkirk, Mardyke, Gravelines, Oudenarde and Ypres. At the Peace of the Pyrenees in 1659, Mazarin secured advantageous terms. Roussillon was ceded, making the ridge of the Pyrenees the new border, along with Artois and its capital Arras, Gravelines, Montmédy and Thionville. In return, France abandoned the Catalan rebels and terminated her formal alliance with Portugal. France had succeeded Spain as the major power in Western Europe.

Brandenburg–Prussia dedicated herself to regaining Western Pomerania from Sweden, whilst the latter's rivalry with Denmark for supremacy in the Baltic remained intense. Denmark's economy had been shattered by the occupations of Jutland in 1627–8 and 1643–4, and she only had sufficient strength to act defensively. Sweden was also in economic difficulties because 'war had not fed war' to the anticipated extent, resulting in high domestic taxation. Oxenstierna

sought salvation either through attacking Denmark to obtain control of the Sound and its lucrative dues or by fighting Poland to regain the Prussian ports and their valuable tolls – one third of Baltic trade passed through Danzig and 50 per cent of all Baltic shipping traded with Polish ports.

Although she had avoided the ravages of war since 1629, Poland under King John II Casimir (r. 1648–68) was descending into internal disorder following the nobility's acquisition of the right to raise troops. Despite this, the Crown Army was reasonably efficient, having emulated the Swedes in adopting both the musket and infantry guns. It suppressed a Cossack revolt in south-east Poland in 1648, but in 1654 the Cossacks sought protection from the Russian tsar, Alexis (r. 1645–76), who promptly invaded Poland and advanced rapidly towards the Vistula. Should Russia have succeeded in reaching the Baltic via the Polish coastline, Sweden's schemes would have been jeopardized, particularly as there was a danger that the forty-four warships belonging to Duke Jakob of Kurland

A Spanish army commanded by Condé and Don Juan of Austria attempted to lift the French siege of Dunkirk. They deployed on sand dunes east of Dunkirk but were attacked on 14 June 1658 by Turenne (on the white charger), whose corps incorporated Sir William Lockhart with 6,000 troops from the New Model Army. Despite initial success by the Spanish cavalry, Turenne's infantry drove the Spaniards from the field and Dunkirk capitulated shortly after.

Alexis Mikhailovich Romanov (1630–76), Tsar of Russia 1645–76. In 1649 he published a set of infantry regulations based on the Dutch model but was unable to achieve sustained military reforms. His army, largely mercenary, was worsted by the Poles, 1654–67, although Kiev and the line of Dnieper were gained in 1667.

Charles X Gustav (1622–60), King of Sweden 1654–60, whose reign was dominated by war against Denmark, Poland and Russia in an effort to consolidate and expand Sweden's Baltic empire. He initiated the reduktion, under which nobles had to surrender alienated crown lands, thus establishing the fiscal basis that made possible the military reforms of Charles XI.

(r. 1642–81) might pass into Russian hands. After Alexis's capture of Smolensk and Vilna in the autumn of 1654, Livonia was directly threatened. Charles X Gustav of Sweden had two choices: either to abandon his claims on the Polish ports in return for an alliance against Russia, or to revoke the Truce of Stuhmsdorf of 1629 and deal first with the Poles and then with the Russians. In conjunction with the royal council, Charles determined upon the latter course and mobilized the army and navy.

In July 1654 Marshal Arvid Wittenberg led 14,000 men out of Pomerania across the Oder and invaded Poland. A second force under Magnus de la Gardie entered Lithuania from Livonia and occupied Samogitia. The main army landed at Wolgast before marching through Great Poland to join Wittenberg's corps at Konin on 24 August. The combined forces blasted south into central Poland: Warsaw, undefended, fell on 8 September; the principal Polish army was beaten at Zarnów; Cracow surrendered in October; and John Casimir fled into Silesia. At the end of 1655 Charles left Wittenberg to command in Poland and turned north to deal with Brandenburg. In January 1656 Frederick William, the Great Elector, submitted to the Treaty of Königsberg, by which Sweden received half the tolls from the East Prussian ports plus the use of Pillau and Memel.

Tsar Alexis declared war on Sweden in May 1656, seeking to acquire direct links with the Baltic. Russia first occupied parts of Swedish Ingria and northern Livonia between Viborg and Narva and established a base on the Baltic at Nyen whilst naval squadrons patrolled Lake Ladoga. More threatening was the advance along the line of the Dvina: Dünaburg and Kokenhusen fell during June and July, and by the end of August the Russians had besieged Riga.

The timing of the assault was fortuitous. A Swedish attack on the monastery of Jasna Góra had presented John Casimir's propagandists with the opportunity to exploit religion and patriotism. Guerrilla warfare had already flared up in Swedish-occupied Poland, forcing Charles to dissipate his strength in garrisons and strongpoints: earlier Swedish assaults on Lvov and Lublin had failed because of epidemic disease after guerrilla operations had interrupted food and forage supplies. Desperation obliged Charles to conclude the Treaty of Marienburg with Frederick William in June 1656, giving Brandenburg four Swedish-occupied counties in Great Poland in return for the use of the entire Brandenburg Army for twelve months and 4,000 men thereafter.

Charles was forced to withdraw from Warsaw, but as soon as the 13,500 Brandenburg troops arrived, he returned to the attack with 18,000 men and defeated the Poles in the three-day battle of Warsaw, which took place on 28–30 July 1656. From his camp outside Riga, Alexis promptly formed an alliance with Denmark and Emperor Ferdinand III and arranged a truce with Poland (the Armistice of Hadziacz, October 1656). Charles also sought allies. An agreement with George Rákóczy resulted in a Transylvanian invasion of southern Poland

King John Casimir and Stefan Czarniecki's Polish army retreats across the Vistula after the battle of Warsaw, 28–30 July 1656. Charles X's Swedish–Brandenburg army of 18,000, including 12,500 cavalry, had frontally attacked the Polish army of 35,500 horse and 4,500 foot in their field fortifications on 28 July, resulting in stalemate. On 29 July, Charles's cavalry absorbed a charge by Polish hussaria as it moved around the Polish right flank through the Bialolecki Forest. Charles was unable to profit from victory because Brandenburg promptly ended its military co-operation.

early in 1657. By the Treaty of Labiau of November 1656, Frederick William received full sovereignty over East Prussia, together with all the port tolls, in return for extended military assistance to Sweden. Thus reinforced, Charles advanced deep into Poland during 1657.

Supported by the Dutch, Frederick III of Denmark (r. 1648–70) entered the war on 1 June 1657 intent on capturing the bishoprics of Bremen and Verden. The last thing that the commander of the Danish army in Holstein, Anders Bille, expected was a Swedish attack, but by 9 July Bremervörde had succumbed to Swedish troops from Bremen and Pomerania whilst Stade was blockaded. Charles withdrew most of his men from Bromberg in the depths of Poland on 26 June and marched rapidly, reaching Western Pomerania within a fortnight. Without pause, he drove across the Holstein frontier with 9,000 men, and the indecisive Bille retreated.

During the autumn all of Jutland was overrun and Bille's army took refuge in the fortress of Fredriksodde. Charles had to defeat Denmark swiftly because Gustav Horn was having difficulty in holding Russian attacks in Ingria and Karelia whilst Rákóczy had been driven from southern Poland.

More serious was the Treaty of Wehlau (September 1657) between Frederick

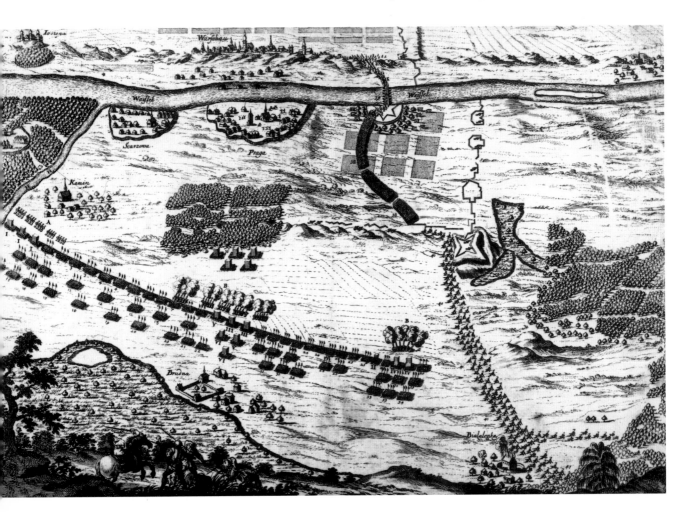

William and John Casimir. Brandenburg received East Prussia and Elbing in return for 6,000 troops to assist in a Polish invasion of Swedish Pomerania. The Poles also undertook to operate against Swedish Livonia.

In response, Charles stormed Fredriksodde in October before preparing to invade the Danish islands. Aided by an exceptionally hard winter, the Swedes crossed the frozen sea to Fyn in January 1658 and then marched over the ice to Langeland, Lolland and Sjelland. Denmark sued for peace. By the Treaty of Roskilde (18 February 1658), Frederick ceded the provinces of Scania, Halland, Blekinge, Bohuslän, and the island of Bornholm in perpetuity, together with the whole of central Norway, providing Sweden with an Atlantic port at Trondheim.

The Roskilde settlement was still inadequate for Swedish needs. Tolls from the Prussian ports remained vital to the continuation of the Swedish war effort, but attacking Brandenburg in order to regain them would have antagonized England, France and the Netherlands. Instead, Charles decided to conquer and subjugate Denmark totally so that Sweden could control access to the Baltic via the Sound. Early in August 1658 a Swedish fleet transported an army corps from Kiel to Korsor harbour on Sjelland. The fortress of Kronborg surrendered in October and the Swedes proceeded to besiege Copenhagen. Seriously concerned about the disruption to Baltic shipping, in October 1658 the Dutch sent thirty-five warships and seventy provision vessels to relieve Copenhagen, whilst Frederick William led 30,000 Brandenburg troops into Holstein. Charles launched an unsuccessful assault on Copenhagen in February 1659, but his position was tenuous. Forty-four British warships under Admiral Edward Montagu (1625–72) arrived in the Sound during May to support the Dutch fleet, forcing the Swedish Navy to retire into Karlskrona. In the same month the Brandenburg Army took Fredriksodde. During October a Brandenburg corps sailed from Kiel to Fyn and forced the Swedish garrison to surrender after defeat at the battle of Nyborg. The Brandenburg Army also occupied all of Pomerania up to the very gates of Stettin and Stralsund.

Early in 1660, whilst planning a campaign into Norway, Charles X died. His son, Charles XI, was only 4 years of age, and regents immediately opened peace negotiations. In May 1660 the Dutch, who had no wish to restore Danish domination of the Sound, mediated the Peace of Copenhagen. Bornholm and Trondheim were restored to Denmark but otherwise the Roskilde terms remained intact. In May 1660 the French, keen to retain a Swedish presence in Germany, negotiated the Peace of Oliva between Poland, Sweden, Brandenburg and the emperor, whereby Frederick William returned Elbing to Poland but was confirmed in his possession of East Prussia. More important, Frederick William had used the war to augment his standing army to 22,000 men. Russia concluded a peace with Sweden by the Treaty of Kardis on 21 June 1661 on the basis of *status quo ante bellum*, whilst Poland and Russia agreed the thirteen-year Truce of Andrussovo in January 1667.

Civil war in England

As a cavalry commander Oliver Cromwell had few equals. Stern discipline allowed him to control his men both during and after a charge, factors that saved the Parliamentarian cause at Marston Moor and Naseby.

The civil wars that plagued Great Britain between 1642 and 1651 were fought and conducted in the same manner as contemporary European conflicts. There was no standing army in England in 1642. Both Parliament and King Charles I raised their forces from volunteers and wholesale recruiting amongst the militias of loyal counties. Some military experience existed amongst those who had participated in the Bishops' Wars with Scotland (1639–40), but the majority of martial expertise derived from officers who had served as mercenaries in the Dutch, Swedish, Russian, Imperial and various German armies. Prince Rupert and his brother Prince Maurice (1620–52) ventured to England in June 1642,

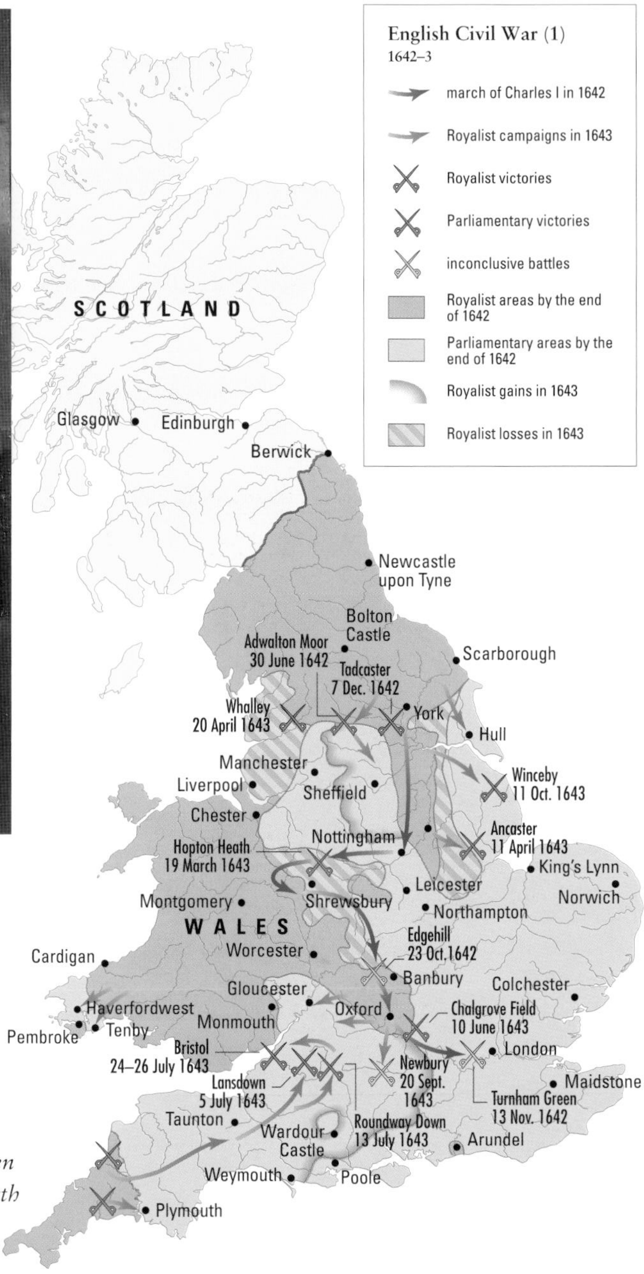
English Civil War (1)
1642–3
march of Charles I in 1642
Royalist campaigns in 1643
Royalist victories
Parliamentary victories
inconclusive battles
Royalist areas by the end of 1642
Parliamentary areas by the end of 1642
Royalist gains in 1643
Royalist losses in 1643
SCOTLAND
Glasgow
Edinburgh
Berwick
Newcastle upon Tyne
Bolton Castle
Adwalton Moor 30 June 1642
Tadcaster 7 Dec. 1642
Scarborough
Whalley 20 April 1643
York
Hull
Manchester
Liverpool
Sheffield
Winceby 11 Oct. 1643
Chester
Nottingham
Ancaster 11 April 1643
Hopton Heath 19 March 1643
King's Lynn
Leicester
Norwich
Montgomery
Shrewsbury
Northampton
WALES
Edgehill 23 Oct.1642
Cardigan
Worcester
Banbury
Colchester
Gloucester
Haverfordwest
Oxford
Chalgrove Field 10 June 1643
Monmouth
Pembroke
Tenby
Bristol 24–26 July 1643
London
Lansdown 5 July 1643
Newbury 20 Sept. 1643
Maidstone
Turnham Green 13 Nov. 1642
Taunton
Wardour Castle
Roundway Down 13 July 1643
Arundel
Weymouth
Poole
Plymouth

The First English Civil War, 1642–6

The English Civil War was essentially an affair of bickering local garrisons, most too feeble to dominate an area unless supported by a field army. Once that army moved on, apparently conquered territories again fell into dispute. Thus the war was fought and refought in the zone between Royalist Wales and the North and the Parliamentarian South East.

THE BATTLE OF NASEBY
14 JUNE 1645

Fairfax's close-run victory at Naseby is often described as the decisive battle of the English Civil War but the contest still had another year to run. The New Model Army proved itself little better than its predecessors and only Cromwell's disciplined cavalry prevented disaster.

accompanied by over 100 professional officers from the Dutch and German armies. Nearly all the senior commanders in the civil wars had gained military experience in Europe: Sir William Verney, Sir John Meldrum, Philip Skippon, Sir Charles Lucas, Sir Charles Wheeler, Sir Jacob Astley, Edward and Richard Fielding, the Earl of Oxford, the Earl of Essex, George Goring, John Byron. Even Thomas Fairfax had seen active service, although Oliver Cromwell had yet to discover his martial talent. These officers rapidly imparted some method and discipline into the levies.

By abandoning London in 1642 Charles I surrendered vital economic and human resources. Parliament assumed control of the centre of population (London contained about 12.5 per cent of the total population of around 4,500,000), the navy, and the wealthy south-east and East Anglia. Thereafter, the recapture of London was Charles's principal strategic aim. He made his first attempt after defeating the Earl of Essex at Edgehill on 23 October, but was checked by the London

Naseby
phase 1

1. The Royalist army advanced. Despite harassing fire from Okey's dragoons behind Sulby Hedge, Rupert's cavalry charged and broke Ireton but Rupert could not rally his men, who rode on to plunder the enemy baggage train. At 'push of pike', the Royalist infantry forced back the Parliamentarian foot until it was close to disintegration

militias at Turnham Green on 13 November. Through a truce with the Irish rebels, Charles released forces for use in England, but Parliament countered by allying with the Scots. Following the indecisive first battle of Newbury on 20 September 1643, the Scots invaded England in January 1644. At Marston Moor near Tadcaster, on 2 July 1644, the Scottish army under David Leslie and the Parliamentary forces under Sir Thomas Fairfax and Oliver Cromwell beat the Royalists under Prince Rupert. When York fell on 16 July, followed by Newcastle on 19 October, the Royalists had lost the north of England. Over the winter of 1644–5 Parliament reorganized its various corps into the New Model Army,

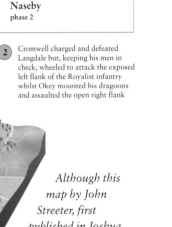

Naseby
phase 2

② Cromwell charged and defeated Langdale but, keeping his men in check, wheeled to attack the exposed left flank of the Royalist infantry whilst Okey mounted his dragoons and assaulted the open right flank

Although this map by John Streeter, first published in Joshua Sprigge's Anglia Rediviva *(London, 1647), was compiled with reference to published accounts and in consultation with Sprigge, Fairfax's chaplain, the initial deployment of the armies is inaccurate.*

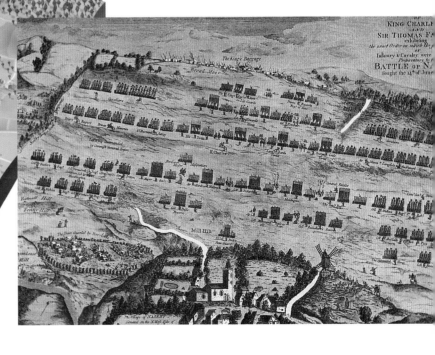

Oxford was Charles I's headquarters from 1643 until 1646, the colleges serving as barracks and quarters. Sir Bernard de Gomme (1620–85), chief engineer and quartermaster general of the Royalist Army, who had learned his trade in the Netherlands under Prince Frederick Henry, designed the fortifications but, as shown, the circuit was never completed. Jan Wyck's (1640–1700) painting depicts Fairfax's low-intensity siege, 19 May – 5 June 1645.

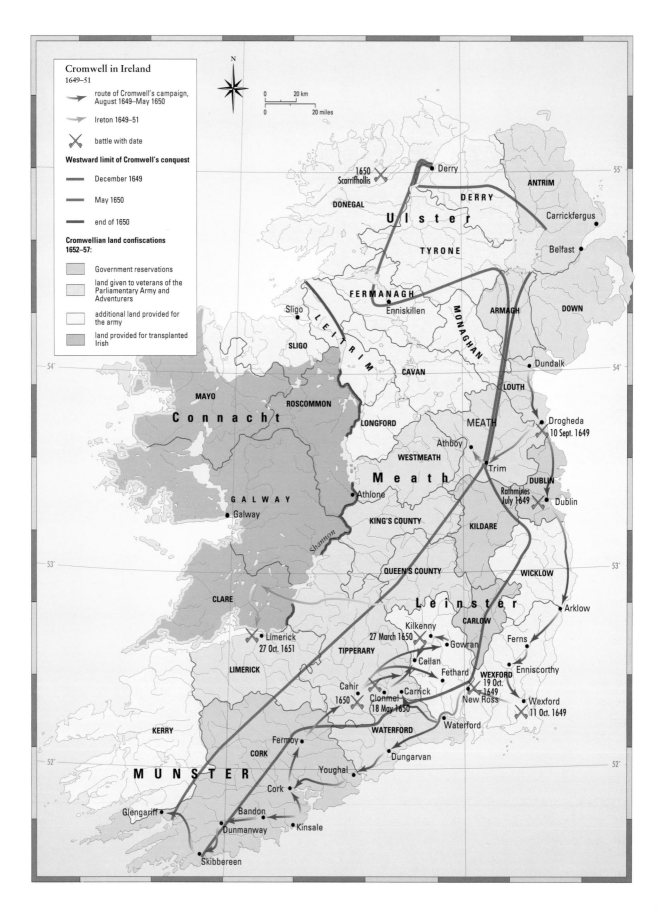

Cromwell in Ireland
1649–51

→ route of Cromwell's campaign,
   August 1649–May 1650

→ Ireton 1649–51

✕ battle with date

Westward limit of Cromwell's conquest

—— December 1649

—— May 1650

—— end of 1650

**Cromwellian land confiscations
1652–57:**

Government reservations

land given to veterans of the
Parliamentary Army and
Adventurers

additional land provided for
the army

land provided for transplanted
Irish

N

0   20 km
0   20 miles

1650
Scarrifhollis ✕

● Derry

ANTRIM

DONEGAL

DERRY

● Carrickfergus

U l s t e r

TYRONE

● Belfast

DOWN

FERMANAGH

● Sligo

● Enniskillen

MONAGHAN

ARMAGH

LEITRIM

SLIGO

CAVAN

● Dundalk

LOUTH

MAYO

ROSCOMMON

C o n n a c h t

LONGFORD

MEATH

● Drogheda
10 Sept. 1649

● Athboy

WESTMEATH

● Trim

DUBLIN

GALWAY

● Galway

● Athlone

M e a t h

Rathmines
July 1649 ✕ ● Dublin

KING'S COUNTY

KILDARE

Shannon

QUEEN'S COUNTY

WICKLOW

L e i n s t e r

● Arklow

CLARE

Kilkenny
27 March 1650 ✕ ● Gowran

CARLOW

● Ferns

● Limerick
27 Oct. 1651 ✕

TIPPERARY

● Callan

● Fethard

WEXFORD
19 Oct.
1649 ✕

● Enniscorthy

LIMERICK

Cahir
1650 ✕

Clonmel
18 May 1650 ✕

● Carrick

New Ross

● Wexford
11 Oct. 1649 ✕

KERRY

Fermoy ●

WATERFORD

● Waterford

● Dungarvan

CORK

● Youghal

M U N S T E R

Glengariff ●

● Cork

Bandon ●

Dunmanway ●

● Kinsale

● Skibbereen

55°

54°

53°

52°

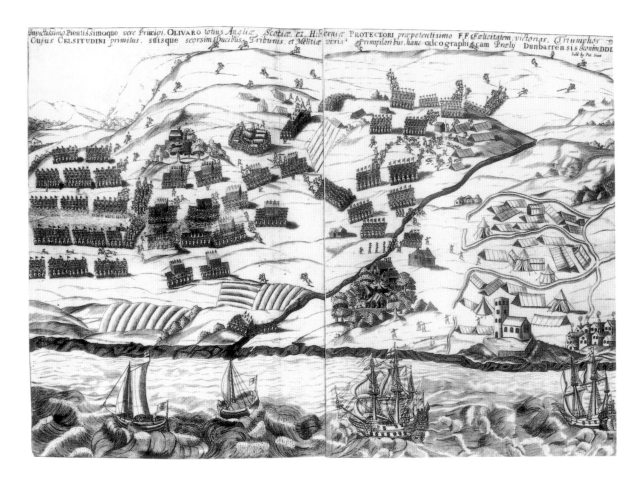

At the battle of Dunbar, 3 September 1650, Cromwell, trapped by the numerically superior army of the Scottish Covenanters under General David Leslie, seized victory by a surprise attack on Leslie's cavalry, aided by Scottish disorganization and incompetence.

which defeated Charles at Naseby on 14 June 1645. In May 1646 Charles surrendered to the Scots. A second civil war flared up in 1648, but the New Model Army under Cromwell defeated the Scottish forces at Preston on 17 August and the Royalists were forced to surrender Colchester to Fairfax. Charles was executed in 1649 but his son, Charles II, came to terms with the Scots, and Cromwell promptly launched an invasion of Scotland in 1650 and beat Leslie at Dunbar on 3 September. During 1651 Charles marched into England, hoping to spark another Royalist rising, but on 3 September was cornered and crushed at Worcester by 30,000 men under Cromwell. Massacres at Wexford and Drogheda characterized Cromwell's savage and ruthless campaigns in Ireland, supposedly revenge for atrocities committed by the Irish rebels in 1641. Irish Catholics were harried from their lands into a reservation in Connacht, west of the Shannon. The phrase 'ethnic cleansing' is not inappropriate.

OLIVER CROMWELL IN
IRELAND, 1649–51

The Irish Catholic Confederation, which had successfully rebelled against Charles I in 1641, was defeated at Rathmines by Michael Jones in 1649. Cromwell, landing shortly afterwards with reinforcements, rapidly returned Ireland to English, Protestant rule.

OTTOMAN THREATS TO VIENNA

There was a contrast between Europe and Asia-in-Europe. Following the 'Long War' with Austria (1593–1606), during which superior logistics had been decisive, Ottoman military prowess declined. Although the Turks had possessed artillery in 1389 and the janissaries were equipped with firearms by 1500, a weakening economy made it difficult for them to keep pace with West European

The Turkish siege of Candia (Iraklion) in Crete (1648–69) lasted for twenty-one years despite the city's obsolete sixteenth-century inner enceinte. Turkish siege technique was equally antediluvian and the siege more closely resembled a blockade than a sustained attack. Candia only succumbed when its sea communications were seriously interdicted.

developments in artillery manufacture and stellated fortification. Their command structure and military organization grew outmoded, the 'Turkish crescent' battle formation reflecting the racial and geographical divisions within the Ottoman Empire rather than modern military requirements. Although the janissaries constituted an Ottoman standing army after 1453, the majority of the Turkish wartime forces were composed of militia and conscripts. By 1600 the janissaries had become politicized, and the resultant nepotism and corruption had diminished their fighting capabilities. On 24 June 1645 Sultan Ibrahim attacked the Venetian island of Crete with 400 ships and 100,000 men. Canea soon fell and the capital, Candia, was besieged in 1648. The Venetians sent 33,000 reinforcements, including mercenaries from Hanover, Celle and Brunswick, whilst their ships blockaded the Dardanelles. The Ottoman fleet was heavily defeated

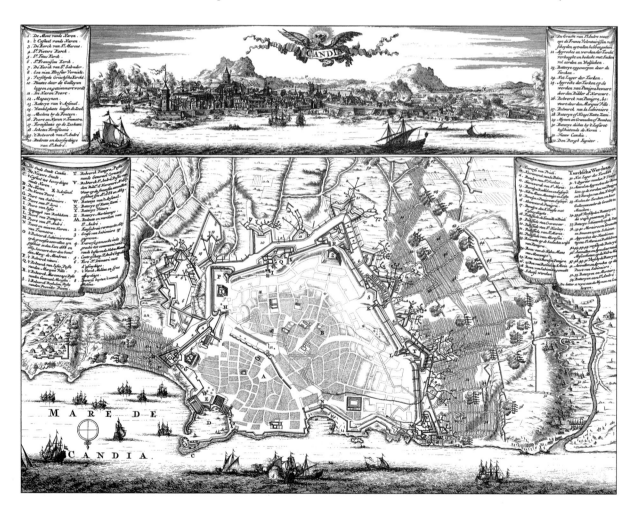

off Naxos in 1651 and in the Dardanelles during June 1656, but Grand Vizier Mehmet Köprülü rebuilt the navy and broke the blockade in 1657. The Turks renewed their efforts to take Candia during the mid 1660s, their warships cutting off the flow of reinforcements from mainland Europe. Candia fell in 1669 after a siege lasting over twenty years.

Habsburg efforts to challenge Ottoman hegemony in Transylvania led to war in April 1663. The Turkish army, consisting of 10,000 cavalry plus 40,000 musketeers recruited from Anatolia and Rumelia, was slow to assemble and did not take the 'Ottoman Road' from Constantinople to Hungary until the spring of 1664. Montecuccoli, the Imperial commander-in-chief, concentrated 30,000 men in mid July 1664, by which time Grand Vizier Ahmed Köprülü was threatening both Vienna and Graz. Montecuccoli intercepted the Turks at Kormend on the River Raab where he was joined by an expeditionary force of 6,000 French soldiers under Jean de Coligny. On 1 August the Turks began crossing the Raab near the Abbey of St Gotthard, east of Graz. Montecuccoli could not intervene immediately as Coligny and the Margrave Leopold of Baden-Baden, commanding the Imperial contingents, had difficulty in co-ordinating their

AUSTRIA, HUNGARY AND THE BALKANS IN 1648

The frontier between Christian Europe and the Empire of the Ottoman Turks ran through the eastern Mediterranean and northern Balkans. Constant friction was interspersed by major campaigns, mostly following the line of the Danube and its principal tributaries.

Austria and the Balkans
1648

  Spanish Habsburg territories

  Austrian Habsburg territories

  Ottoman territory

  border of Holy Roman Empire

operations. The Imperial army was thrown back from the riverbank into woodland, where Montecuccoli persuaded Coligny and Baden-Baden to launch a joint attack. Caught while conducting a river crossing, the Turks were badly beaten. Just ten days later Emperor Leopold I (r. 1658–1705) and the sultan signed the Peace of Vasvár.

Taking advantage of a revolt in Habsburg Hungary, Grand Vizier Kara Mustafa invaded with 100,000 men in May 1683. Leopold's commander, Duke Charles V of Lorraine, had only 33,000 men and was forced to fall back and

Leopold I, Holy Roman Emperor. Cautious, dithering and indecisive, when the Turks approached Vienna in 1683 he deserted his capital and fled in panic to Passau whence he governed from 17 July to 25 August. He re-entered Vienna on 14 September in less than ceremonial glory, his prestige seriously tarnished.

permit the Turks to besiege Vienna on 16 July. While Count Ernst Rüdiger von Starhemberg conducted a vigorous defence, a relief army assembled in answer to Pope Innocent XI's appeal for an international crusade. Contingents from Bavaria and Saxony joined Lorraine and on 31 August King John III Sobieski of Poland (1674–96) arrived with 18,000 men and assumed overall command. Starhemberg was desperate for assistance, and on 9 September Sobieski and Lorraine advanced on the Turkish camp through the Wienerwald and attacked on 12 September. The battle of the Kahlenberg was a complete success and Vienna was relieved.

The recapture of Esztergom (Gran), an important economic centre on the Danube in Hungary 40 kilometres north-west of Budapest, by the Austrian–Imperial–Polish army, 19 October 1683, following 150 years of Turkish occupation (1543–1683). Esztergom's fortress at the top of Castle Hill remains largely intact.

THE SIEGE OF VIENNA, 1683

The army with which Lorraine relieved Vienna comprised 11,000 Austrians; 8,000 from the Army of the Circles commanded by Waldeck; 600 Hanoverian cavalry; 9,000 Saxons led by Elector John George III; and 18,000 Poles under King John III Sobieski, half of whom were cavalry including 3,300 hussaria.

The siege of Vienna
1683

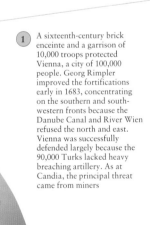

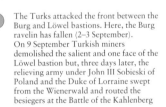

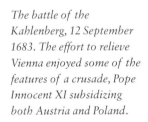

1 A sixteenth-century brick enceinte and a garrison of 10,000 troops protected Vienna, a city of 100,000 people. Georg Rimpler improved the fortifications early in 1683, concentrating on the southern and south-western fronts because the Danube Canal and River Wien refused the north and east. Vienna was successfully defended largely because the 90,000 Turks lacked heavy breaching artillery. As at Candia, the principal threat came from miners

2 The Turks attacked the front between the Burg and Löwel bastions. Here, the Burg ravelin has fallen (2–3 September). On 9 September Turkish miners demolished the salient and one face of the Löwel bastion but, three days later, the relieving army under John III Sobieski of Poland and the Duke of Lorraine swept from the Wienerwald and routed the besiegers at the Battle of the Kahlenberg

The battle of the Kahlenberg, 12 September 1683. The effort to relieve Vienna enjoyed some of the features of a crusade, Pope Innocent XI subsidizing both Austria and Poland.

Charles V, Duke of Lorraine (1643–90), brother-in-law of Emperor Leopold I, besieged Buda on 18 June 1686. On 22 July a lucky cannon shot exploded the Turkish magazine and killed 20 per cent of the garrison. Despite this, Buda did not fall until an assault was launched on 2 September. With the city given over to plunder, a fire broke out which reduced Buda to ashes. Here, Lorraine accepts the surrender of the citadel.

In 1684 Poland, the emperor, Venice and the Pope formed the Holy League against the Turks, to be joined by Russia in 1686. Although an attack on Buda failed in 1684, a renewed assault in 1686 was successful after a shell exploded the Turkish powder magazine. On 12 August 1687 Lorraine beat the Turks at Szegedin, and by the end of 1688 Belgrade and most of Hungary were in Imperial possession. Under Louis of Baden the Imperial army reached Bucharest in 1690, but as more and more troops were required to defend the empire against the French and a new grand vizier, Fazil Mustafa, reorganized and reinvigorated the Turkish Army, the Imperial effort slackened. Fazil Mustafa retook Belgrade in 1690.

Relatively indecisive campaigning followed during the 1690s, but in 1696 the defection of Savoy released Imperial troops from northern Italy, and the end of the Nine Years War in 1697 allowed Leopold to devote all his martial energies to defeating the Turks. At Zenta on 11 September 1697 Prince Eugene of Savoy (1663–1736) caught the Ottoman army as it was crossing the River Tisza,

inflicting 30,000 casualties at a cost of only 300. Peace was signed at Karlowitz in 1699, Austria gaining Transylvania and most of Hungary, whilst the Turks retained the Banat of Temesvár but ceded most of the Morea to Venice. Partial reform of the Ottoman Army began after 1699 when a series of European advisers made limited progress in their attempts to modernize the artillery and military education, measures that only affected the small core of standing troops. Most of the Turkish Army remained undisciplined, untrained, badly armed conscripts, incapable of standing against regular soldiers. When the Turks renewed the war in 1716 they were heavily defeated by Prince Eugene at Peterwardein, 5 August 1716, before losing Belgrade on 22 August 1717.

THE BATTLE OF ZENTA

The army of Sultan Mustafa II was intercepted by Eugene of Savoy, commanding 50,000 Imperial troops, as it crossed the Tisza in Serbia. Stranded on the left bank behind feeble defences, the Turkish infantry was routed by the Imperialists while the Grand Vizier was murdered by mutinous janissaries. Taking advantage of low water, the Imperialists then assailed the sultan's camp. This defeat cost the Turks 30,000 men, eighty-seven cannon and the royal treasure chest, leading to the Peace of Karlowitz, 1699.

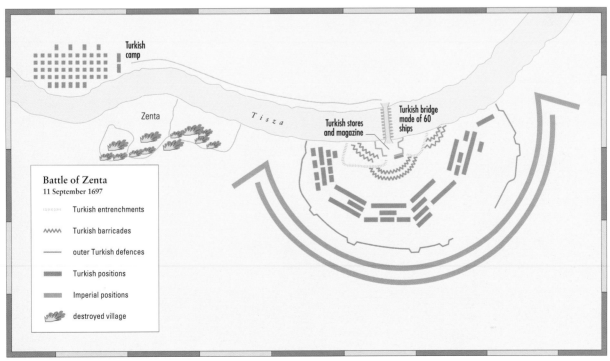

Battle of Zenta
11 September 1697

Turkish entrenchments

Turkish barricades

outer Turkish defences

Turkish positions

Imperial positions

destroyed village

Turkish camp

Zenta

Tisza

Turkish stores and magazine

Turkish bridge made of 60 ships

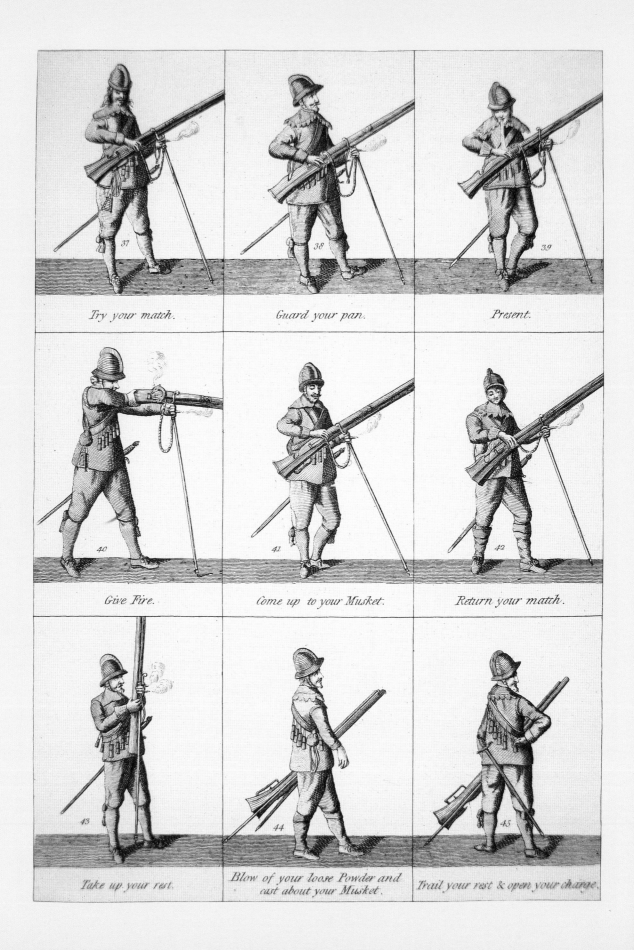

Try your match.	*Guard your pan.*	*Present.*
Give Fire.	*Come up to your Musket.*	*Return your match.*
Take up your rest.	*Blow of your loose Powder and cast about your Musket.*	*Trail your rest & open your charge.*

CHAPTER FOUR

THE CONDUCT OF WAR
1650–1700

EARLY SEVENTEENTH-CENTURY drill books, such as Johann Jacobi von Wallhausen, Manuale Militare, oder Krieggs Manual (1616), prescribed complex and complicated drills for handling the matchlock musket. By the mid century these had been simplified and shortened: in action the drills were further reduced. The adoption of the flintlock again attenuated drill movements, greatly improving rates of fire and enabling infantry to better protect itself against cavalry.

THE CONDUCT OF WAR 1650–1700

ALREADY POTENT STATES fought either to increase their own power or diminish that of rivals, whilst the weaker sought to protect themselves. Although the outcome of war depended principally upon the ability to mobilize resources, it was physically expressed through the gain or loss of territory. The keys to military success were thus aptitude for siege warfare and skill in the design and location of fortresses. Battle, which was unpredictable and usually indecisive, produced tangible results only when victory could be exploited to seize enemy fortifications and land. Occupation of economically vital territories also improved the prospect of ultimate ascendancy through attrition.

Even religious wars were territorial. According to *cuius regio, eius religio*, the faith of the ruler determined that of his people, so both Catholic and Protestant states viewed conversion and reconversion as a function of territorial conquest. Despite the abandonment of this principle at the Peace of Westphalia, princes continued to believe that conformity to a single national confession was essential to maintain internal harmony. Thus in 1685 Louis XIV ended the experiment of two faiths in France by revoking the Edict of Nantes (1598), forcing the Huguenots either to convert or to emigrate. Similarly, militant Catholicism was a prime weapon in Emperor Leopold I's reconquest of Hungary after 1683.

England moved tentatively towards breaking this received wisdom with the passage of the Toleration Act in 1689. In an age where the sanctity of property ranked above that of human life, war was concerned with possessions; people were simply pawns who were mobilized to fight for their ruler's personal and dynastic interests. However, the situation was not entirely bleak. The constitutional monarchy in England and the republican government of the Netherlands increasingly used war to foster the broader national interest. Also, many sections of society – aristocrats, mercenaries, merchants, farmers, manufacturers, ship owners, and the unemployed – benefited from war.

Seventy per cent of the earth's 96 million square kilometres of land – 30 per cent of its total surface area – is devoid of military history because it is too high, low, cold, hot, wet or dry. Of the remaining 30 per cent, strategic geography has determined that the same key regions have been fought over repeatedly. Where armies have been obliged to operate across barren or inhospitable terrain, campaigns have clung to coastal margins or navigable rivers. Generals tended to campaign across territories that both were capable of supporting their armies and would provide political and economic assets when conquered. Because roads were either bad or non-existent, obliging reliance upon boats to convey supplies and heavy equipment, the presence of navigable waterways was vital.

The few regions that fulfilled some or all of these requirements – the Low Countries; the Rhine, Danube and Po valleys; Bohemia and Moravia; and the coastal margins of the Baltic and Iberia – were regular seats of war, their towns and cities fortified, and populations attuned to the needs of armies. No other region in Europe possessed so many fortified towns, detached fortresses and strongpoints as modern Belgium, the southern Dutch Republic and north-eastern France. It had been the theatre of the Eighty Years War between Spain and the Netherlands and was to be the centre of dispute between France, Spain and the Dutch during the reign of Louis XIV.

Commanding the junctions of most important land routes and waterways was a fort or defended town, which an advancing army dared not ignore for fear of endangering its communications. Attackers had to proceed methodically, besieging one fortress after another, while defenders regrouped and redeployed behind the screen of their fixed fortifications. Most engagements derived from attempts to relieve besieged fortresses. In Eastern Europe, Catalonia and the Baltic lands, where the density of population and economic activity were lower, there were fewer towns and roads, but the nodal points – Barcelona, Narva, Reval, Riga, Warsaw, Prague and Vienna – were frequently attacked.

Because navigable waterways constituted the main military thoroughfares, campaigns often aimed to capture all the forts along a 'river line' in order to secure a conduit for supplies and the siege train. In the Low Countries, Ghent, Courtrai and Menin were the keys to the River Lys; Tournai, Oudenarde and Antwerp commanded the Schelde; Ath, Alost, Grammont and Dendermond governed the line of the Dender. Brussels, Mechlin and Hal covered the River Senne, whilst the Meuse, the most vital artery, was protected by some of the strongest fortresses in Europe: Venloo, Maastricht, Liège, Huy and Namur. The crossing points on the Upper and Middle Rhine were guarded at Old and New Breisach, Strasbourg and Kehl, Philippsburg, Mainz and Koblenz/Ehrenbreitstein, whilst the Danube flowed past Ulm, Donauwörth, Ingolstadt, Regensburg, Passau, Vienna, Budapest and Belgrade.

FORTIFICATIONS AND SIEGES

Modern fortifications, evolved from the *trace italienne*, comprised low-level, geometric earthworks that enabled relatively small garrisons to withstand

The defences of Vienna in 1672, drawn by George Matthaus Vischer (1628–96), illustrating the low silhouette presented by artillery fortifications. This worm's-eye view looks northwards across the glacis and the zone non-aedificandi. In the centre before St Stephen's Cathedral is the Kärntner bastion, flanked by two ravelins.

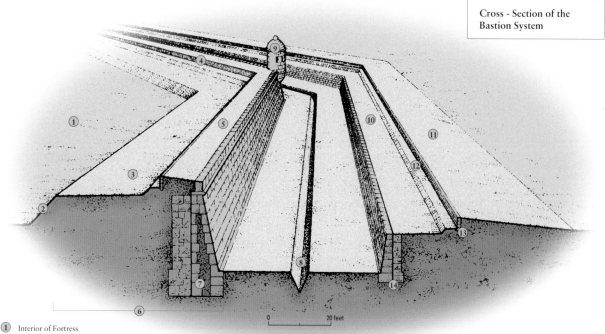

①   Interior of Fortress

②   Talus

③   Terreplein

④   Banquette

⑤   Parapet

⑥   Rampart

⑦   Scarp (masonary ditch)

⑧   Cuvette

⑨   Gurite (sentry box)

⑩   Covered Way

⑪   Glacis

⑫   Banquette

⑬   Palisades

⑭   Counter-Scarp (masonary)

THE ESSENTIALS OF
BASTIONED FORTIFICATIONS

*Section through a simple
fortification of rampart,
ditch and glacis. Because a
clear field of fire was
required, it was forbidden
to build within the zone
non-aedificandi of a
fortified town. When a siege
was imminent, offending
buildings, often substantial
suburbs, were demolished
without compensation.*

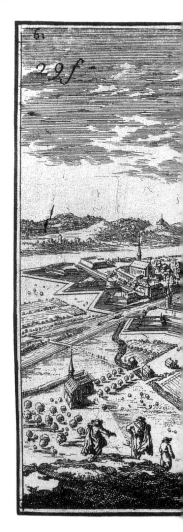

prolonged sieges by larger armies. The ground
plan, or 'trace', was polygonal with a pentagonal
bastion at each salient angle. Some detached forts,
such as Lillo to the north of Antwerp, Bourtange
in Groningen, Lille citadel, and the purpose-built
fortress town of New Breisach in Alsace, were
constructed as regular polygons and assumed the
classic stellar trace. This, however, was rare, and
most fortifications were thrown around existing
settlements, requiring numerous outworks to
compensate for the irregularity of the resultant
polygons.

A bastion possessed an all-round field of fire:
into the country, along the face of the curtain wall,
or back on to the ramparts and into the fortress
itself. Bastions were arranged within mutually
supporting distance so that if attackers assaulted
the curtain wall at any point between two bastions
they could be engaged by crossfire. This was the
essential – to ensure that attackers would be
flanked and enfiladed should they penetrate the
defences; not a metre of 'dead ground' was
permitted within the effective range of the
defenders' guns.

Bastions alone were insufficient and had to be

Plan of the Bastion System with Fields of Fire

—— Cannon fire
—— Musket fire

① Glacis
② Ditch
③ Ravelin
④ Bastion

STRASBOVRG

D. Perelle fe.

CROSSFIRES WITHIN TYPICAL BASTIONED FORTIFICATIONS

Crossfires developed by a regular polygonal system of fortification consisting of bastions, ravelins, ditch and glacis. The salient (point) of a bastion was, to some extent, defiladed and thus often selected as the focus for attack. Engineers paid considerable attention to fires within the fortification, particularly from the main ramparts into the ditch and covered way, in order to contain lodgements.

LEFT: *An engraving by Adam Perelle (1638–95) of the fortifications of the Imperial Free City of Strasbourg in 1659. Vauban refortified the city following its capture by France in 1681, adding a citadel towards the Rhine. Note the new suburbs between the medieval town walls and the artillery fortifications.*

COEHOORN'S 'SECOND MANNER' OF FORTIFICATION

Military engineers were eclectics whose designs reflected the necessities of each site rather than principles imposed by pre-determined systems, most of which have been identified subsequently by historians. Coehoorn maximized the natural defence of the Netherlands, water, and compensated for the low, flat landscape by building double-storeyed bastions and ravelins, a concept borrowed from Wilhelm Dilich, Peribologia *(1640).*

covered by works beyond the curtain wall – ravelins, hornworks, crownworks, demi-lunes – guarding all approaches. By 1700 some of the larger towns, such as Namur, Lille, Bergen-op-Zoom, Dunkirk and Wesel, resembled martial mazes, and the over-complexity of their designs reduced efficiency by requiring considerable garrisons. Another feature was the revival of the citadel, or fort-within-a-fort. At many of the larger fortified complexes – Lille, Namur, Strasbourg, Casale, Barcelona and Turin – a separate fort of considerable strength was erected, repeating the sequence of defences. Once the town had been captured, the garrison withdrew into the citadel, which then had to be separately reduced. This occurred at Namur in 1692 and 1695.

Italian engineers – Antonio da Sangallo the Younger (1483–1546) and Michele Sanmicheli (1484–1559) – had developed the bastion and *trace italienne* during the sixteenth century when Italy had been the seat of war between France and Spain. During the seventeenth century the torch passed to French military engineers, principally Jean Errard de Bar-le-Duc (1554–1610), Blaise François, Comte de Pagan (1604–65), and Vauban, plus the Dutchman Coehoorn. Theory was expounded in the influential *Fortifications de Comte de Pagan* (Paris, 1640),

Coehoorn's 'Second Manner'

1 the glacis

2 the salient place d'arnes

3 the re'entrent salient place d'arnes

4 traverses

5 covered way

6 envelope providing counter-guards to the salients of the bastions and ravelins

7 ravelin

8 redoubt within a ravelin (at a higher level)

9 lower level of two storey bastion

10 upper level of two storey bastion

11 curved flanks or orillons (double decked)

12 gorge, or throat, of bastion

13 interior of fortress

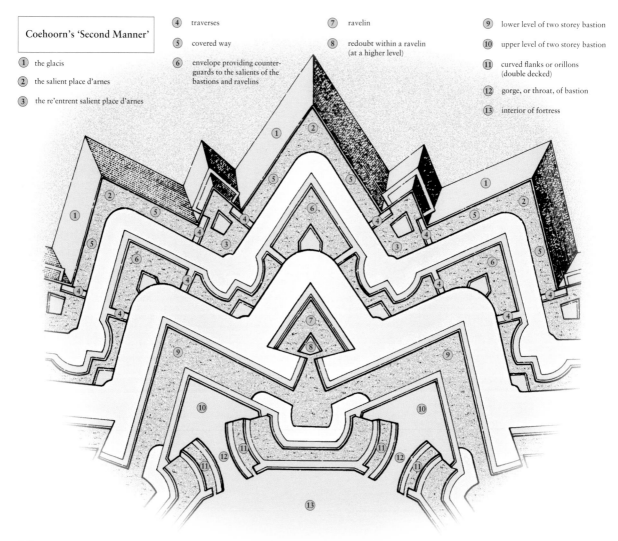

and put into practice by Pagan's protégé Vauban. Vauban built or redesigned 160 fortresses, mostly along the French frontiers. Only Coehoorn and the Swede Erik Dahlberg approached Vauban's eminence. Within the immutable geometrical principles, these great engineers had their individual trademarks. Coehoorn, working in the swampy Netherlands, built in brick and excavated double water-filled ditches in his major fortresses at Coevorden, Nijmegen, Breda and Bergen-op-Zoom, whilst Dahlberg, who repaired and constructed over fifty fortresses, displayed a penchant for casemated artillery towers.

The French invasion of the Dutch Republic in 1672 involved six sieges and no battles, whilst the Nine Years War included seventeen major land actions but twenty-one important sieges. When tied to a siege, a blockading army was vulnerable because the surrounded garrison usually represented only a fraction of the available enemy forces. There were two methods of self-protection: first, the attacker could divide his own strength between a besieging corps and a 'covering' force, and secondly, he could surround his encampment with field fortifications, 'lines of circumvallation'. Should the garrison be aggressive, then the besiegers might also dig 'lines of contravallation' facing towards the fortress. Thus the

IDEALIZED DIAGRAM OF
COEHOORN'S THIRD
SYSTEM OF FORTIFICATION

*Coehoorn's 'Third Manner'
in which the envelope has
been replaced by free-
standing ravelins and demi-
lunes within the wet ditch.
The major works have been
extended from two to three
storeys in order to increase
height and thus the number
and range of cannon.*

Coehoorn's 'Third Manner'

1. the glacis
2. covered way
3. counter-guard
4. demi-loune (three level)
5. ravelin with recessed flanks (three level)
6. bastion with curved orillons (three level)
7. tenaille

attackers' camp and siege works could be sandwiched between two belts of entrenchments, a system perfected during the Eighty Years War by the Dukes of Alva and Parma. At 's-Hertogenbosch in 1629 it took eleven hours to make a circuit of the Dutch siege works.

To capture a fortress, a breach had to be blasted in the main rampart wide enough for the passage of infantry. According to the unwritten yet widely accepted customs of war, at that point the governor could sue for honourable terms. Pointless heroism was incongruous because fortresses were intended not to be impregnable, but merely to delay and obstruct by withstanding a minimum specified duration of siege. They were components within a defensive system, or planned battlefield, capable of delaying an attacker for a predictable time in a manner similar to the crumple zones in a modern car. Only heavy siege artillery –

Sebastian le Prestre de Vauban (1633–1707), whose designs were extravagant and expensive, was accused by Louvois of wasting the king's money on such ephemera as elaborate ceremonial gateways instead of concentrating on military essentials. Cynics suggested that he attacked the most difficult fronts of his own fortresses so as to present his designs in a favourable light.

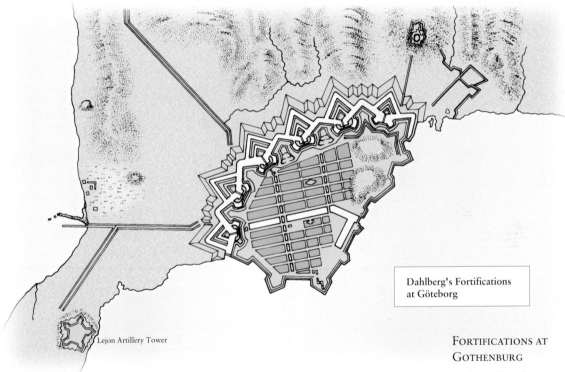

Dahlberg's Fortifications at Göteborg

Lejon Artillery Tower

24-, 32- and 64-pounders – firing solid shot from less than 100 metres could breach earthworks. To achieve this, besiegers had to grind through the outworks, destroying the defenders' cannon, until their own artillery had reached the glacis. 'Sieges in form' were thus slow and methodical unless the garrison's morale collapsed, as at Dixmuyde and Deynze in 1695, or there was treachery afoot, as was probably the case at Mons in 1691 and Namur in 1692. At Venlo on 18 September 1702, three battalions commanded by John, Lord Cutts (1661–1707), stormed the covered way but achieved such momentum that they pursued the defenders over the ramparts into the main body of Fort St Michael and took the surrender of 1,500 Frenchmen. This was most unusual.

FORTIFICATIONS AT GOTHENBURG

Erik Dahlberg began the fortification of Gothenburg (Göteborg) in 1687. The harbour was included within the defences, as were two potentially commanding hills to the east and south-west. Dutch-style bastions, with curved orillons, and ravelins reinforced by counter-guards and tenailles, defended the landward front.

Roman legions had approached beleaguered places via oblique trenches. By the 1620s Maurice and Prince Frederick Henry of Nassau had improved the technique by zigzagging the trenches, 'saps', and achieving close co-operation between infantry and artillery. 'Sapping' was dangerous but volunteer 'sappers' were handsomely rewarded. Learning from Ottoman methods at the siege of Candia, Vauban perfected his own system at the siege of Maastricht in 1673 by linking the saps with three wide trenches dug at intervals parallel to the selected 'front'. Sappers and civilian pioneers – Catinat conscripted 16,000 for the siege of Ath in 1697 – 'broke ground' at a distance of 600 or 700 metres before driving forward a series of saps. Some 400 metres from the glacis, just within the effective

range of heavy cannon, a deep, wide trench was excavated at right angles connecting all the advancing saps: the 'first parallel'. Along its length were constructed batteries for the siege artillery plus *places d'armes* manned by sufficient horse and infantry to repulse sallies from the surrounded garrison. Vauban so spaced his batteries that their fire converged on the target from several angles. At this extreme range the heavy cannon were fired at maximum elevation, causing the shot to veer off line towards the end of their flight, finding out concealed targets amidst the defences. At Namur in 1692 and Ath in 1697, as soon as the garrison cannon on the ramparts and bastions had been dismounted, Vauban ordered his guns and howitzers to fire with reduced charges at maximum

An entirely fictitious scene from the unsuccessful siege of French-occupied Maastricht by the Confederates, 7 July – 29 August 1676, from a painting by Jan Wyck. The figure on the white horse is William III of Orange. Cavalry rarely operated so close to siege works.

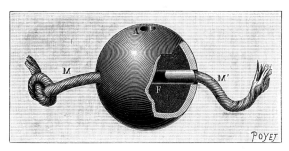

TOP: *An explosive mortar bomb/shell/carcass (1651). The mortar having been charged with propellant, the fuse was ignited and the bomb dropped down the tube. The length of fuse determined the point of explosion, usually an airburst. The case disintegrated into shrapnel.* BOTTOM: *An experimental globe pyrotechnique (1651) fused to achieve a delayed explosion and useful for attacking the inner recesses of fortifications.*

BELOW: *The front and side view of a mid seventeenth-century mortar, probably French or German. Mortars, exclusively siege weapons which travelled with the siege train, employed relatively light charges to lob explosive bombs amidst fortifications.*

RIGHT: *The gunner's quadrant, a set-square and protractor that allowed the gunner to elevate his piece to achieve a desired range and azimuth. Tables were printed which listed quadrant settings for given weights of charge and shot and varying calibres of cannon. On the right, the front and rear view of a double battery, designed to give cannon and gun crews the greatest possible protection from counter-battery fire.*

elevation. Thus was born 'ricochet fire' in which the balls fell into the works, bouncing and bounding, forcing the garrison underground into bombproof casemates and tunnels.

Saps were then pushed to within 200 metres of the foot of the glacis, where the 'second parallel' was dug and the cannon moved forward; at this range the cannon made some impact on the earthworks. Forward again went the saps, the zigzags more frequent and acute to prevent the trenches from being enfiladed by musketry.

Within pistol-shot of the foot of the glacis, the 'third parallel' was constructed and the cannon advanced. Having lost most of its guns and mortars, the garrison was now largely dependent upon musketry and grenades, enabling the attacking artillery to begin the serious business of blasting a breach in the 'covered way' along the top of the glacis.

A breach in the covered way heralded the most bloody and dangerous part of the attack: the infantry assault on the counterscarp. Some generals preferred to march their men up the glacis from the third parallel; others recommended

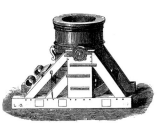

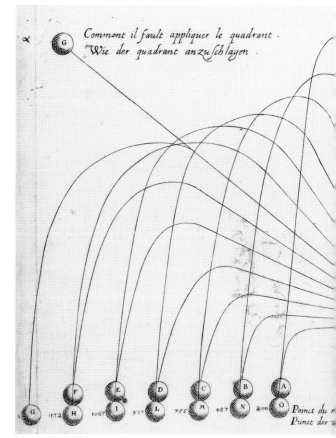

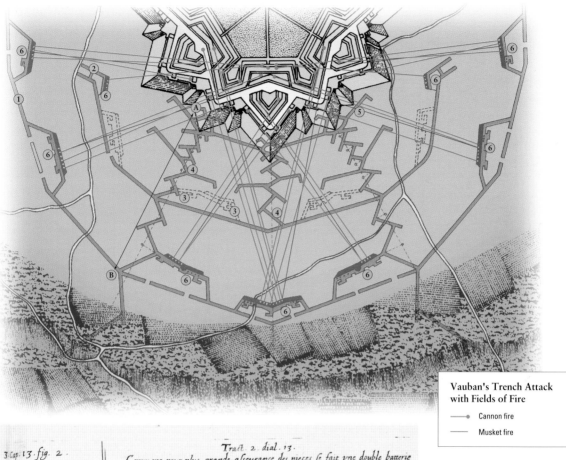

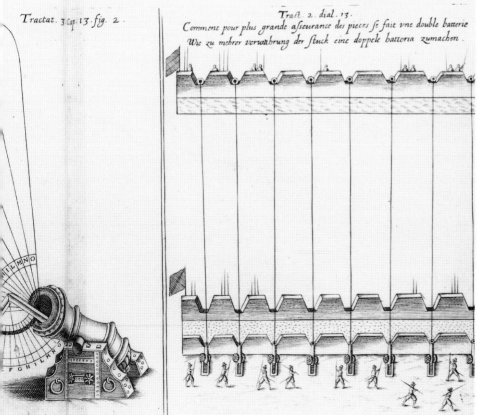

**Vauban's Trench Attack
with Fields of Fire**

━━━● Cannon fire

━━━ Musket fire

① First Parallel

② Second Parallel

③ Places D'armes

④ Saps

⑤ Third Parallel

⑥ Batteries

Ⓐ ←→ Ⓑ c.500 metres

A SIEGE IN FORM

*Stylized diagram of an
attack according to Vauban's
method of three parallels,
on the covered way before
the salients of two bastions
and a ravelin of a regular,
polygonal fortress. The
batteries enfilade the points
of attack. Besieged towns
usually suffered extensive
damage because much of
the artillery fire overshot
into the built-up areas.*

VAUBAN'S SIEGE OF ATH
15 MAY – 5 JUNE 1697

On the ramparts of Ath, a bastioned heptagon refortified by Vauban between 1668 and 1672, stood guérites, *decorated with golden fleurs de lys, and ranks of lime trees, planted to shelter the town from overshooting bombs. To reach any of the four gates, each protected by a double portcullis, involved crossing four drawbridges over the wet ditch.*

sapping up the glacis to attack from a shorter distance. Advancing across open ground in the face of concentrated musketry and grenades launched from the covered way, the ramparts, and flanking ravelins and bastions, casualties amongst the assaulting infantry were usually high whichever method was adopted. *Cavaliers de tranchées* were erected along the third parallel, earthen towers from which supporting fire was delivered against the covered way. Even so, it was a daunting task, the equivalent of 'going over the top'.

A successful assault – and repeated attempts were often needed – secured a lodgement on the covered way. Behind earthen parapets and breastworks thrown up to face the rampart, artillery was advanced to the top of the glacis to begin breaching the curtain wall while engineers blasted sections of the covered way into the ditch to level a passage for the infantry into the fortress. Once the rampart had been breached and the ditch partially filled, the infantry possessed a clear path into the town obstructed only by hastily dug retrenchments in the rear of the breach.

Should the besieging army attack successfully at this stage, then it enjoyed the historic right to put the garrison to the sword and plunder the town for three days, but such a conclusion was rare. Normally, once a lodgement had been made on the covered way, it was accepted that the game was over and the garrison troops were allowed to surrender on honourable terms in recognition of the fact that they had not caused the attackers unnecessary bloodshed and expense by resisting the inevitable. Prisoners of war were expensive embarrassments, so garrisons were usually paroled and allowed to march to a specified destination.

Variations occurred according to local conditions. When the ditch was full of water it had to be either drained, as at Namur in 1695, or crossed on rafts and pontoons. Mining was important, except amidst the high water-tables in the Netherlands. From the third parallel, engineers and specialist miners tunnelled beneath the glacis seeking to position explosives under the counterscarp and covered way, a procedure that was sometimes quicker than waiting for the bombardment to take effect. Subterranean warfare developed when the garrison excavated counter-mines to intercept incoming tunnels or blow up the third parallel. Larger fortresses were equipped with masonry-lined and vaulted counter-mines that ended below the anticipated location of a third parallel.

Vauban and Coehoorn were expert at both fortress construction and reduction. European engineers rapidly imitated the system of three parallels, and a 'siege in form' became synonymous with an attack according to the Vauban method. Because they were of considerable duration and played upon a stationary stage, sieges were grand theatre. Louis XIV 'commanded' as many sieges as possible, taking with him his court, ladies and government. Gentlemen volunteers and travellers attended sieges as part of their education, witnessing great events in relative safety spiced with a hint of danger. The unfortunate Michael Godfrey, deputy governor of the Bank of England, went to the siege of Namur in 1695 to converse with King William III on financial matters. He entered

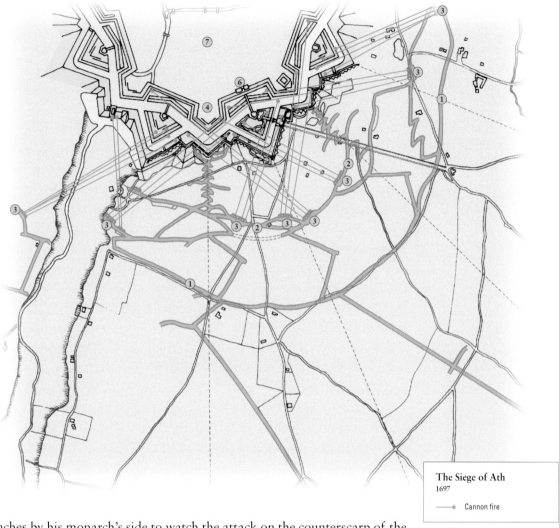

The Siege of Ath
1697

——●—— Cannon fire

1 Second Parallel

2 Third Parallel

3 'Ricochet' Batteries

4 Bastion de Namur

5 Bastion de Limboourg

6 Brussels Gate

7 Ath

the trenches by his monarch's side to watch the attack on the counterscarp of the town only to be struck down by a cannon ball.

SUPPLY AND FINANCE

Military economics continued to determine strategy. The French attacks on the Dutch Republic in 1672 and Philippsburg in 1688 were unsuccessful attempts at mounting rapid campaigns in order to achieve decisive results without becoming involved in attrition. Such 'blitzes' nearly always failed (William of Orange's assault on England in 1688 was the only example of success), condemning to a long war the belligerent who could not rapidly extricate himself by securing peace. When faced with attrition, there was little option but to seek ways of exporting military costs, making conflicts extended and self-perpetuating: French retention of the southern Spanish Netherlands during the Nine Years War (see Chapter 5) was essential in order to extract contributions to support the troops.

As in the Thirty Years War, both to preserve the home economy and to wreck the opponent's it was essential to take winter quarters on enemy territory. In addition, wars were long and frequent because soldiers rarely delivered decision.

Armies were incapable, except in extraordinary circumstances, of destroying an opponent in battle; could operate only during the growing season; engaged in serial sieges; and were hamstrung by inadequate transport, communications and supply. Accordingly, wars seldom reached a strategic conclusion. Conflicts ended not in victory but in compromise settlements caused by economic exhaustion, leaving the frustrated protagonists anxious to renew hostilities.

Wars were also prolonged because states usually belonged to coalitions; only France had sufficient population and assets to fight alone. England and the Dutch Republic, the richest European nations, invariably fought within confederations. The satisfaction of numerous conflicting objectives caused coalition wars to be lengthy, whilst combined resources provided extended endurance. Also, since issues tended to be dynastic and political rather than racial or ideological, wars within Europe were not fought *à l'outrance*. Even religion ceased to be a *casus belli* after 1648, although remaining a factor within it. These were not savage contests of annihilation but wars of territorial adjustment in which armed forces were political instruments, not machines of extermination.

Away from Western Europe different rules applied. Contests against the Turks and colonial wars against native populations in America and Asia were racist and ideological, usually conducted with maximum violence and pursued to a logical conclusion.

Battle tactics are embarrassingly simple; skill lies in devising and applying systems capable of persuading ordinary men to execute them. The first requirement was an adequate supply of food. William III's armies in the Low Countries during the Nine Years War consumed annually 400,000 tons of supplies, mostly food for men and horses. Except at sieges, armies burned little powder and field equipment was durable. In peacetime, soldiers catered for themselves, usually through release from duty to earn a civilian wage. So undeveloped was state bureaucracy that it could shoulder only part of the burden of feeding soldiers in wartime. To minimize difficulties, governments concentrated on providing bread; meat, vegetables, liquors and tobacco could all be purchased from the hordes of semi-official sutlers and camp followers that trailed behind armies. When marching through enemy lands, an army lived off the country. Should an area be occupied for any length of time, contributions were gathered. In friendly or home territory, supplies were drawn from local markets or magazines of flour and grain stored in frontier fortresses.

Provided that an army kept moving, sufficient victuals could usually be found. However, when it halted, in camp or at a siege, it rapidly devoured the locally available comestibles and had either to march or to draw supplies from magazines. Armies could not operate far from their magazines and had to ensure secure communications, preferably by navigable waterway. Green fodder for the horses was the major item that had to be garnered from the countryside on campaign. Each of the 80,000 horses with William III's forces in the Netherlands munched daily between 18 and 30 kilos of green fodder and half that weight of corn during the winter. On the march, horses grazed, but in camp, 'foraging'– gathering hay – occurred every third or fourth day. Armies foraged to the front and flanks of their camps, leaving the rear intact to sustain a retreat. Because opposing camps were frequently close together, foraging grounds were disputed and foraging parties had to be escorted by large formations of cavalry and dragoons to ward off opposing patrols. A 'grand forage' could involve virtually the whole army either as mowers and gatherers or as covering formations. It was the insatiable requirement for green fodder that restricted campaigning to the growing season. Men might fight and march during cold weather but horses could not easily be fed away from their stables. This ended large-scale manoeuvres and limited winter operations to raids and patrols.

To save money, the military relied upon civilian victuallers. Army provisioning was founded on the Antwerp and Amsterdam grain trades and developed through the omnipresence of war in the Low Countries. By the 1650s the business was dominated by Sephardic Jews, mainly of Portuguese origin, who were regarded as neutrals, enabling them to travel freely in search of sources of cheap supply.

Amongst the principal contractors was Samuel Oppenheimer of Heidelberg (1630–1703), who began as financial agent and victualling contractor to the garrisons of Elector Karl Ludwig of the Palatinate. In 1673 he formed a consortium to provision Leopold I's Austrian Army of the Rhine. Oppenheimer supplied the entire Austrian war effort in Hungary after 1683, whilst his son, Emmanuel, victualled the Imperial garrisons in western Germany during the Nine Years War.

Second only in scale to the Oppenheimers was the Dutch Sephardic partnership of Antonio Alvarez Machado and Jacob Pereira. From their office in the Lange Voorhout in the Hague they provided and distributed bread to the Spanish and Dutch armies throughout the Franco-Dutch War (1672–8). In 1678 they also supplied basic victuals and transport to the British corps in Flanders. Following the Peace of Nijmegen (1678), Machado and Pereira continued to supply the peacetime Dutch Army before receiving the contract to victual William's expedition to England in 1688, enjoying the title of providiteurs-general. Their retention of the supply contract in 1689 was a formality, and Jacob Pereira's younger son, Isaac, accepted the contract to supply bread to William's forces in Ireland between 1690 and 1691. Machado and Pereira also supplied the English Army in the Low Countries, plus all its mercenaries, throughout the Nine Years War. Via a host of subcontractors, Machado and Pereira provided a complete service, in a manner reminiscent of Wallenstein.

These great Jewish enterprises were the multinational companies of their day. At a time when only three towns in England had populations in excess of 20,000 people, the army victuallers fed moving armies of 100,000 men and 80,000 horses under the most adverse conditions.

WEAPONRY

Weaponry further restricted military effectiveness. Experiments with newfangled guns were commonplace – multi-barrelled muskets, rifles, rifled pistols, grenade throwers, multiple mortars, and giant mortars that hurled 225-kilo bombs – but soldiers were conservative and cautious: field equipment had to withstand harsh treatment, and well-proven designs were preferred. As late as the 1670s, infantry fought in formations little changed from those of Gustav II Adolf except that the number of pikes had declined and the proportion of matchlock muskets increased, a reform strongly advocated by Montecuccoli. Around 1600 there had been one musket for every five pikes on the battlefield, but by 1680 this ratio had been reversed.

Although improved since 1648, the matchlock musket remained cumbersome and was best fired with the butt pressed against the chest. Ignited by lowering a slow match into the priming tray, it was useless in wet weather, and at night, when the glow of matches revealed positions. It was inaccurate even within its effective range of less than 100 metres.

The flintlock musket, sometimes referred to as the snaphance or the fusile,

SEVENTEENTH-CENTURY MUSKETS

(From the top): An Austrian matchlock caliver, c. 1600. Because a caliver could not pierce iron armour, it was superseded by the heavier musket, *which appeared around 1540; American dog-lock musket, c. 1640; A richly decorated Swedish flintlock rifle, c. 1650. Rifles were largely reserved for hunting* *and sport. Loading was too slow for military adoption; A German wheel-lock carbine, c. 1675. Carbines were issued to cavalry and dragoons.*

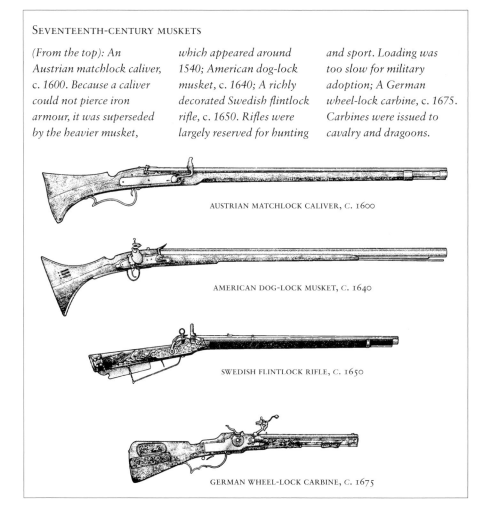

AUSTRIAN MATCHLOCK CALIVER, C. 1600

AMERICAN DOG-LOCK MUSKET, C. 1640

SWEDISH FLINTLOCK RIFLE, C. 1650

GERMAN WHEEL-LOCK CARBINE, C. 1675

represented an advance. It was lighter, could be fired from the shoulder, was more accurate, and had double the rate of fire. Soldiers could also carry more ammunition because the flintlock was of smaller calibre, taking sixteen balls from a pound of lead as opposed to twelve. Simultaneously the cartridge was introduced, in which a ball plus the correct amount of powder were pre-wrapped in a paper cylinder, substantially reducing loading time.

Over fifty years the new firearm replaced the old. It was first used in England late in the reign of Charles II, whilst his successor, James II, formed a special regiment of fusiliers in 1685 to guard the ammunition train, where the absence of lighted matches increased safety. Brandenburg–Prussia adopted the new musket in 1689, Russia in 1700, and the French were halfway through their programme of modernization by 1693, although it was not completed until 1708. Nearly all European armies had been rearmed by 1714 with the exception of the Ottoman Army, which continued to use antiquated weaponry well into the second half of the eighteenth century.

The unwieldy pike fatigued the soldier and hampered close-formation drill. Throughout the previous hundred years various devices had been tried to enable pikeless infantry to cope with cavalry. Gustav Adolf occasionally protected his foot with sharpened stakes driven into the ground, after the manner of fifteenth-century longbowmen, but this was possible only in defensive actions. In 1647 the French introduced the 'plug bayonet', in which a knife blade mounted on a tapered hilt was inserted into the muzzle of a musket. British forces in Tangier were equipped with this weapon in 1663. Although the plug bayonet enabled musketeers to engage cavalry with cold steel, it had a serious drawback: once it was inserted, the musket could not be discharged. At Killiecrankie in 1689 the English battalions fixed plug bayonets after giving the Scots rebels a volley only to be routed partly because of their inability to return fire.

Vauban had found the answer in 1669. His socket bayonet, similar to the weapon now in universal service, consisted of a blade welded to a collar that fitted over the muzzle and was locked in place by a lug, converting the musket into a short pike but leaving it capable of fire. The new pattern was issued to French infantry in 1689: Brandenburg–Prussia switched in the same year, Denmark in 1690 and Russia in 1709. France abolished the pike in 1703, England

A collar of bandoliers, or the 'Twelve Apostles' (English, c. 1650). Each wooden tube contained a musket ball plus sufficient powder to fill the chamber and flash pan. Bandoliers were principally associated with the matchlock musket; the flintlock's higher rate of fire required soldiers to carry more than twelve rounds and so the cartridge box became standard equipment.

in 1704 and the Dutch Republic in 1708. By 1700 most European armies had almost erased the distinction between pikeman and musketeer, although Russia continued to employ the pike into the 1720s, finding it efficacious against charging Turkish horsemen.

Grenades, 'pomegranates', hollow iron shells filled with gunpowder, first appeared in the late Middle Ages and were known to have been used at the siege of Arles in 1536. Ineffectual in battle, grenades were reserved for sieges. In 1667 four men from each French foot company were trained in throwing grenades and termed 'grenadiers'; after 1671, infantry regiments added one company of grenadiers to each battalion. Grenadier companies were introduced into English regiments in 1678, and most European armies had followed suit by 1690. Tall,

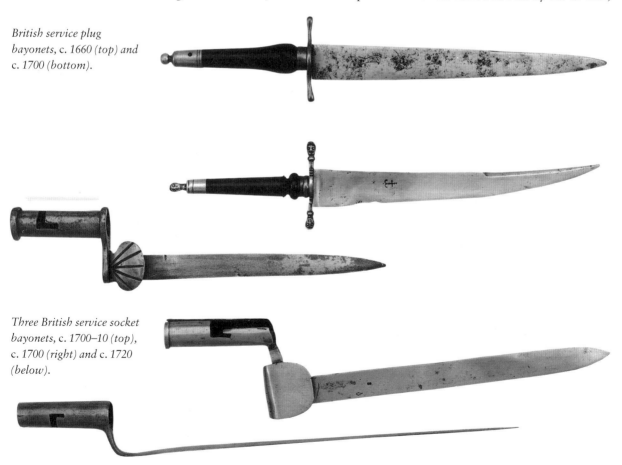

British service plug bayonets, c. 1660 (top) and c. 1700 (bottom).

Three British service socket bayonets, c. 1700–10 (top), c. 1700 (right) and c. 1720 (below).

A wheel-lock pistol from the early seventeenth century, decorated with steel inlays. This type of weapon formed part of officers' field equipment.

strong, agile men were selected and formed a *corps d'élite;* equipped with flintlock musket, bayonet, sword, hatchet, and a pouch of twelve to fifteen grenades, they were charged with difficult and dangerous tasks. After 1714, grenades were transferred from the infantry to the artillery and engineers.

FORMATIONS AND TACTICS

Dragoons moved on horseback to fight as infantry. Although the dragoon was supposedly 'invented' by Marshal Charles de Cossé-Brissac in 1554, heavy feudal cavalry had frequently operated on foot, and in 1537 Count Peter Strozzi commanded arquebusiers who fought dismounted. The nomenclature 'dragoon' did not appear until the beginning of the seventeenth century and probably

WHEEL-LOCK, DOG LOCK AND FLINTLOCK PISTOLS

TOP LEFT: *A wheel-lock 'over and under' double-barrelled and double-locked pistol, c. 1600. Pistols with straight hilts were known as dags or tacks. Such* ingenious novelties were too costly and delicate for military use.
BOTTOM LEFT: *A flintlock pistol, c. 1700. The bulge at the breech end of the barrel* shows this to have been specially strengthened to discharge two or three balls simultaneously – 'double' or 'triple shotting'.
TOP RIGHT: *An English dog-*lock cavalry pistol, c. 1640. The lock is of the snaphance type.
BOTTOM RIGHT: *A French flintlock cavalry pistol, c. 1680.*

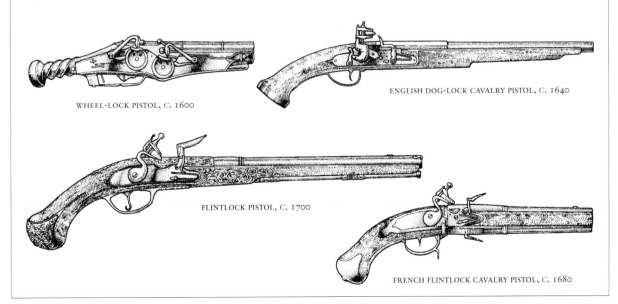

WHEEL-LOCK PISTOL, C. 1600

ENGLISH DOG-LOCK CAVALRY PISTOL, C. 1640

FLINTLOCK PISTOL, C. 1700

FRENCH FLINTLOCK CAVALRY PISTOL, C. 1680

Cavalry in a square defending itself with pistol and carbine fire against attacking lancers, from John Cruso, Militarye Instructions for the Cavallerie According to the Moderne Warrs *(Cambridge, 1632). Military manuals sold well amongst the English gentry during the 1620s and 1630s because of interest in the Thirty Years War and improvements to the militia initiated by Charles I.*

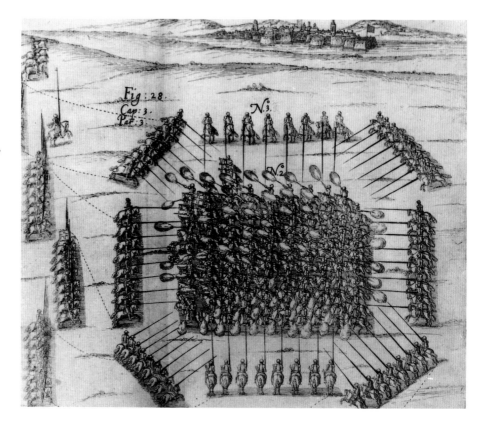

derived either from the dragon on their standards or their dragon-like, fire-breathing flintlock musketoons. In France, where dragoons had been extensively employed during the Wars of Religion, fifteen independent companies were combined into six regiments in 1635 and the term 'dragoon' passed into official usage three years later.

Armed with muskets, sabres and hatchets, and riding small, cheap nags, dragoons were employed by both Wallenstein and Gustav Adolf either to reconnoitre and secure defiles during an advance or to cover a retreat. The New Model Army's single regiment of 1,000 dragoons, under Colonel John Okey, lined the hedges on the Parliamentary left at Naseby in 1645 and took Prince Rupert's advancing cavalry in the flank. At the battles of Sinzheim and Enzheim in 1674, Turenne rode his dragoons on to the field before ordering them to operate dismounted along the flanks of the army. However, by 1700 dragoons were losing their special identity and changing into general-purpose cavalry.

As infantry rose in importance during the sixteenth and seventeenth centuries, so cavalry suffered a relative decline. In 1494, 34 per cent of the French Army consisted of heavy cavalry; thirty years later, the proportion had fallen to just 10 per cent. Firearms reduced the efficacy of the charge until heavy horse was able to perform only against infantry whose cohesion had already been broken. Moreover, infantry was both cheaper to equip and maintain and more versatile,

A German musket range of the early seventeenth century, equipped with moving target. The Royal Armouries Museum in Leeds contains contemporary German target rifles, complete with fore and back sights and hair triggers, and an explosive target.

Pike drill based on the illustrations in Jacob de Gheyn, Wapenhandling van roers, musquetten ende spiessen (Arms Drill with Arquebus, Musket, and Pike) *(Amsterdam, 1607). Numbers 16 and 22 show the stances for 'charging' or advancing with the pike, whilst 30 demonstrates the posture for resisting attack by cavalry.*

especially at sieges. However, during the 1660s cavalry returned to fashion, and a mixture of heavy and light horse, plus dragoons, comprised one third of the field armies during the Nine Years War.

In addition to reconnaissance and the war of 'posts and ambuscades', a sufficiency of horse was vital to exploit local successes on the battlefield. During the second half of the century most European armies trained their cavalry in both the aggressive Swedish tactics established by Gustav Adolf and the caracole. Unbroken foot could usually resist cavalry by musketry and the reach of its pikes and bayonets, but once they got to work amongst disorganized infantry, horsemen were deadly. Cavalry, normally deployed on the flanks of the infantry lines, first attacked their opposite numbers: if successful, they were then in position to attack the raw wings and rear of the enemy foot. Turenne usually followed the Swedish model of interspersing bodies of musketeers amongst his cavalry so that volley fire might 'disorder' the opposing cavalry sufficiently to assist the charge.

Just as Wallenstein, Piccolomini and Horn would have felt at home amongst

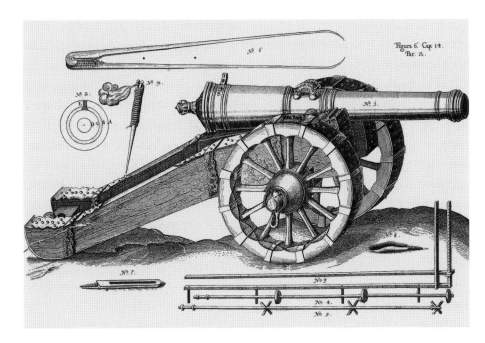

A German field gun, probably a 6-pounder, c. 1660, complete with gunners' tools and equipment.

late seventeenth-century cavalry, so they would have been familiar with infantry tactics. In battle, battalions were arrayed in double or triple lines some 200 metres apart, the gaps between the battalions covered, in echelon, by those in the rearward line. A battalion of 700 men occupied a 200-metre front, the pikes forming a block in the centre flanked by two wings of 'shot'. The grenadier company stood off to the right. The battalion comprised five or six ranks, providing the mass necessary for the pike and bayonet with sufficient depth for the musketeers to give fire according to variations on the counter-march.

Battles were fought at very close quarters. Cheaply manufactured military muskets, ineffective above 100 metres, were not equipped with sights and aiming was approximate. Because only one of the six ranks of musketeers fired simultaneously, battalions could not develop a heavy weight of shot, but they enjoyed the security of having at least half the musketeers always loaded. Infantry could not load and fire on the move, so they engaged when static at a distance of around 50 metres. Even well-trained soldiers – the pikemen were simply observers, and frequently the victims, of the musketry duel – were psychologically incapable of trading volleys at fifty paces while standing unprotected. Usually one side adopted a defensive position, reinforced by field fortifications, and dared the other to attack. Should two lines of infantry meet in the open, then one side quickly became 'disordered' after the exchange of a few volleys and was charged: if in the vicinity, cavalry now came into its own.

Principally a siege weapon, on the battlefield artillery was merely an adjunct to infantry firepower. Britain, France and the Netherlands adopted the Swedish practice of using light, 1½-pounder and 3-pounder cannon as infantry guns. Extremely manoeuvrable, towable by a horse or half a dozen men, they filled the intervals between the battalions of a brigade, giving close support with canister, grape and partridge shot. Larger cannon from the artillery train, usually 12-pounders, were grouped into batteries of between ten and twenty guns to cover weak sectors of the line. Once deployed, the heavier cannon remained stationary, largely because the civilian drivers refused to risk their lives on the battlefield.

During sieges, whether attacking or defending, musketeers operated from the physical security of cover and consequently fired with greater accuracy. In battle, armies thus sought to replicate siege conditions by employing field fortifications: entrenchments, breastworks, *abatis*, *chevaux de frise* and earthen redoubts.

Russia extended this concept to strategy, creating series of fortified artificial frontiers in the featureless steppe to protect and consolidate new settlements and colonies. The practice began in the eighth century but gathered pace during the sixteenth and seventeenth centuries as Russia expanded towards the Black Sea. These fortified lines, 'cherta' – the Tula Line (1533), the Oka Line (1560s), Kromny–Kursk–Voronezh (1594–1600), Kursk–Kharkov (1637), the Simbirskaya (1648–54), the Belgorodskaya (1665) – were up to 1,000 kilometres long, consisting of ditches and earthen ramparts supported by fortresses, blockhouses, watchtowers and signalling posts manned by garrisons varying in strength between 100 and 1,000 men.

In 1605 the Dutch Republic built a string of wooden redoubts connected by a continuous ditch and earthen rampart on the line of the Waal and IJssel rivers to protect Overijssel from invasion by Spínola's Army of Flanders. Mazarin had thirty-eight redoubts constructed along the Meuse to defend France against Spanish attack. During the Franco-Dutch War (1672–8), Louis XIV's generals built continuous defensive lines around occupied sectors of the Spanish Netherlands to secure the collection of contributions. This practice was considerably extended during the Nine Years War. Between 1690 and 1693, conscripted peasants excavated redoubts, ramparts and zigzagged trenches from Dunkirk to Maubeuge on the Sambre, the strongest section lying in Flanders between the rivers Lys and Scheldt. In 1700 and 1701, before the outbreak of the War of the Spanish Succession, the French constructed the Lines of Brabant, which ran for 208 kilometres from Antwerp, through Diest, to the Meuse.

THE LEGALITIES OF WAR

There were few restraints on the conduct of war. Louis XIV blurred the distinction between war and peace when, from 1678 to 1688, he seized more territory (Strasbourg, Luxembourg, Lorraine, Alsace, Orange, Toul, Verdun, Metz and Casale) than during the preceding and succeeding conflicts. For good measure, he bombarded Genoa in 1684 without a declaration of hostilities. The practice of making 'war pay for war' encouraged soldiers to abuse their authority and disregard mitigating rituals.

Efforts were made to resurrect formal practices, especially in relation to the siege, in order to control the excesses of violence that had characterized the Century of Religious War. The Jurists – Hugo de Groot, better known as Grotius

(1583–1645), Richard Zouche (1590–1660), Samuel Pufendorf (1632–94), Cornelius van Bynkershoek (1673–1743) and Emerich de Vattel (1714–69) – attempted regulation through the formulation of natural and international law, but their success was limited. Grotius argued that human rights, discernible in natural law, did not evaporate just because states were at war. On the contrary, war ought never to be conducted unless the belligerents agreed to abide by the conventions suggested by natural law. These guidelines were apparent to reason: decent treatment of prisoners; humanity towards civilians; respect for property; rights for neutrals; honesty in negotiating and abiding by treaties; and resorting to war only for good reason. His ideas reached an audience through his book *De Jure Belli ac Pacis* (1625), and they may have indirectly influenced the peacemakers in Münster and Osnabrück.

Practicality and reciprocity, however, were more potent than philosophy. French and Spanish delegates met at Deynze, near Ghent, from 1676 until 1678 to consider how to make contributions less onerous. Although no formal document resulted, both sides agreed that the total contributions demanded from an area should not exceed the peacetime taxation that had been levied in the base year of 1669. Occupying armies were enjoined to negotiate contributions over a wide geographical area instead of victimizing individual towns and villages. Should a region not be able to pay, then there was to be no burning of property, the demon of '*brandschatzen*', but an orderly exchange of hostages until the debt had been discharged. Such good intentions did not endure, and the French collected contributions throughout the Nine Years War without regard for Deynze. The growth of civilian control over armies also helped to mitigate the burden of military occupation. Tired of marauding troops marching across his lands, in 1690 the Prince-Bishop of Liège appointed a military commissioner to liaise with all foreign troops 'visiting' the principality. He co-operated with their officers and administrators to ensure that the men were housed and fed with minimum disruption to the civilian population.

Louis XIV, the Circle of Swabia and the Duchy of Württemberg concluded a convention in 1692 banning the use of poisoned bullets. It also stipulated that only parties of more than nineteen infantrymen or fifteen cavalrymen, accompanied by an officer, could collect contributions; smaller groups would be treated as robbers. There was little altruism in this. Pillaging and marauding were injurious to military discipline, as the French discovered during the Ravaging of the Rhineland and the Palatinate in the winter of 1688–9.

Hugo de Groot, or Grotius, wrote in the Prologue to De Jure Belli ac Pacis *(1625) that 'I saw prevailing throughout the Christian world a licence in making war of which even barbarous nations should be ashamed; resorting to arms for trivial or for no reasons at all, and when arms were once taken up no reverence left for divine or human law, exactly as if a single edict had released a madness driving men to all kinds of crime.'*

CHAPTER FIVE

THE WARS OF LOUIS XIV 1667–97

THE SECOND ANGLO-DUTCH WAR ended in humiliating defeat for Charles II when the Dutch fleet under Michiel de Ruyter entered the English anchorage in the Medway on 22–23 June 1667. Three capital ships were burned and the Royal Charles towed to the Netherlands. The three Anglo-Dutch Wars (1652–4, 1665–7 and 1672–4) were, unusually, almost exclusively naval contests: normally, sea power was intimately associated with the conduct of land operations.

THE WARS OF LOUIS XIV 1667–97

GUIDED BY LE TELLIER and Louvois, who shared office from 1662, Louis XIV prepared an army and navy capable of dominating the Habsburgs and the Dutch. Although the French Army had shrunk to around 50,000 personnel after the Peace of the Pyrenees, by 1667 it had expanded to 80,000 in readiness for the War of Devolution (1667–8) against the Spanish Netherlands, launched to enforce the territorial claims of Louis's Spanish wife, Marie Thérèse, daughter of Philip IV. In alliance with the Dutch, who were fighting their second naval war

with England (1665–7), Turenne led the troops across the frontier on 24 May 1667 accompanied by the king and queen, two royal mistresses, and the court. Bergues, Ath, Charleroi, Tournai, Douai, Oudenarde and Alost fell quickly but Lille had to be subjected to a major siege, beginning on 28 August, directed by Vauban and Louis-Nicolas, Chevalier de Clerville. A circumvallation, 24 kilometres long, was completed by mid September, and Vauban 'broke ground' three days later. Progress was swift and, at midnight on 25 September, the *Gardes françaises* and the regiments of Picardy and Orléans attacked the covered way. Twenty-four hours later an assault on a demi-lune, a triangular outwork covering the point of a bastion, was sufficient to induce the governor to 'beat the

A panorama of the siege of Namur, 1695, by Jan van Huchtenburgh (1647–1733). Not only was the recapture of Namur the principal military event of the Nine Years War but it has gained a place in English literature through Uncle Toby and Corporal Trim's 'gardening' in Laurence Sterne's Tristram Shandy (1759–67).

chamade', a drum call signalling a willingness to surrender on terms. On the next day 2,500 survivors marched out, heading for Ypres: amidst great ceremony, Louis entered to receive the keys to the city.

Alarmed at French success, the Dutch terminated their war with England and allied with their former enemy and Sweden, the Triple Alliance thereby exerting sufficient pressure to persuade Louis to make peace with Spain.

Although the Peace of Aix-la-Chapelle (1668) rewarded France with Oudenarde, Tournai and Lille, Turenne and Vauban advised that if the Dutch had remained loyal, the entire Spanish Netherlands could have been captured. Louis determined to attack the treacherous Dutch, but first the Triple Alliance had to be dismantled. Charles II of England took French gold in return for an alliance whilst Charles XI of Sweden accepted 600,000 rijksdaler for stationing 16,000 men in Pomerania to dissuade German princes from supporting the Dutch during the coming war. This brought Sweden into conflict with Frederick William of Brandenburg–Prussia, who deployed his strong army in the Rhineland to support the Dutch. However, in June 1673 French bribes induced him to abandon the war and he promptly renewed the 1666 alliance with Sweden.

When the Dutch Smyrna Fleet sailed into English home waters during March 1672, it was attacked off the Isle of Wight by a battle squadron under Sir Robert Holmes. Forty-eight hours later Charles II declared war, followed by Louis within ten days. The French armies numbered 120,000 men nominally commanded by

The defeat of Spanish forces by the French in an action by the Bruges canal, 31 August 1667, by van der Meulen. Louis XIV on the white stallion, is conferring with his field commander, François de Créqui.

the Sun King, although operations were directed by Turenne and Condé with Vauban managing the sieges. Turenne, with 23,000, assembled near Charleroi, whilst Condé's 30,000-strong Army of the Ardennes concentrated at Nancy, where it had spent the winter as an army of occupation in the Duchy of Lorraine. The remainder of Louis's troops garrisoned the fortresses along the frontier with the Spanish Netherlands.

As Turenne marched down the Sambre, accompanied by Louis, Condé advanced along the Meuse: they joined at Visé, the only Meuse bridge between Liège and Maastricht. Anticipating that the latter was the target, the Dutch drained troops from their Rhine fortresses to garrison Maastricht. Condé advocated an immediate siege, arguing that it would secure the passage of the Meuse and deter Spain from assisting the Dutch. Turenne thought otherwise, stressing that because there was no prospect of Spain entering the war in 1672, valuable time should not be lost in besieging such a powerful fortress. Better to mask Maastricht by placing 10,000 men in garrisons at Maaseik, Tongeren, Bilsen, Saint-Truiden, Valkenburg and Sittard, and then traverse the Electorate of Cologne to the Rhine, drawing upon the magazines previously established in the Electoral fortresses of Neuss, Kaiserswerth, Bonn and Dorsten, thus outflanking the principal Dutch fortifications that had been built to resist attack from the south through the Spanish Netherlands.

Turenne prevailed, and the army set off for the denuded Rhenish defences.

The French secured communications between the Meuse and the Moselle by besieging Limbourg in the Ardennes, 10–21 June 1675. Situated on a hill and protected by rings of medieval fortifications plus some modern bastions, Limbourg contained a garrison of 1,000 men under the Count of Nassau. Condé and his son, the Duke of Enghien, took the covered way on 16 June and induced the 700 survivors to surrender by exploding three mines on 20 June.

*The siege of Orsoy,
24 May– 5 June 1672. Prior
to invading the Dutch
Republic, Louis XIV seized
the Dutch-garrisoned Lower
Rhine fortresses in Cleves.
Whilst Condé secured
Wesel, Turenne took Orsoy,
Rheinberg and Büderich.
Like the majority of
threatened towns, they all
fell within a few days:
protracted sieges in form
were exceptional.*

With Condé operating along the right bank of the Rhine and Turenne the left, the fortresses that the Elector of Brandenburg had allowed the Dutch to garrison – Rheinberg, Wesel, Rees and Emmerich – fell rapidly. The corps reunited at Emmerich on 11 June, and the following day Condé's cavalry and dragoons swam the Rhine near the Tolhuis at Lobith and occupied the Isle of Betuwe. Outflanked, the outnumbered and ill-prepared Dutch field army, only 15,000 strong, withdrew first to Utrecht and then into the coastal province of Holland, where the main sluices were opened and the polders flooded. Although the 'Water Line' was a makeshift, comprising inundations, fortresses and temporary earthworks, it halted the French advance, a fact tacitly admitted when Louis left the army on 1 August to return to Saint-Germain. To add to Dutch problems, the armies of the Bishop of Münster and the Elector of Cologne, commanded by Luxembourg, marched into Groningen and Friesland. By the autumn of 1672 the French and their German associates had occupied two-thirds of the United Provinces.

The Dutch raised William III of Orange to the position of stadholder, or national military leader, and began to accumulate allies. Following the French violation of the Duchy of Cleves, Frederick William of Brandenburg joined with the republic during May 1672 and, the next month, initialled a defensive agreement with Emperor Leopold. Whilst Condé's corps, temporarily commanded by Luxembourg, was thwarted before the inundations, Turenne's troops demonstrated in front of Maastricht before crossing the Electorate of

One of the most celebrated military exploits of the seventeenth century: Condé's French cavalry and dragoons swim the Rhine near the Tolhuis at Lobith to invade the Dutch Republic – the water level was exceptionally low following a prolonged drought.

Cologne to the Rhine. Turenne marched south to Koblenz, observing the manoeuvres of the Imperial army under Raimondo Montecuccoli, and then down the Moselle to winter in Lorraine. Having exhausted the magazines in Cologne, Turenne's men plundered and ravaged the Rhine and Moselle valleys. Peasants removed themselves and their possessions into the afforested hills and skirmished fiercely with the starving troops. By thus wasting the countryside,

Maastricht
1673 and 1676

William III of Orange, King of England (r. 1689–1702), led the military alliances against France, 1672–8 and 1688–97, often holding together by sheer force of personality anti-French coalitions of disparate princes, countries, and interests.

MAASTRICHT, 1673 AND 1676

Maastricht, a key fortress on the Meuse, was captured by the Dutch in 1632. During the French siege of 1673, Vauban attacked the front between the Porte de Tongres and the Porte de Bruxelles, concentrating on the

'demi-lune' before the latter. Amongst the casualties was Charles de Montesquiou, Comte d'Artagnan (1620–73), captain of the King's Musketeers, later immortalized by Alexandre Dumas.

ensuring that Imperial forces would be unable to operate close to the Rhine and Moselle, Turenne cleared the flank and rear of Luxembourg's corps in Utrecht and Holland.

Spain grew uneasy because France had virtually surrounded the southern Netherlands with a ring of clients and possessions; towards the end of 1672 Spanish troops were already fighting behind the Water Line. During February and

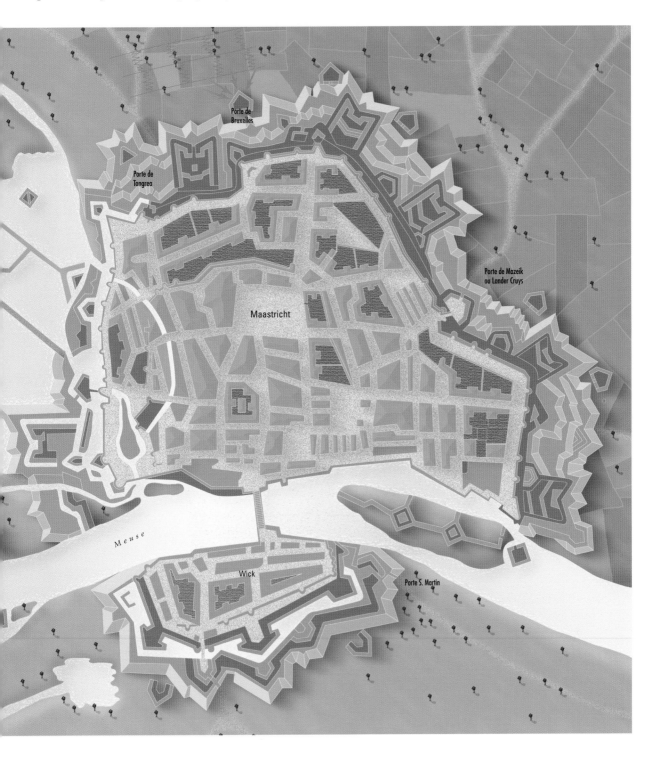

March 1673 Turenne screened Louis XIV's preparations for the siege of Maastricht by threatening the Imperial and Brandenburg forces. Leaving Condé to observe the Dutch, the royal army of 40,000 left its winter cantonments to concentrate at Ghent. After feinting at Brussels, Louis ordered the garrisons of Tongeren and Maaseik to invest Maastricht and a corps from Turenne's army to blockade Wick, the suburb on the east bank of the Meuse. From 8 June, 20,000 conscripted peasants excavated lines of contravallation and circumvallation while engineers bridged the Meuse with the new copper pontoons to link the besiegers. Forty-five thousand Frenchmen equipped with fifty-eight siege cannon surrounded Maastricht's garrison of 5,000 infantry and 1,000 cavalry commanded by Major General Jacques Fariaux. Employing for the first time his system of three parallels, Vauban's attack on the Tongeren Gate forced Fariaux and 3,000 survivors to surrender on 30 June. Late in August Spain, the United Provinces and Leopold signed the Hague Convention. Louis's difficulties multiplied when England terminated her naval war with the Dutch on 19 February 1674.

Condé's 45,000 men withdrew from Holland to an entrenched camp at Seneffe, north-west of Charleroi. General Karl van Rabenhaupt, with 11,000, then besieged the major French base at Grave on the Meuse covered by William commanding 65,000 Dutch, Imperial and Spanish troops. William approached Seneffe on 9 August 1674 but retired two days later, hoping that Condé would follow rather than march to relieve Grave. He obliged, jumping William's rearguard with a body of cavalry. Initially Condé was successful, but gradually the main armies were sucked into a bloody battle of attrition in which the French suffered at least 10,000 casualties and the Allies not less than 15,000. Grave resisted for three months, finally surrendering on 26 October. Turenne was charged with preventing a large German–Imperial army from interfering in either the Spanish Netherlands or Franche-Comté, the principal French objective for 1674. General Caprara had already crossed the Rhine and was near Strasbourg. He dispatched Duke Charles IV of Lorraine south along the right bank to threaten Franche-Comté, but Turenne responded rapidly, forcing Lorraine to return downstream. Intending to 'make war pay for war', the Frenchman sought to subsist his troops at the enemy's expense by operating on the right bank of the Rhine. Hence, his army comprised more horse than foot – 6,000 to 1,500 – to facilitate the collection of supplies over a wide area. In June Turenne departed from Hagenau, crossed the Rhine on a bridge of boats near Philippsburg, from whose garrison he drew a further four battalions, and went in search of Caprara, who was known to be marching north to effect a junction with reinforcements approaching from Frankfurt-am-Main under the cautious Austrian general Duke Alexander de Bournonville. Covering 160 kilometres in five days, Turenne overhauled Caprara's 7,000 cavalry and 2,000 infantry before they had joined with Bournonville and forced them to battle at Sinzheim on 16 June.

Although Turenne's preponderance of cavalry had been ideal for the rapid advance, he lacked firepower for battle. Caprara's infantry lined the hedges and gardens before the village of Sinzheim, but Turenne deployed his foot and dismounted dragoons in small skirmishing parties, which drove in these outposts and forced a passage over the River Elsatz and into the village. Behind a fighting rearguard the Imperialists withdrew through Sinzheim and formed in line of battle on the plateau above. The French now had to advance up a narrow defile in the knowledge that the Imperial horse would pounce on them as they emerged on to the plateau before they could deploy. Turenne, a master of improvisation, pushed his foot and dismounted dragoons up the flanks of the defile to man the numerous hedges as well as a castle on the left and a vineyard on the right. Their flanks secured, the French horse progressed up the defile and arranged itself in order of battle relatively unhindered. Turenne mingled groups of musketeers amongst the horse, in the Swedish manner, to provide additional firepower and lengthen the front. A premature advance by the French right wing nearly resulted in disaster, but well-aimed volleys from the infantry in the vineyard halted the counter-attack. Turenne then ordered a general advance and, supported by musketry, the cavalry steadily pushed the Imperialists back across the plateau. Exhausted and disorganized, Turenne's soldiers allowed the Imperialists to leave the field in good order. Both sides lost around 2,000 men.

Turenne had insufficient strength to exploit his success and, after demonstrating towards Heidelberg, was obliged to recross the Rhine to Neustadt. Early in July, having rebuilt his forces, he returned to the right bank and marched towards the Imperial headquarters at Heidelberg, seeking to force Bournonville to battle, but he refused to be drawn and retreated north of the Main. Remaining on the east bank, Turenne's troops lived off the country, seizing, looting, plundering and levying contributions. Even the dreaded *brandschatzen* reappeared. The peasants retaliated, attacking isolated parties and resisting the marauders.

This 'First Devastation of the Palatinate' continued for the rest of the summer, assisted by the garrison of Philippsburg. Forced from the Palatinate, Bournonville crossed the Rhine at Mainz with 30,000 men at the end of August, threatening Lorraine and Alsace. Concentrating 25,000 men between Wissembourg and Landau, Turenne was confident that Bournonville would have to retire, unable to subsist his troops. As anticipated, on 20 September Bournonville withdrew to the right bank and marched south to seize Strasbourg with its valuable Rhine bridge, thus separating Turenne from supporting forces in Upper Alsace and Franche-Comté. Turenne advanced to the village of Wanzenau to observe the Imperialists' positions around Enzheim, west of Strasbourg.

His front covered by the River Breusch and expecting Frederick William of Brandenburg with 20,000 reinforcements, Bournonville with his 36,000 men appeared secure. Turenne had to risk battle both to reopen his communications with Upper Alsace and to forestall a junction between Bournonville and Frederick William. Through an oversight the Imperialists had not blocked all the

① 14 June 1674: Turenne crosses
the Rhine

② 16 June: battle of Sinzheim,
French victory

③ 7 July: stand-off at Heidelberg

④ August–September: French
reinforcements arrive to join
Turenne's army in the area of the
Moselle

⑤ September: the Imperial army
marches along the Rhine and
besieges Strasbourg

⑥ 4 October 1674: battle of Enzheim,
French victory

⑦ September–November: Turenne
marches south and demonstrates
around Alsace whilst moving his
army into Lorraine

⑧ Turenne marches his army in
scattered detachments concentrating
on Belfort then moves north towards
Colmar

⑨ 5 January 1675: battle of Türkheim,
French victory

crossing-points of the Breusch, and on the night of 3–4 October, Turenne quietly moved over the river and placed his army at Molsheim between Bournonville and Strasbourg. At dawn he attacked. The battle of Enzheim on 4 October was, according to Bournonville, 'one of the longest, most obstinate, and artilleryzed [*sic*] that have ever been seen', the French firing 2,500 cannon balls. At the end of a day of frontal assaults, both Bournonville's flanks were threatened and he withdrew from the field having suffered around 3,500 casualties, mostly from the barrage. Turenne lost about 3,000.

During the manoeuvres around Enzheim the Elector of Brandenburg had been approaching the Rhine with 20,000 men and thirty-three cannon. On 10 October he crossed at Kehl, marched through Strasbourg and linked up with Bournonville, creating a combined force of 50,000. Greatly outnumbered, Turenne fell back to Deittweiler, between the forts of Saverne and Hagenau, where he received sufficient reinforcements to increase his strength to 33,000. Thinking that Turenne had gone into winter quarters, Bournonville and the elector settled down on the plains between the River Ill and the Rhine. Early in

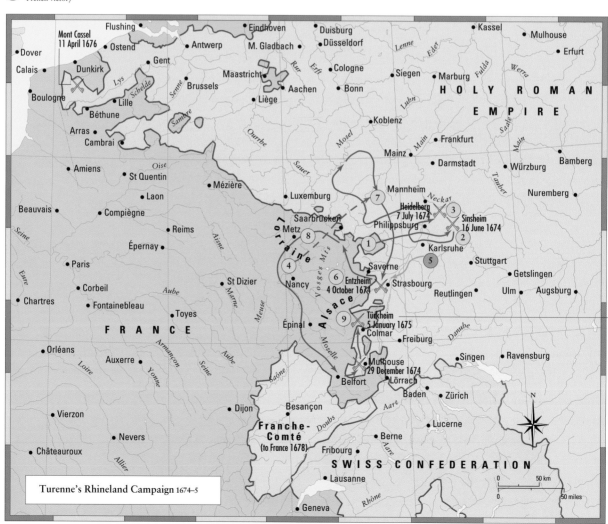

Turenne's Rhineland Campaign 1674–5

December Turenne left nine battalions at Saverne and Hagenau to cover his rear and marched first north, then west. Through snow and heavy frost he next turned south behind the screen of the Vosges before swinging east into the Belfort Gap. On 31 December Turenne debouched on to the plain of the Rhine, taking the Imperialists, scattered in garrisons and cantonments, by surprise. Desperately Bournonville threw his cavalry forward to delay the French whilst attempting to concentrate on Colmar and the little town of Türkheim. Driving rapidly north, Turenne shattered the Imperial horse at Mulhouse on 29 December and arrived at Türkheim on 4 January 1675.

Bournonville and the

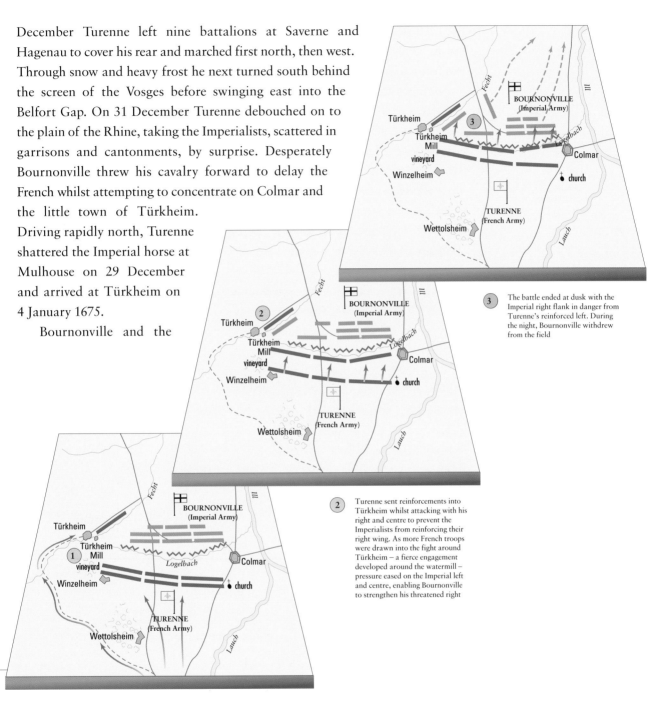

3 The battle ended at dusk with the Imperial right flank in danger from Turenne's reinforced left. During the night, Bournonville withdrew from the field

2 Turenne sent reinforcements into Türkheim whilst attacking with his right and centre to prevent the Imperialists from reinforcing their right wing. As more French troops were drawn into the fight around Türkheim – a fierce engagement developed around the watermill – pressure eased on the Imperial left and centre, enabling Bournonville to strengthen his threatened right

1 Masked by high ground between Winzelheim and Wettolsheim, Turenne threw infantry into Türkheim before advancing the remainder of his troops against the Imperialists between Türkheim and Colmar

TURENNE'S RHINELAND CAMPAIGN 1674–5

Turenne employed several ploys to parry Imperial attempts to invade France: manoeuvre, control over logistics, devastation, and battle, which was accepted only when victory was probable or all other options had failed. The battle of Türkheim ensured the success of the winter march around the Vosges.

elector had assembled 30,000 men between Colmar and Türkheim, but their front was too long to be strongly held along its entire length and Türkheim itself was under-garrisoned. Quick to spot these weaknesses, Turenne denied his opponents the opportunity to improve their deployment by promptly ordering his 30,000 men into order of battle. The French advanced to pin the Imperial left and centre before launching their main effort against Türkheim. Progress through the town was interrupted when Bournonville committed reserves, leading to a severe fight on the outskirts. As more and more Frenchmen were sucked in, pressure on Bournonville's centre and left eased, allowing him to swing his line round to face Türkheim, blocking any further French manoeuvres. After dark, the Imperial army left Turenne in possession of the field and withdrew into Strasbourg and then across the Rhine. Turenne watched them go before sending his troops into winter quarters.

Leopold recalled the veteran Montecuccoli to command during 1675. He decided to capture the Rhine bridge at Strasbourg prior to invading Alsace. Montecuccoli first marched directly on Strasbourg with 35,000 men but was countered by Turenne's 25,000. Next the Imperial commander feinted before turning north to attempt a crossing at Speyer, but once more the French hurried after him and thwarted the effort. True to his principle of seeking to operate in the enemy's territory, Turenne then made the passage of the Rhine, and a campaign of manoeuvre ensued with each side feeling for supply-lines and communications to force the other into an unfavourable stance. At the end of July Montecuccoli had been placed in such a disadvantageous position at Nieder Sasbach that he was compelled to offer battle on terms propitious to the French. Whilst reconnoitring an enemy artillery battery, Turenne was hit by a cannon ball and killed instantly. Lieutenant General the Comte de Lorge (1631–1702) assumed command and decided to withdraw across the Rhine into Alsace. Montecuccoli followed closely and Lorge had to cover his passage by fighting a rearguard action at Altenheim on 1 August 1675.

In the Spanish Netherlands the French concentrated on opening communications with Maastricht by securing the line of the Meuse: the bishopric of Liège was forced into neutrality before Givet, Dinant, Charleroi and Limburg were captured.

France opened the 1676 campaign in the Spanish Netherlands with the sieges of Condé (21–25 April) and Bouchain (2–11 May). June and early July were spent devouring the countryside between Brussels, Mons and Namur preparatory to the next round of sieges. Marshal Herman von Schomberg assumed command when Louis departed for Paris on 4 July; three days later, William of Orange besieged Maastricht with 40,000 men. Schomberg was confident that the garrison led by the energetic Lieutenant General Jean Sauveur de Calvo (1625–93), a Spaniard who had been in French service since 1641, would offer prolonged resistance. Accordingly, on 18 July he detached 18,000 men under d'Humières to besiege the Spanish fortress of Aire. Schomberg successfully covered the siege despite the close attentions of the Duke de Villahermosa and a Spanish corps. Aire surrendered on 31 July, and on 6 August Schomberg marched towards Maastricht.

Calvo's spirited defence had already thwarted three attempts to carry the Dauphin bastion and all assaults on the covered way. When Schomberg arrived on 26 August, William broke off the siege. Calvo's successful defence of a major fortress against a siege in form was a rare achievement. Along the Rhine, Margrave Ludwig of Baden (1655–1707) besieged Philippsburg on 24 June whilst Duke Charles V of Lorraine covered; Luxembourg was too weak to interfere and Philippsburg surrendered on 8 September. Taking advantage of the Imperialists' concern with Philippsburg, Luxembourg crossed the Rhine into the Breisgau to subsist his men at the enemy's expense.

The war of sieges continued during 1677. On the Schelde, d'Humières's feint at Mons enabled Luxembourg to besiege Valenciennes (28 February – 17 March). Cambrai followed (22 March – 17 April), and Saint-Omer, the remaining Spanish fortress in Artois, was attacked simultaneously by Philippe, Duke of Orléans, the king's brother. William mustered 30,000 at Dendermond and marched to relieve Saint-Omer. At the battle of Cassel on 11 April 1677 both sides fielded about 30,000 men: William's left was shattered by d'Humières whilst Luxembourg held the assault by the Dutch right. The Allies departed the field in some disorder, having lost around 8,000 killed and wounded in addition to 2,500 prisoners. They might well have disintegrated under a vigorous pursuit, but the French were too disorganized, and contented themselves with pillaging William's baggage train.

Having achieved their strategic objectives, the French spent the summer observing William until he suddenly concentrated his forces and besieged Charleroi on 6 August. Luxembourg led 40,000 men south of the Sambre to deny the besiegers forage and supply via the Sambre and the Meuse whilst d'Humières threatened their communications with Brussels, obliging William to raise the siege after only eight days. Along the Rhine, de Créqui successfully protected Alsace by outmanoeuvring Charles of Lorraine and, at the end of the campaign, captured Freiburg-im-Breisgau.

Screened by Luxembourg's feints at Ypres, Namur and Mons, the main French army marched north in February 1678 to besiege Ghent (1–10 March) and Ypres (15–25 March). Assuming that these sudden seizures would sufficiently alarm the Dutch, Louis presented his peace terms on 15 April; additional persuasion was applied by Luxembourg's blockade of Mons. William attempted to relieve this pressure but news that a peace treaty had been signed did not arrive in time to prevent a savage battle at the Abbey of Saint-Denis, near Mons, on 14 August, both sides losing about 4,000 men. On the Rhine, Créqui blocked an attempt by Charles of Lorraine to retake Freiburg and then defeated an Imperial corps under Guido von Starhemberg (1663–1737) at Rheinfeld near the Swiss border. He further reduced the threat to Alsace by beating Charles of Lorraine at Ortenbach on 23 July. The gate into Alsace was finally closed when Créqui

An engraving of the battle of Fehrbellin, 28 June 1675. When Wrangel entered Brandenburg with 13,000 Swedes late in 1674 the local inhabitants were ordered to withdraw, taking their supplies with them. The half-starved invaders were camped in two corps separated by the River Havel when they were surprised by Frederick William. Although managing to reunite via the bridge at Fehrbellin, the unbalanced Swedish army suffered 600 casualties and retired into Pomerania. Fehrbellin was an artillery bombardment rather than a closely fought battle.

captured both ends of the Rhine bridge at Strasbourg between 28 July and 11 August. A belated attempt by Charles to invade Alsace via Lauter was parried. In Catalonia the French captured Puigcerda after a siege lasting from 30 April to 28 May. Peace arrived when the Treaty of Nijmegen between France and the Dutch Republic was signed on 10 August. A Franco-Spanish treaty followed on 17 September and France made peace with Leopold I on 6 February 1679. Louis XIV gained Franche-Comté plus Valenciennes, Cambrai, Aire, Saint-Omer, Ypres, Condé and Bouchain. Vauban immediately set to work improving their fortifications.

In the spring of 1674 France increased her subsidies to Sweden on condition that she augmented her Pomeranian garrison to 22,000 men and attacked Brandenburg, which had re-entered the war against France. Even though not anxious for war, Sweden had to agree; there was no other money to pay the troops. At Christmas 1674 Karl Gustav Wrangel, the governor of Swedish Pomerania, marched into the Uckermark of Brandenburg with 20,000 men simply because they could no longer subsist in Pomerania. Elector Frederick William hurried back from the Rhine but not before Wrangel had reached the gates of Berlin. On Frederick William's arrival, Wrangel retired before an army only half

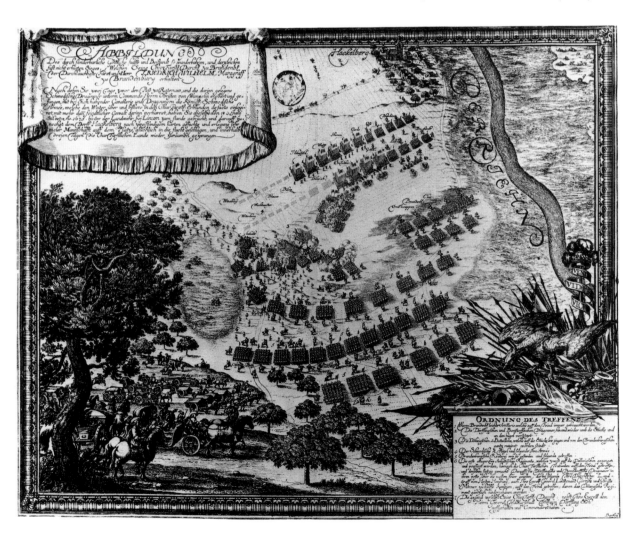

the size of his own but was pursued and defeated at Fehrbellin on 28 June 1675.

On hearing of the first serious Swedish defeat since 1634, Christian V of Denmark declared war, in alliance with the Dutch, against both France and Sweden. Brandenburg overran most of the Swedish possessions in north Germany whilst the Danes captured Wismar in October 1675 and seized the lands of the Duke of Holstein–Gottorp. A combined Dutch–Danish fleet under Cornelius van Tromp seized the island of Gotland and then, in June 1676, defeated the Swedish Navy off Ölond. Danish troops invaded southern Sweden in late summer 1676 but were overpowered at Lund in December. They returned again in 1677 but were finally forced to retire when Charles XI achieved victory at Landskrona.

By the autumn of 1678 Sweden had lost all her German territories. Following the signature of the Treaty of Nijmegen, Sweden tried to pressurize Brandenburg by attacking from Livonia into East Prussia. Gustav Horn's army managed to take Riga but lost 80 per cent of its strength in the process. Sweden was saved from humiliation because France wished to retain a Swedish presence in Germany and Leopold I was strongly opposed to Danish possession of German Baltic ports. By the Peace of Saint-Germain, Brandenburg received a sliver of Pomerania

The siege of Luxembourg City, 29 April – 3 June 1684. Luxembourg occupied a rocky site and could only be attacked on its northern front. Between 22 and 26 December 1683, de Créqui bombarded Luxembourg with 3,000–4,000 mortar bombs but the Spaniards refused to submit. De Créqui later returned to conduct a siege in form against a garrison of 2,500 who conducted a vigorous defence, despite Vauban's extensive employment of mortar fire.

along the right bank of the River Peene plus full control over Pomeranian port tolls. At Lund in September 1678 Denmark and Sweden agreed to return to the *status quo ante bellum*.

Although Louis XIV emerged from the Franco-Dutch War as the most powerful monarch in Western Europe, he immediately set about consolidating and extending his gains in order to acquire defensible frontiers in the Spanish Netherlands, Alsace and the Rhineland. Between 1678 and 1688 the peacetime French Army numbered 140,000 men, enabling Louis to reinforce aggressive diplomacy with armed force. By 1680 his diplomats had reclaimed Alsace, Lorraine, Orange, Toul, Metz and Verdun, whilst troops occupied most of the Duchy of Luxembourg and were blockading Luxembourg City. When, in 1682, the governor of Luxembourg tried to break the blockade, French units invaded Flanders, ruined the countryside, and seized territory around Courtrai. On 30 September 1681 France simultaneously seized Casale in Montferrat and Strasbourg. Spain declared war in 1683 but only succeeded in losing Courtrai in November and Luxembourg City on 3 June 1684, following a formal siege. Under cover of these operations, in May Louis's Mediterranean fleet bombarded Genoa, whose politics were pro-Habsburg and anti-French. No power could stand alone against France.

Although Western Europe was concerned, concerted action was slow to develop. Leopold was distracted, first by revolt in Hungary and then, in 1683, by the Turkish invasion of Austria. At Regensburg (Ratisbon) on 15 August 1684 a truce was concluded between Austria, Spain and France that guaranteed the expanded borders of France for twenty years. In 1685, having secured his frontiers, Louis commenced the climacteric of his campaign against the Huguenots by revoking the Edict of Nantes. Protestant refugees, living evidence of Louis's violence and intolerance, were welcomed into England, the Dutch Republic, Sweden–Finland, Switzerland and Brandenburg–Prussia.

THE NINE YEARS WAR, 1688–97

During the four years following the Truce of Regensburg an anti-French confederation evolved, led by William of Orange. In 1685 a number of German states, including Bavaria, formed the League of Augsburg to defend German soil. Although neither the Dutch nor Frederick William of Brandenburg–Prussia joined the league, they were supportive. The persecution of the Huguenots and the Vaudois finally convinced the Republican party in the United Provinces that Louis could not be trusted, particularly as the accession of the Catholic and Francophile James II of England in 1685 presaged an Anglo-French alliance that would endanger their maritime commerce.

The balance of power was also shifting in Central Europe. Victory at Belgrade in September 1688 allowed Leopold to reduce his commitment against the Turks and direct more forces, particularly the Army of the Circles, towards the defence of the Rhine. Whereas Louis had accepted the Truce of Regensburg on the assumption that twenty years would provide ample opportunity for diplomats to translate his seizures into permanent accretions, the Turkish retreat undermined his calculations. Instead of being coerced into confirming the truce, Leopold was leading a coalition of German princes dedicated to regaining lands forfeited to France. Affairs came to a head in Cologne, where there were two contenders for the throne of Archbishop-Elector Maximilian Heinrich von Wittelsbach, a French client since 1671. The favourite, Cardinal Wilhelm Egon von Fürstenberg, was also on Louis's payroll. When Maximilian Heinrich expired on 3 June 1688, the succession of Fürstenberg, already accepted as coadjutor by the cathedral chapter, seemed assured. The rival candidate was Prince Joseph Clement of Bavaria, a nephew of Maximilian II, Elector of Bavaria, and a younger brother of Maximilian Heinrich. Neither received the necessary two-thirds majority and the impasse was referred to Pope Innocent XI. There was no prospect of Innocent, who had been insulted by Louis, finding in favour of Fürstenberg, and Joseph Clement was duly installed on 26 August 1688. When Brandenburg troops entered the city of Cologne in support of Joseph Clement, 16,000 French soldiers occupied the remainder of the electorate, including Bonn and Kaiserswerth. In return for a Dutch commitment to support Austrian claims to the Spanish succession, Emperor Leopold joined the League of Augsburg.

Instead of waiting to assess the impact, Louis, encouraged by Louvois and aware of the strength gathering beyond the Rhine, determined upon a pre-emptive strike. On 24 September 1688 a French army under the dauphin and the Duc de Duras, attended by Vauban, attacked the Imperial fortress of Philippsburg. Louis hoped that a short, sharp siege would persuade Leopold and the German princes to translate the Truce of Regensburg into a permanent settlement before they could fully mobilize. If the worst occurred – and Louis was not pessimistic – the annexation of Philippsburg would complete the defence of France's eastern frontier. Assisted by heavy rains, Philippsburg held out for two months, but Germany paid for the campaign as French detachments roamed the Rhineland extracting contributions and seizing supplies; Boufflers surprised Kaiserslautern on 2 October before attempting Koblenz.

German reaction was swift. Frederick William of Brandenburg, John George III of Saxony, Ernst Augustus of Hanover, and Karl of Hesse-Kassel agreed to mobilize their forces (at the Concert of Magdeburg on 15 October 1688). The emperor recalled the Bavarian, Swabian and Franconian troops from Hungary and sent them, under the Elector of Bavaria, to defend southern Germany. By the end of October a German army of 20,000 men had concentrated at Frankfurt-am-Main and Boufflers had to withdraw from before Koblenz.

France faced war with Spain and the Anglo-Dutch along her entire frontier from Dunkirk to Basle. Louvois and Louis decided to erode further the military capability of the Rhineland through a campaign of depredation, the 'Second Devastation of the Palatinate'. The resultant systematic destruction of towns, villages, fortresses and supplies in the Palatinate, Trier and Württemberg was designed to create a *cordon sanitaire* along the French border through which German armies would be unable to operate. Tübingen, Heilbronn, Heidelberg, Worms, Mainz, Mannheim, Eslingen, Oppenheim, Pforzheim, Kaiserslautern, Speyer, Koblenz and Cochem were all partially or totally destroyed. Raiding parties reached as far as Nuremberg and Würzburg.

This combination of terror and crude economic warfare characterized the Nine Years War. Catinat in Piedmont and Noailles and Vendôme in Catalonia were to use identical methods; constricting an opponent's freedom of manoeuvre through the consumption or destruction of material resources became a standard operational ploy. In the case of the Palatinate it was particularly successful; although the German princes did not make peace, the Rhineland theatre was relegated to secondary status capable of supporting only limited operations. Whilst their political objectives were defensive, most participants tried to act offensively so that troops could be subsisted through contributions levied upon enemy lands. Exporting military costs involved the occupation of territory, resulting in positional campaigns, the extensive use of fortified 'lines', and the predominance of the siege. Because the rival armies were almost identical in weaponry, tactics, organization and numbers they were almost incapable of inflicting significant defeats on the battlefield. Navies were similarly ineffective. Politicians thus sought only what their generals and admirals could offer and deliver: the capture and retention of territory through siege and fortification.

Following the capture of Philippsburg, Louvois intended to winter the successful corps in the Palatinate but the unexpected reappearance of the Imperial Army in the Rhineland forced these plans to be abandoned and replaced by the Second Ravaging of the Palatinate. The scruples of some senior French officers resulted in only a partial execution of royal orders. Heidelberg (below) was so lightly damaged by Tessé in October 1688 that Louvois dispatched Baron de Montclair (d. 1690) during February 1689 to finish the job.

FORMATION OF THE GRAND ALLIANCE

By attacking Philippsburg, Louis knowingly allowed William of Orange to invade England, calculating that he would become enmeshed in a civil war: at the same time the Turks were encouraged to greater endeavours on the Danube. In the spring of 1688 England was sliding towards a commitment to France, yet the Dutch were determined to secure England's considerable military and economic resources. Exploiting internal disquiet, William of Orange invaded on 15 November 1688. James II fled to France, and William and his wife, Mary, were created joint sovereigns. Louis quickly dispatched James to Ireland, where the Catholics were already in revolt, to play him against the new regime; if William's energies could not be consumed by civil war in England, Ireland was a serviceable substitute. Between March 1689 and October 1690 the Netherlands, England, the Holy Roman Empire, the Spanish Netherlands, the League of Augsburg, Spain, Bavaria, Savoy–Piedmont and the Duchy of Lorraine declared war on France. This 'Grand Alliance' enjoyed further support, in the form of mercenaries, from Denmark, Sweden, Hesse-Kassel, Württemberg and Hanover. Instead of a short war, France faced an attritional struggle against a large coalition.

Following a winter of raiding and destruction the French withdrew from Germany and the Prince-Bishopric of Liège. France, holding the advantage of a central position, formed two main armies: one to operate along the line of the Sambre under the command of d'Humières and a second at Mainz directed by de Duras. Although the Grand Alliance was numerically superior, its campaigns were ill-coordinated. Not until 1691, when William III was able to leave England and Ireland and assume personal command, did strategy grow more coherent.

The campaign of 1689 opened in the Rhineland. The smallest of three German armies, commanded by the Elector of Bavaria, held the 'Lines of Stollhofen' between the Black Forest and the Rhine, guarding central Germany against an attack from Strasbourg and Kehl. The Army of the Middle Rhine consisted of 50,000 Austrians, Bavarians, Saxons and Hessians around Frankfurt-am-Main directed by Charles V of Lorraine. He besieged Mainz on 5 June, Marshal d'Huxelles resisting for fifty-two days. A victory at Herderbosch on 11 March by 40,000 Brandenburg and Hanoverian forces, commanded by General Hans Adam von Schöning, over the Marquis de Sourdis and the Comte de Vertillac forced the French to evacuate most of the Electorate of Cologne: Neuss fell on 14 March, Siburg and Kempen on 16 March, quickly followed by Zons and Soest. Kaiserswerth was bombarded on 23 May and besieged from 21 to 26 June, and then Bonn received similar treatment, surrendering on 10 October.

The eastern flank of the Anglo–Dutch–Spanish army in the Spanish Netherlands, commanded by Waldeck, was thus cleared and the danger removed of a French attack on the United Provinces along the Rhine. Accordingly, Waldeck crossed the Sambre and invaded France. Despite winning an engagement at Walcourt on 25 August, Waldeck found that his advance was effectively blocked by d'Humières and he withdrew north of the Sambre.

ITALY AND SWITZERLAND, C. 1648

Although the Austrian Habsburgs dominated northern Italy, France sought to increase her influence in the region by exerting pressure on the Duchy of Savoy–Piedmont.

James II's Catholic forces occupied most of Ireland, except Londonderry and Enniskillen in Ulster. Although aware that the war would be decided in the Low Countries, William had to divert resources to Ireland to secure his new crown. A French squadron under the Comte de Château-Renault was surprised by an Allied squadron under Admiral Edward Herbert on 11 May while landing supplies and reinforcements in Bantry Bay. Both claimed victory, but Herbert withdrew. Londonderry withstood a low-intensity siege of 105 days (28 April – 10 August), and on 23 August Marshal Herman von Schomberg landed near Bangor with 14,000 Allied troops but was unable to make progress.

Scotland also rose in support of James. Led by John Graham of Claverhouse, Viscount Dundee, the rebels scattered a small Williamite army under General Hugh Mackay at Killiecrankie on 27 July but defeat at Dunkeld on 21 August marked the effective end for the Scottish Jacobites.

During the spring of 1689 France reignited a Catalonian peasant rising against Charles II of Spain that had initially broken out in 1687. Exploiting the situation, Marshal Noailles invaded Catalonia during May with 9,000 men and took the fortress of Camprodon against feeble resistance. Insufficient troops were available to develop this success even though Barcelona was open to attack, so at the end of June Noailles withdrew into Roussillon whilst the Spaniards advanced to besiege and raze Camprodon before turning to suppress the revolt.

A fifth theatre of war opened in 1690. Sandwiched between France and Habsburg Milan, and dominated by the French fortresses of Pinerolo in the west and Casale in the east, Duke Victor Amadeus II of Savoy–Piedmont 'could not afford to be honourable'. From the spring of 1687 he edged closer to Spain and the emperor, but the outbreak of war along the Rhine presented him with greater opportunities. Although France initially treated it as a subsidiary theatre, William regarded Piedmont as the sole stage where the Allies might act decisively by invading southern France to capture Toulon and fomenting rebellion amongst the Huguenots of Dauphiné, the Cevennes and Languedoc. Victor Amadeus was less ambitious, wishing only to free himself from France, avoid domination by Spain and Austria, and regain Pinerolo and Casale.

A light, mule-transportable mountain gun from the reign of Louis XIV. The French Army operated extensively in the Alps during the persecution of the Vaudois in Piedmont, 1685–6, and the Nine Years War. Campaigns were also conducted through the southern Pyrenees and Catalonia, 1689–97.

A ferment of religious animosities and Savoyard hatred of the French produced a brutal war characterized by massacres, atrocities, and the burning of towns and villages. French troops suffered constant guerrilla attacks by an armed populace, both Catholics and Protestant Vaudois. In return they inflicted draconian reprisals: by 1696 Savoy and most of southern and western Piedmont had been ruined. During the first weeks of 1690, French troops overran all of

Zürich

Berne

SWISS CONFEDERATION

Geneva

46°

Innsbruck

Inn

T y r o l

Trento

S t y r i a

C a r i n t h i a

Villach

Udine

I M P E R I A L   H U N G A R Y

Drave

PIEDMONT

Turin

Pinerolo

MILAN

Milan

Casale

Savoy

FRANCE

Po

MANTUA

PARMA

MODENA

REP. OF GENOA

Genoa

LUCCA

Pisa

Florence

Volterra

Siena

TUSCANY

Elba

PRESIDIOS

Orbetello

42°

Corsica
(to Genoa)

Aleria

Antibes

Nice

L i g u r i a n

S e a

Bologna

Ravenna

San Marino

Ancona

Tiber

PAPAL

Orvieto

STATES

Rome

Ostia

Terracina

Civitella

Pescara

R E P U B L I C   O F   V E N I C E

Piave

Verona

Venice

Adige

Trieste

Pola

C a r n i o l a

Save

OTTOMAN

EMPIRE

A
d
r
i
a
t
i
c

S
e
a

Zara

Spalato

Mostar

Foggia

Barletta

Bari

Taranto

Sardinia

Olbia

Sulcis

T y r r h e n i a n

S e a

Naples

Salerno

K I N G D O M   O F   N A P L E S

Gulf of
Taranto

Croton

38°

Palermo

Reggio

S i c i l y

Catania

Syracuse

N

Italy
c.1648

Spanish Habsburg
territories

Austrian Habsburg
territories

Ottoman territory

border of the Holy
Roman Empire

0   50 km

0   50 miles

12°

12°

16°

Savoy, except the fortress of Montmélian, and Victor Amadeus withdrew to Turin.

On 3 June 1690 Spain agreed to provide military assistance from Milan, and a similar deal with the emperor was concluded on 4 June. Victor Amadeus then declared war on France, formally joining the Grand Alliance on 20 October. From his base in Pinerolo, Catinat ravaged the countryside and, by threatening the key town of Saluzzo, forced Victor Amadeus to accept battle on 18 August at the abbey of Staffarda. Surprised and defeated, the Savoyard army lost 5,000 men and fell back to Carmagnola to absorb reinforcements.

Catinat exploited his victory by levying contributions across southern Piedmont. Early in November he moved northwards to besiege and capture Susa on the River Dora Riparia, a vital fortress controlling communications with Briançon in Dauphiné.

In the northerly theatres French prospects were promising. William and most of the British troops were tied down in Ireland, whilst the emperor was heavily committed in Hungary. There was also an unexpected French naval success. So many English and Dutch ships had already been lost to French privateers that

William III's polyglot army of British, French Huguenots, Dutch and Danes successfully performed the difficult feat of fording the Boyne against a strongly defended far bank. The fighting was fierce until further crossings threatened to trap James II's Franco-Irish force within a bend of the river, forcing it to retire. Although casualties were light – the Williamites lost about 500 men, the Jacobites 1,000 – King James fled to France and the Jacobite fires in Ireland slowly died. Jan Wyck's painting closely follows that of Dirck Maas (1659–1717), an eyewitness to the action.

merchants demanded greater protection, which could only be provided by denuding the Channel Fleet. While Vice Admiral Henry Killigrew's twenty-four warships escorted merchantmen towards Cadiz, the Comte de Tourville entered the English Channel with many more ships than the combined Anglo-Dutch fleet of Arthur Herbert, now Earl of Torrington. Torrington, who wished to evade battle until Killigrew could rejoin, was instructed to fight. On 10 July, off Beachy Head, English vessels failed to support the Dutch, and the Allied fleet was defeated, losing five ships. As they withdrew to the Nore, Tourville ruled the Channel, but an outbreak of disease restricted exploitation of the victory to the burning of the fishing village of Teignmouth.

Although Tourville stood across his communications with England, William campaigned vigorously in Ireland. Landing at Carrickfergus on 24 June with enough reinforcements to augment the army to 40,000 men, he assumed command from Schomberg and marched south towards Dublin. James moved north with about 25,000, including 6,600 French infantry, and took position along the River Boyne but was defeated on 11 July. While the Jacobite army withdrew

At Fleurus, 1 July 1690, Luxembourg took advantage of Waldeck's faulty deployment to mass his army obliquely against the Confederate right. This scene shows the French cavalry driving off the Dutch horse, exposing the right of Waldeck's infantry, which was then assaulted to the front, rear and flank. Only by forming a huge hollow square was the Dutch foot, supported by Spanish cavalry, able to retire from the battlefield. Both sides lost about 20 per cent of their strength.

to Limerick, James left Ireland for France, command passing to the Duke of Tyrconnel (1630–91). Bad weather saved Limerick from capture. To improve communications with England and boost his own prestige, the Earl of Marlborough launched an amphibious operation that captured Cork (29 August) and Kinsale (15 October).

Waldeck again commanded the Allied army in the Spanish Netherlands, but d'Humières had been relegated to supervise the garrison of the Lines of the Lys and the Scheldt, the chief command in Flanders passing to Luxembourg, France's most capable general. Taking a central position, he rapidly combined with Boufflers's corps east of the Meuse and advanced with 40,000 men against Waldeck's 30,000. Waldeck was beaten in a day-long battle at Fleurus on 1 July although both sides suffered about 7,000 casualties. Intelligence that a German attack might materialize from Koblenz along the line of the Moselle prevented Luxembourg from taking advantage of his success. The Turkish recapture of Belgrade in October forced the emperor to recall troops from the Rhineland, whilst a further 6,000 went to northern Italy. Another setback was the death of the Duke of Lorraine; the less able Elector of Bavaria was appointed in his stead. Fleurus allowed the French to reinforce their corps in the Rhineland to 40,000, against which the German armies were unable to take significant action.

During the winter of 1690–91 William provided reinforcements sufficient to increase the Piedmontese Army to 20,000 men, but plans to invade France through Savoy had to be abandoned after Catinat's pre-emptive capture of Nice early in March. He then prepared to attack Turin, taking Avigliana as a preliminary, but his forces were inadequate and he turned southwards. Carmagnola fell on 9 June and Catinat then besieged Cuneo, the principal fortress of southern Piedmont. The arrival of Imperial reinforcements under Prince Eugene of Savoy enabled Victor Amadeus to force Catinat to abandon the siege and assume the defensive, but Savoyard schemes for an invasion of France were obstructed by the Austrians. Already sensing that he might not achieve his political objectives by military means, in October Victor Amadeus made diplomatic contact with France; during December Giovanni Gropello (1650–1722) opened negotiations with the Comte de Tessé (1651–1725), commandant of Pinerolo. Nothing resulted, because Louis only offered Savoy neutral status for the remainder of the war.

In Catalonia, whilst the army remained inactive until Noailles had established magazines at Cardona, the navy assumed the initiative. Employing bomb ketches, which had proved effective against Genoa, thirty-six French ships bombarded Barcelona on 10 July, destroying over 300 houses. They next proceeded to Alicante on 25 July and fired 3,500 bombs into the town over four days; 90 per cent of the buildings were damaged. These terror attacks helped to unite Spain, including Catalonia, behind Charles II in Madrid.

In Ireland William handed command to Godard van Reede, Baron van Ginkel. Emerging from winter quarters, he secured a crossing of the Shannon at

Athlone (29 June – 10 July) before defeating the Jacobite army under its French commander, the Marquis de Saint-Ruth, at Aughrim on 22 July. The Jacobites withdrew into Limerick. Without prospects of further French assistance, the Jacobites signed the Treaty of Limerick (13 October), which ended hostilities on surprisingly generous terms.

Along the Rhine little was achieved, epidemics debilitating both the French and the Imperialists. Again the main theatre was the Spanish Netherlands. In an operation carefully planned by Louvois, Luxembourg surprised the Allies by besieging the fortress of Mons (15 March – 10 April). William hurriedly concentrated at Halle, south of Brussels, but was unable to intervene. Boufflers raided Liège in June, bombarding the city and burning some of the suburbs, but he was unable to effect a siege. William left the army in Waldeck's care before the campaign was concluded, whereupon Luxembourg embarrassed the rearguard as it decamped from Leuse on 19 September.

Anti-government factions in England had become disillusioned with both the cost and the unimpressive results of fighting the French in Flanders; instead, the Elizabethan strategy of mounting amphibious 'descents' upon the enemy coast was resurrected, employing infantry returned from Ireland. The initial target (January 1692) was Dunkirk, but secrecy was compromised and the operation

The siege of Mons was a masterpiece of logistical planning, Louvois achieving complete operational secrecy and tactical surprise. Mons guarded a direct route to Brussels but its fortifications were old and weak – 'sodworks … not very uniform'. After three weeks had been spent draining the inundations, the siege progressed quickly. According to the French account, Mons fell when a hornwork was breached but the Confederates insisted that the Prince de Berghes (1650–1704) was induced to surrender by the townspeople to prevent further damage.

The French siege of Namur, 1692. Directed by Vauban and Jean-Claude de Bressé (d. 1704) and taking advantage of the poor morale of the understrength garrison, the French captured the town on 5 June but heavy rain hampered an attack on the citadel. Eventually the French seized a hornwork and the panicked governor sued for terms.

cancelled. The principal French objective for 1692 was the vital Sambre–Meuse fortress of Namur (29 May – 1 July). To deter William from marching to its relief, Louis arranged a simultaneous landing upon the south coast of England using 12,000 Irish troops, released under the terms of the Treaty of Limerick, leavened by an equal number of Frenchmen.

An essential preliminary was the acquisition of naval supremacy in the English Channel. During a five-day battle between the capes La Hogue and Barfleur on the northern coast of the Cotentin peninsula (29 May – 3 June), Edward Russell's Anglo-Dutch warships shattered Tourville's fleet and the invasion was cancelled.

The fall of Namur opened the line of the Sambre–Meuse and threatened Liège. William sought to restore the situation through battle. After sowing false

intelligence that the army was engaged upon a grand forage, William marched at night from his position at Halle and surprised Luxembourg's camp at Enghien. However, inadequate reconnaissance reduced the Allied assault to a tangential blow against the French right wing around the village of Steenkirk (3 August). Each side suffered 8,000 casualties, although only half the troops were engaged.

The Imperialists in the Rhineland numbered 47,000 but were slow to enter the field. Two limited offensives across the Rhine brought no enduring success. They failed to capture Ebernberg on the River Nahe, near Bingen, whilst a counter-attack by Marshal de Lorge (1630–1702) seized Pforzheim. Lorge then brushed aside a small corps on the borders of Württemberg and proceeded to levy contributions throughout the duchy. Because Catinat's army had been drained to provide troops for other theatres, Victor Amadeus was persuaded by William to

Seapower as an adjunct to land warfare. Edward Russell's victory over Tourville's fleet at the battle of La Hogue (Barfleur) prevented a French corps from invading southern England and restored Anglo-Dutch command of the Channel.

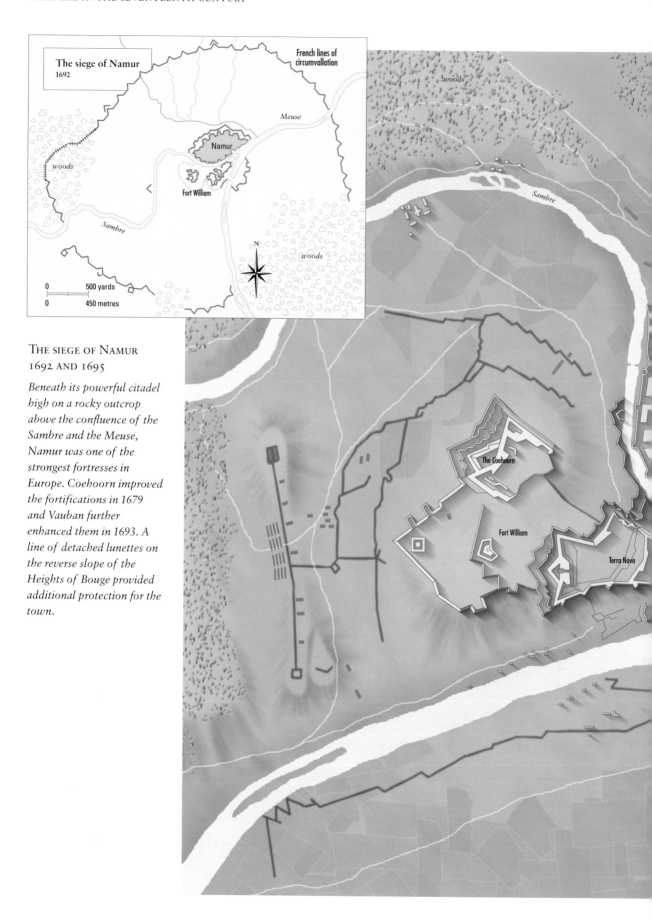

The siege of Namur
1692

French lines of
circumvallation

Meuse

Namur

Fort William

woods

Sambre

woods

N

| 0 | | 500 yards |
| 0 | | 450 metres |

THE SIEGE OF NAMUR 1692 AND 1695

Beneath its powerful citadel high on a rocky outcrop above the confluence of the Sambre and the Meuse, Namur was one of the strongest fortresses in Europe. Coehoorn improved the fortifications in 1679 and Vauban further enhanced them in 1693. A line of detached lunettes on the reverse slope of the Heights of Bouge provided additional protection for the town.

woods

Sambre

The Coehoorn

Fort William

Terra Nova

The siege of Namur
1695

siege lines

Namur

Heights of Bouge

Meuse

del

woods

invade France, although his personal preference was either to recapture Pinerolo and Susa or enter Savoy to relieve Montmélian. In the spring a detachment was sent to blockade Casale, whilst the main Piedmontese army entered Dauphiné, where, during July, it captured Guillestre, Embrun and Gap, ruining the countryside en route. This, however, was the limit of the advance, and all attempts to foment a rising amongst the Huguenots failed. The campaign was already languishing when Victor Amadeus contracted smallpox and the troops recrossed the Cottian Alps in the autumn. During the winter, as he slowly recovered, Victor Amadeus made further diplomatic approaches to Tessé.

Harvests between 1689 and 1692 had been poor but that of 1693 failed completely throughout France and northern Italy. Faced with dwindling resources, Louis gave the army priority in funding over the navy; following a final fleet action off Lagos, when 80 of 400 Anglo-Dutch merchantmen from the Smyrna Fleet were seized (27 June 1693), the navy concentrated on commerce raiding, the *guerre de course*. Louis decided to launch major land offensives in Catalonia, Germany and the Netherlands as a prelude to dangling generous peace terms before the Grand Alliance. A concomitant diplomatic initiative arrested Swedish dalliance with the Grand Alliance and diverted Sweden's good offices to opening fissures amongst the German princes; only the gift of the electoral dignity persuaded Ernst August of Hanover not to desert the Grand Alliance, whilst concessions were also required to retain the wavering John George IV of Saxony.

However, the weight of French diplomacy was directed towards Piedmont, where Victor Amadeus was determined to recapture Pinerolo. After sending detachments under the Spanish general the Marquis de Leganez to mask Casale, he advanced westwards. Catinat left Tessé at Pinerolo and withdrew to Fenstrelle to protect Tessé's communications with Susa. The attack on Pinerolo was half-hearted, more bombardment than siege, and ended with Victor Amadeus renewing his diplomatic overtures to Tessé through Gropello on 22 September. As Victor Amadeus dithered, Catinat counter-attacked. Reinforced with troops from Catalonia and the Rhine, he advanced from the mountains above Pinerolo and was across Victor Amadeus's communications with Turin by 29 September.

Abandoning the bombardment of Pinerolo, the Savoyard army hastened eastwards, encumbered by its siege train. At La Marsaglia on 4 October, the outnumbered, fatigued and out-generalled Piedmontese lost 6,000 men. Although Cuneo and Turin lay open to attack, supply difficulties prevented Catinat from exploiting his victory, and, after levying contributions from as far south as Saluzzo, he retired into winter quarters.

Louis's three land offensives began in Catalonia, where Noailles besieged Rosas (from 28 May to 9 June 1693), the chief Catalan naval base, using both his army and fifty warships. Lorge crossed the Rhine in May with 50,000 men and sacked Heidelberg for the second time in four years. He then advanced cautiously into Franconia, but Ludwig of Baden occupied a strongly fortified blocking

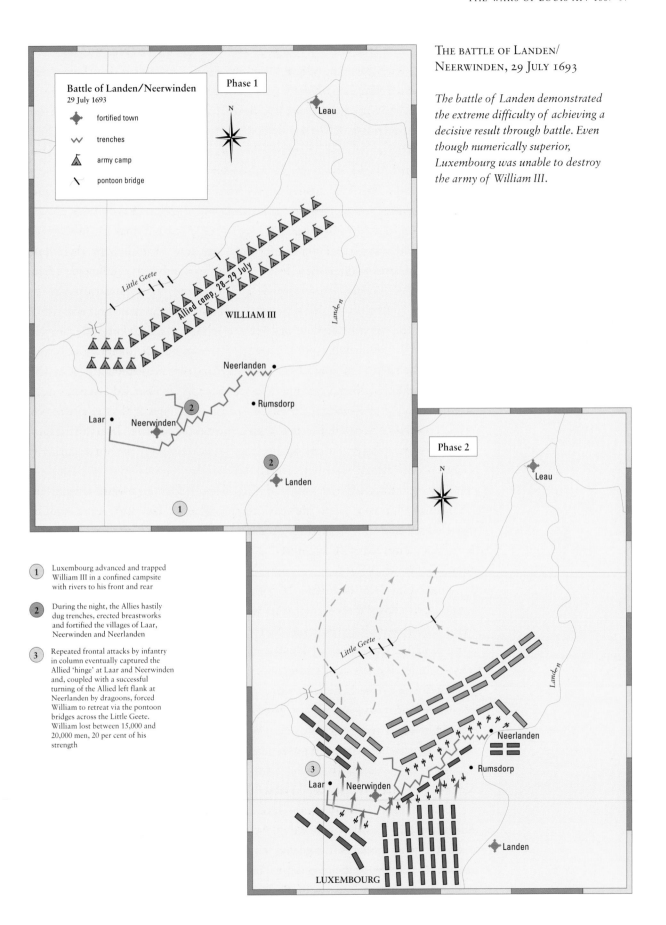

Battle of Landen/Neerwinden
29 July 1693

- ⬥ fortified town
- ᗯ trenches
- ◭ army camp
- ╲ pontoon bridge

Phase 1

N

Leau

Little Geete

Allied camp 28–29 July

WILLIAM III

Landen

Neerlanden •

• Rumsdorp

Laar •   Neerwinden

2

Landen

1

Phase 2

N

Leau

Little Geete

Landen

Neerlanden

• Rumsdorp

Laar •   Neerwinden

Landen

LUXEMBOURG

3

The battle of Landen/ Neerwinden, 29 July 1693

The battle of Landen demonstrated the extreme difficulty of achieving a decisive result through battle. Even though numerically superior, Luxembourg was unable to destroy the army of William III.

1. Luxembourg advanced and trapped William III in a confined campsite with rivers to his front and rear

2. During the night, the Allies hastily dug trenches, erected breastworks and fortified the villages of Laar, Neerwinden and Neerlanden

3. Repeated frontal attacks by infantry in column eventually captured the Allied 'hinge' at Laar and Neerwinden and, coupled with a successful turning of the Allied left flank at Neerlanden by dragoons, forced William to retreat via the pontoon bridges across the Little Geete. William lost between 15,000 and 20,000 men, 20 per cent of his strength

position at Ilzfeldt (26 July – 28 August) which Lorge and the Dauphin could not penetrate. In the Netherlands, Luxembourg, commanding 68,000 men supported by 48,000 under Boufflers, manoeuvred so that William had to split his army of 120,000 into three corps to protect Flanders, Brussels and Liège. Having achieved a local superiority of 66,000 to 50,000, he trapped William in a confined and awkward position around the villages of Landen and Neerwinden, west of Maastricht, on 29 July. Although the Allies lost only 12,000 compared to French casualties of 15,000, William withdrew from the field in some disorder, and Luxembourg was able to profit from victory by besieging and taking the Meuse fortress of Charleroi (on 10 October).

PEACE NEGOTIATIONS BEGIN

The successes of 1693 were insufficient to bring the Grand Alliance to negotiation, and France was now so exhausted by war and famine that she could not resume the general offensive in 1694 and relied upon diplomacy to disunite her opponents. In particular, Louis needed peace in Italy. With Savoy and Nice occupied, much of Piedmont devastated, and his army beaten at La Marsaglia, Victor Amadeus was receptive, and talks reopened in October 1693. As a gesture of goodwill, Victor Amadeus promised to remain inactive for the campaign of 1694. Tessé was empowered to negotiate a truce to be followed by a junction of Franco-Savoyard forces to drive the Imperial armies from Italy before declaring it a neutral zone. By attempting to detach one member, Louis hoped to induce the collapse of the Grand Alliance and thus bring about a general settlement. Accordingly, he also made indirect contact with William. Victor Amadeus manoeuvred between both sides, pressing Louis to make peace on favourable terms but advertising the negotiations to persuade his allies to redouble their efforts on his behalf.

On 17 May 1694 Noailles's 26,000 men defeated 16,000 Spaniards on the banks of the River Ter, French warships providing flanking fire and logistic support. Palamós was stormed on 10 June and Gerona on 29 June, opening the route to Barcelona. Following an ill-conceived and worse-executed 'descent' on Brest (8 June) and the bombardment of Dieppe, Saint-Malo and Le Havre, the powerful Anglo-Dutch fleet was ordered to the Mediterranean: seventy-five vessels under Edward Russell anchored off Barcelona on 8 August. The French ships immediately sailed for the safety of Toulon, obliging Noailles to withdraw to the line of the Ter, harassed by General Blas Trinxería's Catalan guerrillas, the *miquelets*. Sea power had proved decisive.

Instead of returning to home waters, Russell wintered at Cadiz in readiness for operations off Catalonia in the spring. There was also the possibility that the Allied fleet might assist the Duke of Savoy in recapturing Nice, especially since Catinat's army had been depleted to reinforce Noailles, but he demurred, explaining that the season was too far advanced for such complex manoeuvres. Either Victor Amadeus was abiding by his pledge to remain inactive or, more probably, the devastated Piedmontese countryside could no longer support sustained operations, a situation exacerbated by an acute shortage of grain throughout northern Italy during the winter of 1694–5. Late in the year, Imperial envoys proposed Casale as the target for the next year, but this did not accord with Victor Amadeus's aim of regaining Savoyard control over the fortress, and he promptly renewed his negotiations with Tessé.

In both Germany and the Netherlands the French remained on the defensive during 1694. Lorge sallied over the Rhine early in June, but an advance by Ludwig of Baden forced him to recross at Philippsburg on 28 June after a sharp engagement. Baden then occupied a series of fortified camps to deter the French from re-entering Germany. Although able to protect Flanders, Luxembourg could not prevent William seizing the small Meuse fortress of Huy (on 27 September), an essential preliminary to future operations against Namur.

Negotiations over the winter of 1694–5 convinced William that more was to be gained through military action than diplomacy, whilst Louis hoped that Savoy–Piedmont could be detached from the Grand Alliance. Victor Amadeus knew that the Imperial forces intended to attack Casale and, not wishing to encourage the extension of Austrian Habsburg power from Milan, on 15 March 1695 he instructed Gropello to warn Tessé. Instead of letting the emperor conquer Casale, Gropello proposed that the French garrison might surrender to the Piedmontese following a token siege provided that the fortifications were then dismantled and the fortress returned to its rightful owner, the Duke of Mantua. Louis consented on 29 April on condition that Victor Amadeus prevented his allies from attacking any other French possession in Italy. The siege of Casale began on 25 June and, after nominal resistance, the garrison surrendered on 9 July. Despite the suspicions of his allies, Victor Amadeus avoided any further action, and the rest of the summer was spent demolishing the fortifications, a task not completed until mid September, too late to begin further operations. On 23 November Gropello intimated to Tessé that Victor Amadeus might abandon his allies if France would cede Pinerolo. Although Louis was reluctant to abandon territory, he knew that the defection of Savoy–Piedmont could shatter the Grand Alliance, and in February 1696 he instructed Tessé to negotiate.

Luxembourg died in January 1695. His replacement, Villeroi, commanded 115,000 men but was outnumbered by the Allies. William feinted towards Flanders and invested Fort Knokke (17–24 June) to commit Villeroi before hurrying eastwards to besiege Namur (8 July), which was defended by 15,000 men under Boufflers. Villeroi did not march immediately to Namur's relief, confident that the fortress could endure almost indefinitely. He was further delayed by an engagement at Aarsele (14–15 July) with the Prince de Vaudémont's (1649–1723) 37,000-strong shadowing corps. Slowly Villeroi edged towards Namur, bombarding Brussels en route (13–15 August). Some 4,000 shells and red-hot shot were fired, destroying over 2,000 buildings, but William refused to be drawn from the Meuse. Finally Villeroi approached Namur, only to be thwarted

After the capture of Dinant (below) and Huy in 1674, Maastricht remained the only French-held Meuse fortress, dependent for supply upon Liège. On 31 March 1675 French troops 'guaranteed' the neutrality of Liège, de Créqui successfully besieged the Spanish garrison of Dinant 21–30 May, and on 1–6 June Huy succumbed to a siege by de Rochefort.

by William's covering army. Boufflers surrendered on 22 September. The recapture of Huy and Namur restored the Allies' position on the Meuse and secured communications between their armies in the Low Countries and those on the Rhine and the Moselle.

Taking advantage of the presence of the Anglo-Dutch fleet, the Marquis de Castañaga unsuccessfully attacked Palamós on 15–25 August 1695. When the warships left the Mediterranean in the autumn, the French were free to resume their advance towards Barcelona.

The campaign of 1696 was dominated by a financial crisis in England and the defection of Savoy–Piedmont from the Grand Alliance. Without money to pay his troops in the Netherlands, William was unable to mount significant operations;

without distractions, the Imperial armies in the Rhineland could not manoeuvre. Louis threatened an invasion of England. William III's murder by Jacobites as he travelled to Windsor was to be the signal for a landing in Kent by 14,000 soldiers commanded by Boufflers and d'Harcourt. The uncovering of the assassination plot on 2 March terminated the invasion scheme, which could not in any case have succeeded because the Anglo-Dutch fleet retained command of the English Channel. The sole operation of note was a raid on the French magazine at Givet on 15–17 March by Menno van Coehoorn; the destruction of 4 million rations forced Louis to abandon plans to retake Namur. The Givet operation possibly induced Louis to seek economic salvation in the New World, and in 1697 the Baron de Pointis led a naval expedition that captured and looted Cartagena.

Determined to capture Pinerolo through either diplomacy or war, Victor Amadeus prepared to attack. He was pre-empted by Louis's offer of peace, and on 30 May 1696 Tessé and Gropello drafted a treaty. The final version of the Treaty of Turin was signed on 29 August and ratified by Louis on 7 October. France ceded Pinerolo, its fortifications demolished, plus the land corridor into Dauphiné, and promised to restore Savoyard territory seized during the war as soon as all Allied forces had evacuated Italy. An immediate truce was preliminary to the combination of the French and Savoyard armies, which would force Savoy's ex-allies to accept the neutralization of northern Italy. Victor Amadeus's daughter Marie Adelaide was betrothed to the Duke of Burgundy. On 12 July Catinat's

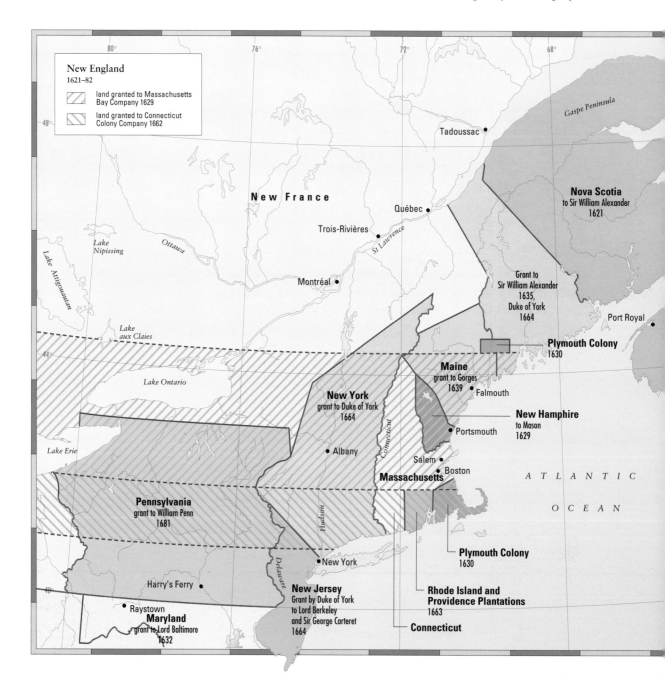

army, suitably reinforced, advanced on Turin as if to attack, offering Victor Amadeus the pretext to sue for peace. He did so, and pulled out of the Grand Alliance.

Early in August the remaining Allied forces left Turin and withdrew towards Lombardy. When the truce expired, French and Savoyard armies marched into the Milanese and besieged Valenza, obliging the Allies to seek a peace. A truce was proclaimed at Vigevano on 7 October, declaring Italy to be a neutral zone. During the next two months the Allied armies departed. Although Victor Amadeus had secured his war aims of capturing Pinerolo and neutralizing Casale, the price, both to his reputation and to the economy of the duchy, was high.

FIGHTING OUTSIDE EUROPE

Although not affecting the campaigns in Europe, there was fighting in the Americas and India, mainly to protect trades in sugar, tobacco, fish and precious metals. These petty operations, usually raids conducted by local militias occasionally supported by small detachments from Europe, were strategically insignificant. The French seized St Kitts on 15 August 1689, but it was recaptured on 22 July 1690.

A British attempt to take Guadeloupe in April 1691 was unsuccessful. During 1695 the British attacked French bases on Hispaniola following raids on Jamaica. In 1697 the Baron de Pointis and the Marquis de Château-Renault brought a squadron into the Caribbean in search of the Spanish treasure fleet. Unable to locate the *flota*, they looted Cartagena, the entrepôt for the South American silver traffic.

Also in 1697, a British squadron tried to regain control of Newfoundland but achieved little. Whereas the war in the Caribbean was mostly conducted by white settlers, in North America the Nine Years War relied upon vicious frontier raiding by Native Americans: the Five Nations of the Iroquois were allied to the British and the Algonquin tribes to the French. The capture of Port Royal by Sir William Phips, governor of New York, on 21 May 1690 and the unsuccessful attack on Quebec later in the same year were the only formal military operations.

In India Admiral Duquesne-Guiton sailed in

NEW ENGLAND, 1621–82

The European populations of New England and New France were minute, clinging to the coastal fringes and the valleys of the Hudson and St Lawrence. Each sought to embarrass the other's territory by irregular operations along the Trois Rivières–Albany corridor.

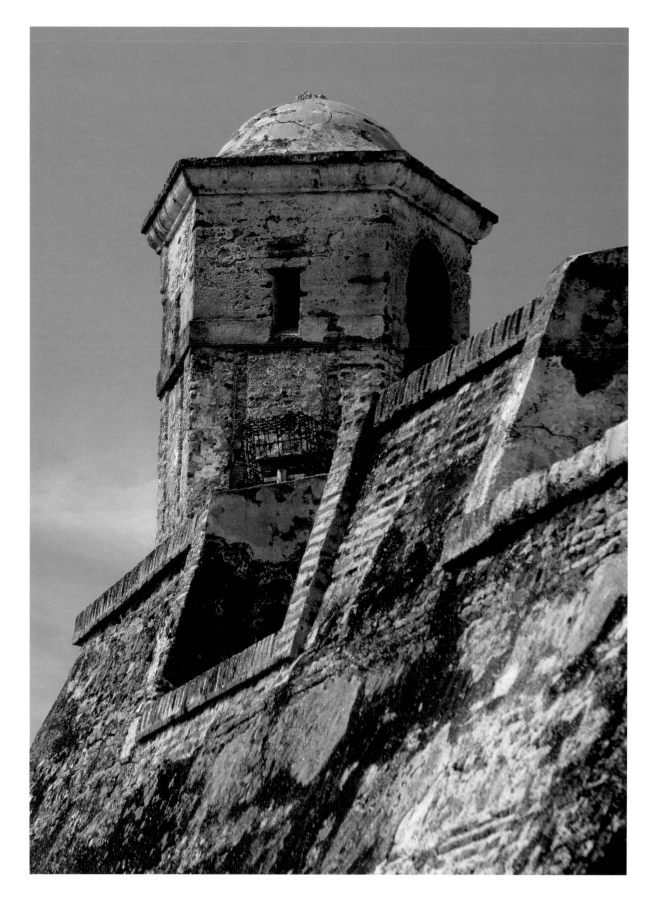

October 1690 into Madras harbour and bombarded the Anglo-Dutch fleet. Three years later, in September 1693, the Dutch besieged and captured the tiny French garrison at Pondicherry.

THE PEACE OF RIJSWIJK

Financially exhausted, England, the United Provinces and Spain did not want another campaign. Peace had seemed within reach in 1696 when the defection of Savoy wrecked their expectations and encouraged France to further military effort. Catinat's 40,000 men were redeployed to reinforce the French armies in Catalonia and the Netherlands; success in either or both theatres would oblige the Grand Alliance to make peace on French terms. The Allies did not enjoy such riches. The Savoyard Army was forfeit whilst the Spanish troops that had fought for Savoy–Piedmont had to stay in northern Italy to police the truce and cover Milan.

Before the campaign in the Netherlands opened, peace plenipotentiaries met in the palace of Rijswijk on the outskirts of The Hague on 6 May. Nevertheless the French attacked, besieging Ath from 7 May to 5 June 'to make a noise' during the negotiations. Three French armies, under Villeroi, Boufflers and Catinat, then threatened Brussels, but the Allies retreated through the night of 22–23 June to take up a blocking position around Koekelberg near Anderlecht; here the armies remained until the signature of peace. In Catalonia, where the Duc de Vendôme had succeeded Noailles, the French advanced during June and besieged Barcelona (from 12 June to 10 August) with 25,000 troops and a sizeable fleet. This determined the Spanish king, Charles II, to make peace.

Negotiations were formally conducted at Rijswijk but proceedings were hastened by private conversations between the Earl of Portland and Boufflers, beginning on 8 July at Brucom, near Halle. Peace was signed at Rijswijk on 20 September, the emperor adding his signature on 30 October when he finally realized that his allies would not support his request for the return of Strasbourg. The settlement represented a modest victory for the Grand Alliance. William III was recognized as King of England and Louis XIV undertook not to support actively the candidature of James II's son. The forward defence of the United Provinces was improved by permitting them to garrison a line of fortresses in the south of the Spanish Netherlands from Nieuport to Namur, including Charleroi, the 'Dutch Barrier'. The territorial settlement observed the *status quo ante bellum*. France surrendered Philippsburg, Breisach, Freiburg-im-Breisgau and Kehl, whilst the new French fortresses at La Pile, Mont Royal and Fort Louis were to be demolished. However, France retained Alsace and Strasbourg. The Duke of Lorraine was restored to his duchy. With an eye on the Spanish succession, Louis allowed Charles II of Spain to recover Luxembourg, Chimay, Mons, Courtrai, Charleroi, Ath, Barcelona and Catalonia. Dinant was returned to the Bishop of Liège. With the question of the Spanish succession unresolved, the Peace of Rijswijk was simply a truce in the long struggle between France and the Habsburg–Dutch coalition.

A guérite *on the ramparts of the Spanish-built Castillo de San Felipe de Barajas at Cartagena, Colombia. Similar artillery fortifications defended most European colonies in Africa, India and East Asia – Manila, Corral in Chile, Malacca, Panama, Colombo, Batavia (Jakarta), Madras – and helped Russia to expand into the Ukraine and Siberia and the British, French and Spanish to colonize North America.*

CHAPTER SIX

REFLECTIONS

FRENCH DRAGOONS, c. 1697. Guidon of the
Régiment du Dauphin (left); officer (centre) and
trooper (right) of the Régiment de la Reine.

REFLECTIONS

HISTORIANS FREQUENTLY STRAIN to hear the first cuckoo of the modern world. Except for the introduction of the battalion, which has remained the basic organizational building-block of all armies, seventeenth-century warfare was not modern, nor did it give birth to the modern. Soldiers fought at hideously close quarters and battles were more akin to the hand-to-hand struggles of the Middle Ages than the long-distance encounters of the nineteenth and twentieth centuries. Even by 1700, military discipline and command and control were more approximate than actual. The new standing armies were not national after the manner of the conscript forces of the later nineteenth century where compulsory military service was a duty performed in return for citizenship. Those states that introduced variations of limited conscription, principally Sweden and Denmark, produced territorial rather than standing armies. The standing armies of other states were mixtures of volunteers, mercenaries, pressed men and prisoners of war from myriads of races and creeds. They were certainly not national formations but more properly 'state mercenary armies' whose principal identity was the fact of their service for a particular ruler or government. Service was motivated by the same economic considerations that had inspired the mercenary of the Thirty Years War; there was little to choose between the social background and motivation of soldiers whether in 1600 or 1700. Similarly, senior officers shifted their allegiances nearly as frequently in the Nine Years War as they had before 1648. What changed was the transition from temporary armies raised by private military entrepreneurs to standing armies recruited from amongst individual mercenaries – anyone for whom money is the motivation to fight can be described as a mercenary – and mercenary formations hired from other governments.

Another temptation when listening for the first cuckoo of modernity is to apply twenty-first-century standards and expectations of combat-effectiveness, or 'professionalism', to seventeenth-century soldiers. They were worlds apart. In the first place, it is generally unclear what criteria contemporaries applied to judge military proficiency but one thing is abundantly obvious: the martial ideal of the seventeenth century was the antithesis of that of the twenty-first century. In the earlier period, a good soldier was a solid and reliable member of a close-knit team who held his place in the formation without flinching. There was no requirement or scope for individual heroism or initiative. A good modern soldier, on the other hand, is the opposite: an individual, valuable because of his own skill and independent judgement. Expectations of military efficiency during the seventeenth century were evidently below those current in the eighteenth century, where from 1740 the army of Frederick the Great set the standard. Even the apparently well-drilled and disciplined Swedish army that Gustav II Adolf took to Germany in 1630 was a nine-day wonder. It was badly damaged by the pyrrhic

victory at Lützen in 1632 and shattered two years later at Nördlingen. Subsequently the Swedish Army consisted mostly of German mercenaries, and reverted to battle tactics that were a compromise between Gustavian methods and those of the old tercios. Thereafter, fighting methods changed little until the end of the century; Gustav would have been comfortable on the battlefield of Neerwinden in 1693.

Generals floundered amidst uncertainty caused by inadequate intelligence and inaccurate, or non-existent, maps. Christian IV of Denmark blundered into Germany in 1625; Gustav II Adolf did not possess a clear strategy when he landed on Usedom in 1630; and William III had only the haziest notion of how to proceed on invading England in 1688. Communications were poor and exceptionally slow, making the co-ordination of operations across wide theatres, such as the strategy of the Hague Convention in 1626, difficult, if not impossible. One of the reasons why fighting was limited to certain key theatres – Flanders, the north Italian plain, the Rhineland – was that senior officers became acquainted with the landscape. The paucity of usable routes, the omnipresence of fixed fortifications, and the fact that armies had to hug major waterways limited

King Charles XII of Sweden (r. 1700–21) at the battle of Narva, 30 November 1700. Between 1700 and 1706 the mentally unstable Charles achieved a series of victories over the Russians, Poles and Saxons. However, the invasion of Russia in 1708 was undertaken without a coherent strategy and stumbled to disaster at Poltava, 8 July 1709, where the army created by Charles XI was wrecked.

operational options, providing some relief to the harassed commander. Usually, rival armies maintained physical, and often visual, contact throughout a campaign. To lose touch, as Wallenstein did before Lützen, was unwise. Generals and monarchs frequently gave the impression of not knowing what they were doing. Strategy was vague, operations uncertain, and methods conventional and unimaginative. Again, nothing in the fields of strategy and operations was revolutionary or modern.

Neither did the conduct of war alter significantly after the Peace of Westphalia in 1648. Standing armies and improved logistics only partially reduced the social and economic impact of campaigning soldiers. Up to the end of the Nine Years War, contributions were collected aggressively and troops plundered and lived off the land. The Devastations of the Palatinate in 1674 and

French troops pillaging a village during the invasion of the Dutch Republic, 1672, by Romeyn de Hooghe (1645–1708). Produced as anti-French propaganda – Hooghe was William of Orange's principal political artist – the design, subject matter and sense of movement reflect the influence of Callot. August Coppens published a series of etchings illustrating the damage to Brussels caused by the French bombardment in 1695.

1688–9 were equal in severity to any depredations suffered during the Thirty Years War. The French invasion of the Dutch Republic in 1672 was ferocious and rapacious, whilst destruction and atrocity dominated the Nine Years War in Catalonia and Savoy–Piedmont. Perhaps military violence against the civilian was slightly less random and haphazard, but the citizens of the Rhine valley, the Netherlands, Livonia and Piedmont would not have noticed much difference between warfare in 1600 and that in 1700. Wars were still caused by monarchical and dynastic ambition, and determined by acquisition and retention of territory. Whether at the end or beginning of the century, the prime concern for a state was to export its military costs by making 'war pay for war'.

Change did, of course, occur, primarily in weaponry – the pike was largely replaced by the socket bayonet; tercios and pike squares evolved towards the

Uniforms of the Gardes Françaises, 1697. Pikeman (left); three grenadiers (centre); sergeant (right).

linear battalion; and cavalry regained some of its battlefield importance – but battle tactics and formations adjusted to accommodate these developments, they did not radically alter. Uniform was widely adopted and governments continued to improve bureaucratic and revenue-gathering machinery, thus increasing their centralized authority. During the second half of the century both field armies and national establishments grew considerably in size. Fashion also changed. In the early part of the seventeenth century the model was the Dutch Army, but Sweden assumed this mantle during the 1620s and retained it until defeat at Fehrbellin in 1675. Thereafter the French Army of Louis XIV was emulated across much of Western Europe. However, none of these changes amounted either to a Military Revolution or to the birth of the modern.

GLOSSARY OF MILITARY TERMINOLOGY

BANQUETTE A raised firing step at the foot of a **parapet**.

BASTION A fortification with two angles and two faces, built where the **curtain wall** makes an angle.

CASEMATE A stone vault built into the **curtain wall** or the flank of a **bastion**. It housed mortars, cannon or musketeers.

CAVALIER A small earthen tower used for observation or to mount light cannon.

CHEMIN DE RONDE A continuous road around the top of the **rampart**.

CHEVAUX DE FRISES Sharpened stakes driven into the ground to obstruct attackers.

CIRCUMVALLATION A **parapet**, preceded by a ditch, facing the open country and enclosing a besieger's lines.

CONTRAVALLATION A **parapet**, preceded by a ditch, dug around a besieger's lines facing the beleaguered fortress.

COUNTER-GUARD A small, triangular work built in the ditch to cover a gate or the point of a **bastion**.

COUNTER-MINE A mine tunnel dug by the defenders.

COUNTERSCARP Properly, the outer slope of a moat or ditch. Commonly used to describe that part of the fortifications including the **counterscarp**, **covered way** and top of the **glacis**.

COVERED WAY A continuous, wide walkway around the **counterscarp**. It was 'covered' by the **parapet** formed by the apex of the **glacis**.

CROWNWORK An outwork similar to a **hornwork**, with two long flanks and two **bastions** at the head. The shape resembled a crown.

CURTAIN WALL The straight line of the **rampart** between two **bastions**.

DEFILADE Protection against enfilading fire.

DEMI-LUNE A small, detached **bastion** built before the apex of a **bastion** or a weak sector of the **curtain wall**.

ENCEINTE The main belt of fortifications around a fortified place, excluding outworks.

ENFILADE Crossfires capable of sweeping a target from end to end.

ESPLANADE An open space between a citadel and town.

FASCINE Bundle of brushwood used to fill moats and ditches.

FRONT A section of fortifications between two **bastions**.

GABION Conical basket, packed with earth; protected batteries and trench **parapets**.

GLACIS The **parapet** of the **covered way** which sloped gradually towards the open country.

GUÉRITE A stone sentry box projecting over a ditch.

HORNWORK A rectangular outwork built on the **glacis** with long flanks and a bastioned head. Hornworks provided enfilading fire along the length of the **curtain wall** and flanked attackers.

LODGEMENT The result of a successful assault on the **covered way**.

MARÉCHAL DE CAMP A rank in the French Army equivalent to major general. Occasionally used in the Imperial, Spanish and Portuguese armies.

PARAPET An earthen breastwork running along the top of a fortification to protect infantry and artillery.

PLACE D'ARMES A troop concentration area within either a besieger's works or a fortress.

RAMPART The main defence line of a fortress, comprising the **curtain wall** and attached **bastions**. It accommodated the heaviest cannon.

RAVELIN A triangular work with two faces built in the moat before the **curtain wall**. It was positioned between two **bastions**.

REDAN Zigzagged work shaped like the teeth of a saw. Often positioned to cover the vulnerable point at which a waterway pierced the fortifications.

REDOUBT A small, square, detached fort.

RETRENCHMENT An emergency work dug by the defenders in the rear of a breach.

SAP A zigzagged approach trench.

SCARP The inner slope of the ditch.

TENAILLE An infantry position built into the ditch before the **curtain wall**.

TERRE-PLEIN The flat top of the **rampart** providing space for both the recoil of the heavy artillery and the *chemin de ronde*.

TOUR BASTIONÉE A tower **bastion**. Invented by Vauban and used at Neuf-Brisach, Besançon and Belfort. At the foot of each **bastion**, where it joined the **curtain wall**, he constructed a strong, low stone tower equipped with heavy guns and magazines.

BIOGRAPHICAL NOTES

ARNIM, HANS GEORGE VON (1581–1641)
Born in Boitzenburg, Brandenburg. Served under Gustav II Adolf 1613–17; with the Poles 1621; field marshal under Wallenstein 1626; general of Saxon Army 1631–5 and 1638–41.

BANÉR, JOHAN (1596–1641)
Swedish. Entered Swedish Army in 1613 and fought under Gustav II Adolf in Russia, Poland, Livonia and Germany; field marshal 1634; commander of Swedish forces in Germany 1634–41; victor at Wittstock 1636.

BOUFFLERS, LOUIS-FRANÇOIS, DUKE OF (1644–1711)
French. Served in Africa 1662, and invasion of Dutch Republic 1672; brigadier 1675; *maréchal de camp* 1677; colonel general of dragoons 1678; lieutenant general 1681; marshal of France 1693.

BOURNONVILLE, ALEXANDER, COMTE DE HENNIN
Marshal general of the Imperial armies. Fought against Turenne in the Rhineland 1674. He had previously served as viceroy of Catalonia for which service the King of Spain had created him Prince of Bournonville in 1658.

CAPRARA, COUNT AENEAS (1631–1701)
Born in Bologna. Imperial field marshal. Fought in a total of forty-four campaigns mostly against the Turks, whom he defeated at Neuhausel 1685. An experienced diplomat, he was a plenipotentiary at the negotiations leading to the Peace of Nijmegen 1678, and Imperial ambassador to the Porte in 1682 and 1685.

CATINAT, NICOLAS (1637–1712)
Frenchman trained as a lawyer. Directed the campaign against the Vaudois 1686. Lieutenant general 1689; led French forces in Savoy–Piedmont 1690–6. Created marshal of France for his victory at La Marsaglia 1693. Served in Italy during the War of the Spanish Succession.

CHARLES II (1630–85)
King of Great Britain and Ireland 1660–85. Conscious of the insecurity of his restored throne, Charles was the first English monarch to maintain a significant peacetime standing army. It was intended as a robust police force to maintain domestic order.

CHARLES IX (1550–1611)
King of Sweden 1604–11. When Duke of Södermanland, Charles acted as regent in Sweden for his nephew Sigismund III, King of Poland–Sweden. Sigismund, whose invasion of Sweden was defeated in 1598–9, was deposed as King of Sweden in 1599 but Charles waited until 1604 before accepting the crown.

CHARLES X GUSTAV (1622–60)
Son of John Casimir, Count Palatine of Zweibrücken, and Catherine, the eldest daughter of Charles IX of Sweden. As Prince Charles Gustav of Zweibrücken he served under Torstensson in Germany 1645, and was commander of Swedish forces in Germany 1648; King of Sweden 1654–60.

CHARLES XI (1655–97)
King of Sweden 1660–97. He achieved his majority in 1672 and took control of Sweden's armed forces and foreign policy following the defeat at Fehrbellin 1675. As well as totally reorganizing the Swedish Army, he greatly enhanced the economic and political power of the monarchy and achieved a degree of absolutism.

CHRISTIAN IV (1577–1648)
King of Denmark 1596–1648. Although an effective domestic ruler, particularly in economic affairs – he founded several new towns, included Kristiania, now Oslo – Christian was a poor strategist and field commander whose misjudgements led to the invasion of Jutland in 1627–8 and 1644.

COEHOORN, MENNO VAN (1634–1704)
Dutch military engineer. Brigadier 1690. He conducted the successful siege of Namur 1695, and was promoted to lieutenant general. He designed a small, light mortar (first used at the siege of Grave 1674) which thereafter carried his name.

CONDÉ, LOUIS II DE BOURBON, PRINCE DE (1621–86)
French. Entered French Army in 1640; victor at Rocroi 1643, and Lens 1648; served with Spanish Army 1651–9, losing to Turenne at the battle of the Dunes 1658; major commands in French Army 1667–8 and 1672–5.

CRÉQUI, FRANÇOIS, CHEVALIER DE, MARQUIS DE MARINES (1624–87)
A capable French general, apprenticed during the Thirty Years War. He was promoted *maréchal de camp* 1650; lieutenant general 1654; and marshal of France 1668. Went into exile when Turenne was raised to marshal general but returned in 1675 although he was heavily defeated by Charles V of Lorraine at Conzer Brück 11 August 1675, and then surrendered Trier, 6 September.

CROMWELL, OLIVER (1599–1658)
Lieutenant general 1645; Lord Protector of England 1653–8. Cromwell was without military experience until 1642 but then demonstrated considerable aptitude for war. He rose rapidly to command first the cavalry of the Eastern Association and then that of the New Model Army. He succeeded Sir Thomas Fairfax (1612–71) as commander-in-chief of the New Model Army in 1650.

EUGENE, PRINCE OF SAVOY (1663–1736)
Born in Paris, a cousin of the Duke of Savoy. Entered Austrian Army 1683; major general 1685; lieutenant field marshal 1688; served in Italy as general of cavalry 1690–3; Imperial commander-in-chief in Italy 1694; commander-in-chief in Hungary 1697–9; defeated Turks at Zenta 1697; Imperial commander-in-chief in Italy 1701–7; victor, with Marlborough, at Blenheim 1704, and Oudenarde 1708. Defeated Turks at Peterwardein 1716 and Belgrade 1717. President of the Imperial War Council after 1702.

FERDINAND II OF AUSTRIA (1578–1637)
Born in Graz. Archduke of Inner Austria 1590; King of Bohemia and Hungary 1617; Holy Roman Emperor and ruler of Austria 1619–37. Ferdinand was a fervent Roman Catholic who conducted the Thirty Years War to advance the Counter-Reformation and extirpate Protestantism within the empire.

FERDINAND III OF AUSTRIA (1608–57)
Born in Graz. King of Hungary 1625; King of Bohemia 1627; king of the Romans 1636; Holy Roman Emperor and ruler of Austria 1637–57. Ferdinand was a realist who knew that he was losing the war and began the slow movement towards peace in the empire.

FERNÁNDEZ DE CÓRDOBA, DON GONZALO (1585–1635)
Apprenticed in the Army of Flanders, he was Spanish commander in the Palatinate 1621–3; commanded the Army of Flanders 1623–6; and the Spanish Army of Milan during the War of Mantua 1626–30.

FREDERICK V (1596–1632)
Elector Palatine 1610–32; King of Bohemia 1619. Frederick fled to the Netherlands in 1622 where he lived on English and Dutch subsidies. He emerged to follow Gustav II Adolf across Germany in 1630–2 but died before he could reclaim his electorate.

FREDERICK HENRY, PRINCE OF ORANGE (1583–1647)
The youngest son of William I of Orange, he succeeded his brother Maurice as Prince of Orange and captain-general of the Dutch Republic in 1625. A specialist in siege warfare – he intended every campaign to recapture an important fortress – he is reputed to have said, 'God deliver us from pitched battles'.

FREDERICK WILLIAM VON HOHENZOLLERN (1620–88)
The 'Great Elector' of Brandenburg 1640–88, who restored Brandenburg following the Thirty Years War by centralizing the political administration, reorganizing state finances, developing a strong army, rebuilding towns and cities, and acquiring Ducal Prussia.

GALLAS, MATTHIAS, COUNT VON CAMPO AND DUKE VON LUCERA (1584–1647)
Born at Trento, South Tyrol. Served under Wallenstein 1631–3; implicated in Wallenstein's murder 1634, and took over his army. Victor at Nördlingen 1634. A drunk and careless. His campaigns of 1637, 1638 and 1644 destroyed the Imperial cause.

GARDIE, JACOB PONTUSSON DE LA, COUNT (1583–1652)
Born in Reval, Swedish Estonia. Served under Maurice of Nassau 1606–8, and largely responsible for introducing Dutch military methods into Sweden. Commanded Swedish forces in Russia 1608–13, but defeated at Klushino 1610; field marshal 1620; commander-in-chief in Latvia 1626–8; regent during Queen Christina's minority 1632–44.

GEORGE WILLIAM VON HOHENZOLLERN (1595–1640)
Elector of Brandenburg 1620–40. George William, a Calvinist, stayed neutral in the Thirty Years War until Sweden invaded the electorate in 1631. Sweden remained in occupation until 1641, devastating Brandenburg's lands and economy.

GUSTAV II ADOLF, BETTER KNOWN AS GUSTAVUS ADOLPHUS (1594–1632)
King of Sweden 1611–32. Gustav extracted the maximum from his Swedish subjects without driving them to rebellion by stressing the danger posed by Catholicism, embodied in Poland–Lithuania and the Austrian Habsburgs. Even so, the human and economic demands of involvement in the Thirty Years War were enormous.

HATZFELD, MELCHIOR, GRAF VON (1593–1658)
Born at Castle Powitzko, Silesia. Fought with Wallenstein 1625–32. Imperial field marshal 1632–46. Defeated by the Swedes at Wittstock (1636) and Jankov (1645). Retired 1646. Recalled in 1657 to lead Imperial army into Poland.

HENRY IV (1553–1610)
Henry of Navarre, King of France 1589–1610. An inspirational leader who ended the French Wars of Religion by the Edict of Nantes in 1598. During the final twelve years of his reign, France enjoyed considerable economic prosperity.

HOLCK, HENRIK (1599–1633)
Danish. Served in Danish Army until 1629 and with Wallenstein 1629–33. By 1627 he had earned enough money from war to buy extensive estates on Funen.

HORN, GUSTAV KARLSSON (1592–1657)
Swedish. Privy councillor 1625; general in Swedish Army 1628; captured at Nördlingen 1634, and imprisoned until 1642.

HUMIÈRES, LOUIS DE CREVANT, DUC D' (1628–94)
A childhood companion of Louis XIV. Lieutenant general 1656; marshal of France 1668. For his unimaginative performance at Walcourt 1689, he earned the sobriquet 'marshal sans lumières'.

JAMES II (1633–1701)
King of England 1685–8. In his quest to establish a Catholic absolute monarchy, James relied heavily upon an expanded army but he was unable to secure the loyalty of its politicized officer corps. When the Dutch invaded in 1688, sufficient officers deserted or remained neutral to emasculate the army.

JOHN GEORGE I (1585–1656)
Elector of Saxony 1611–56. A lazy, drunken prince concerned only to 'drink his beer in peace'. Adhered to the Habsburgs and consequently surrendered leadership of the German Protestants first to Frederick V of the Palatinate, then Gustav II Adolf of Sweden, and finally Frederick William of Brandenburg.

LEOPOLD I OF AUSTRIA (1640–1705)
Holy Roman Emperor 1658–1705. A scholarly, cultured man who derived little enjoyment from the duty of government. However, he presided over the reconquest of Hungary and the final removal of the Turkish menace to eastern and central Europe. A devout Catholic, he took the opportunity aggressively to reintroduce the Roman Church into Hungary, thereby inducing serious aristocratic revolts.

LE TELLIER, MICHEL (1603–85)
French. Secretary of state for war in France 1643–77; chancellor 1677–85. Creator of the French standing army. Father of Louvois (q.v.).

LORRAINE, CHARLES IV (1604–75)
Duke of Lorraine 1608–75. Charles IV doggedly but unsuccessfully resisted the steady French assimilation of his duchy, a process effectively completed between 1662 and 1670. He ended his days as a mercenary in Germany.

LORRAINE, CHARLES V (1643–90)
Duke of Lorraine 1675–90. Born in Vienna. Entered Austrian Army 1664; victor over Turks at the Kahlenberg 12 September 1683 and Mohács 1687; captured Mainz and Bonn 1689.

LOUIS XIV (1638–1715)
King of France 1643–1715. Not only did Louis consolidate the work of Richelieu and Mazarin in centralizing and modernizing French institutions but also established a model of absolute monarchy that was imitated throughout Western Europe.

LOUVOIS, FRANÇOIS MICHEL LE TELLIER, MARQUIS DE (1641–91)
French. Secretary of state for war in France 1677–91, and a principal military and political adviser to Louis XIV. Son of Michel Le Tellier (q.v.).

LUXEMBOURG, FRANÇOIS-HENRI DE MONTMORENCY, DUC DE (1628–95)
French. Lieutenant general 1668; marshal of France 1675; commander-in-chief of the French armies in the Low Countries 1677–8 and 1690–5. Trained by Condé, Luxembourg was patient yet quick to discern and seize the slightest advantage. He was a master of positional warfare.

MATTHIAS OF AUSTRIA (1557–1619)
Archduke of Upper Austria 1593; King of Hungary 1608; King of Bohemia 1611; Holy Roman Emperor 1612–19. Matthias had considerable sympathy for the Protestants in Bohemia but his adherence to the Letter of Majesty caused the Bohemian Revolt of 1618.

MAURICE, PRINCE OF ORANGE (1567–1625)
The second son of William I of Orange, he became captain-general of the Dutch Republic in 1588 and Prince of Orange 1618. Although he was famous for his reform of the Dutch Army, his mastery of siege warfare was more significant in bringing victory in the Eighty Years War with Spain.

MAXIMILIAN I VON WITTELSBACH (1573–1651)
Duke of Bavaria 1597–1623 and Elector 1623–51. Maximilian, the leading Catholic prince of the empire, supported the rival Habsburgs in return for the forfeited Palatine Electorate. Maximilian forced the downfall of another competitor, Wallenstein, in both 1630 and 1634. Although the Swedes occupied Bavaria 1632–4, Maximilian reclaimed it following Nördlingen. He concluded an armistice with France and Sweden in 1647.

MAXIMILIAN II EMMANUEL VON WITTELSBACH (1662–1726)
Elector of Bavaria 1680–1736. Joined Austrian Army 1683; made his reputation at the siege of Belgrade 1688; governor of the Spanish Netherlands 1691–1714.

MAZARIN, CARDINAL JULES (1602–61)
Born in Italy, he assumed French nationality in 1639.

Cardinal 1641; chief minister in France 1642–61, in succession to Richelieu. Mazarin acquired Alsace and the bishoprics of Toul, Verdun and Metz at the Peace of Westphalia, made an advantageous peace with Spain in 1659, and defeated the last attempts (the Frondes) of the nobility and parlements to resist absolute monarchy.

MERCY, FRANZ VON (1590–1645)
Born in Longwy, Lorraine. Entered Austrian Army in 1606; defended Breisach against Bernard of Saxe-Weimar 1636; entered Bavarian service 1638; killed at Allerheim 1645. A highly skilled and successful general.

MONTECUCCOLI, RAIMONDO (1609–80)
Born in Modena. Entered Austrian Army in 1625; fought at Breitenfeld, Lützen, Nördlingen and Wittstock; general 1645; field marshal 1658; generalissimo of Imperial armies and victor over the Turks at St Gotthard 1664; president of the Hofkriegsrat 1668; fought against Turenne on the Rhine front 1672–5; retired 1675. Writer and theorist of war.

NASSAU, WILLIAM LOUIS OF (1560–1620)
Born in Dillenburg, Hesse. Cousin of and principal military adviser to Maurice of Orange (q.v.). Began military career 1579; captain-general and stadholder of Friesland 1584; stadholder of Groningen and Drenthe 1594.

NOAILLES, ANN-JULES, DUC DE (1650–1708)
French. Governor of Roussillon 1678; governor of Languedoc 1682; French commander in Catalonia 1689–95; marshal of France 1693; viceroy of Catalonia 1694. He fell seriously ill in 1695 and was replaced by Vendôme (q.v.).

OXENSTIERNA, AXEL (1583–1654)
Chancellor of Sweden 1612–54, to both Gustav II Adolf and Queen Christina. After Gustav's death in 1632, Oxenstierna was the effective ruler of the Swedish empire in Germany 1632–6, and then of Sweden itself from 1636 until Christina achieved her majority in 1644. A critic of Gustav's strategy, he thought that the Swedes should have marched on Vienna following their victory at Breitenfeld.

PAPPENHEIM, COUNT GOTTFRIED (1594–1632)
Born in Bavaria. Cavalry colonel under Tilly and the Catholic League 1620; captured Wolfenbüttel 1627; stormed Magdeburg 1631; killed at Lützen 1632.

PETER I, 'THE GREAT' (1672–1725)
Tsar of Russia 1682–1725. After breaking the reactionary power of the *streltsy* in 1699, Peter began modernizing Russia's government and armed forces. He introduced a system of national conscription, revised in 1705; training schools; and a War College. Fleets were developed for the Baltic, the Caspian and the Black Seas.

PHILIP III (1578–1621)
King of Spain 1598–1621. Philip was a weak monarch who allowed Spain to be governed by his favourite, the Duke of Lerma. When the Thirty Years War broke out, the Austrian Habsburgs were given Spain's unconditional support.

PHILIP IV (1605–65)
King of Spain 1621–65 and Portugal 1621–40. Ineffectual, he was dominated from 1621 to 1643 by his first minister, the Count-Duke of Olivares. Philip's reign saw the outbreak of

the Portuguese Revolt in 1640, which eventually led to independence in 1668; the loss of the Netherlands 1648; and a disadvantageous peace with France 1659.

PICCOLOMINI, OTTAVIO (1599–1656)
Born in Florence. Entered Austrian Army in 1616; fought in Bohemia 1618; joined Wallenstein 1627, but implicated in his murder 1634; fought for Spain against France 1635–9; victor at Thionville 1639; commander-in-chief of Imperial armies 1648; head of Imperial delegation at Congress of Nuremberg 1649; prince of the empire 1650.

RICHELIEU, ARMAND JEAN DU PLESSIS, CARDINAL AND DUC DE (1585–1642)
French. Bishop of Luçon 1607; secretary of state 1616–17 and1619–24; chief minister to Louis XIII and effective governor of France 1624–42. Richelieu's anti-Habsburg policy laid the foundations for the subsequent rise of France under Mazarin and Louis XIV.

RUPERT, PRINCE OF THE RHINE (1619–82)
Born in Prague, the third son of Frederick V, Elector Palatine. Fought in Thirty Years War 1638; commander of Charles I of England's cavalry 1642; commander-in-chief of the Royalist armies 1644; commander of the Royalist fleet 1648–53; privy councillor 1660; held senior naval commands in the Anglo-Dutch wars 1665–7 and 1672–4.

SAXE-WEIMAR, BERNARD, DUKE OF (1604–39)
Born in Weimar. A mercenary who fought with the Protestants in Germany 1621–3 and 1625–7; the Dutch 1623–5 and 1627–30; the Swedes 1630–5. Transferred to French service in 1635.

SIGISMUND III VASA (1566–1632)
King of Poland 1587–1632; King of Sweden 1592–9. Following deposition as King of Sweden in 1599, Sigismund initiated a long war with Sweden (1600–29) in an attempt to regain his inheritance. In Poland, Sigismund adopted a militant Catholic and pro-Habsburg stance.

SPÍNOLA, AMBROGIO DI FILIPPO, MARQUÉS DE LOS BALBASES (1569–1630)
Genoese mercenary. Entered Spanish Army in the Netherlands in 1602, commanding 9,000 men raised at his own expense; took Ostend 1604; commander-in-chief in the Netherlands 1604; occupied the Palatinate 1620; captain-general of the Spanish armies in the Netherlands 1621; captured Breda 1625.

TILLY, JOHANN TSERCLAES, GRAF VON (1559–1632)
Born in Brabant. Served in a Walloon regiment at the siege of Antwerp 1585; fought against the Turks 1594; commander of the Bavarian Army 1610; commander of the army of the Catholic League 1618; victorious at the White Mountain 1620 and Lutter 1626; commander of both the Imperial and the Catholic League armies 1630; captured Magdeburg 1631; defeated at Breitenfeld 1631; killed at Rain 1632.

TORSTENSSON, LENNART (1603–51)
Swedish. Artillery expert. Fought with Gustav II Adolf in Livonia 1621–3; with the Dutch 1624–5; with Sweden in Prussia 1626–9. Colonel of the first Swedish artillery regiment 1629; commander of the field artillery in the Swedish army in Germany 1630; general 1631; chief of staff

to Banér 1635; conquered Denmark 1643; victor at Jankov 1645; retired because of ill health 1646. Ennobled 1647.

TURENNE, HENRI DE LA TOUR D'AUVERGNE, VICOMTE DE (1611–75)
Born in Sedan, a grandson of William I of Orange. Arguably the greatest soldier of the seventeenth century. Fought in the Dutch Army 1623–32; *maréchal de camp* in the French Army 1635; marshal of France 1643; commanded French armies in Germany 1643–8; took Arras 1654; victor at the battle of the Dunes 1658; commanded in Flanders 1667–8; commanded on the Rhine 1672–5.

VAUBAN, SÉBASTIAN LE PRESTRE DE (1633–1707)
French military engineer. Commissary-general of the fortifications 1678; lieutenant general 1688. In 1705 he was promoted marshal of France, the first non-noble, the first engineer, and the first officer who had never commanded a victorious army in battle to be so honoured.

VENDÔME, LOUIS JOSEPH, DUC DE (1654–1712)
French. Brigadier 1677; lieutenant general 1688; marshal of France 1695. He succeeded Noailles in command of the French forces in Catalonia 1695, and captured Barcelona in 1697.

VICTOR AMADEUS II (1666–1732)
Duke of Savoy 1675–1730; King of Sicily 1713–20; King of Sardinia 1720–30. A master of intricate diplomacy who succeeded, not only in preserving his duchy from predatory France, but also in greatly extending his domains. He abdicated in favour of his son, Charles Emmanuel III, in 1730; changed his mind in 1731; was arrested; and died, deranged, in Rivoli Castle.

VILLEROI, FRANÇOIS DE NEUFVILLE, DUC DE (1644–1730)
French. Lieutenant general 1677; marshal of France 1693; commander of French armies in the Low Countries 1695–7 and 1703–6.

WALDECK, GEORG FRIEDRICH, GRAF VON (1620–92)
German. Entered Dutch Army in 1672 after service with Brandenburg and Brunswick; commanded a Franconian detachment at the siege of Vienna 1683; Imperial field marshal in Hungary 1683–5; marshal general of the Dutch armies 1688; commander of the Anglo-Dutch forces in the Low Countries 1688–90.

WILLIAM III OF ORANGE (1650–1702)
Stadholder of the Dutch Republic 1672–1702; King of Great Britain and Ireland 1689–1702. Despite his sharp intellect and exceptional skills in politics and diplomacy, William was a poor soldier because he lacked the supreme virtue of a contemporary general – patience. Instead of progressing incrementally by manoeuvre, he tried to cut corners in his desire for quick decisions and tangible results.

WRANGEL, KARL GUSTAV, COUNT (1613–76)
Swedish. Commander-in-chief of Swedish forces in Germany 1646–8; governor of Swedish Pomerania 1648; grand admiral 1657.

FURTHER READING

This guide presents modern, accessible works published in English. A good treatment of the period, written with military developments in mind, is by Thomas Munck, *Seventeenth Century Europe, 1598–1700* (London, 1990). Despite its importance, there are no recommendable general works devoted to seventeenth-century warfare but it is included within several broader surveys – Jeremy Black, *European Warfare, 1660–1815* (London, 1994); Frank Tallett, *War and Society in Early Modern Europe, 1495–1715* (London, 1992); M. S. Anderson, *War and Society, 1618–1789* (Leicester, 1988); Robert I. Frost, *The Northern Wars, 1558–1721* (Harlow, 2000); and John Childs, *Armies and Warfare in Europe, 1648–1789* (Manchester, 1982). On the Military Revolution debate, see Michael Roberts, 'The Military Revolution, 1550–1650', *Essays in Swedish History* (London, 1967); Geoffrey Parker, *The Military Revolution, 1500–1800* (Cambridge, 1988); Jeremy Black, *A Military Revolution? Military Change and European Society, 1550–1800* (London, 1991); and C. J. Rogers ed., *The Military Revolution Debate* (Boulder, CO, 1995).

The impact of war on localities is the subject of C. R. Friedrichs, *Urban Society in an Age of War: Nördlingen, 1580–1720* (Princeton, 1979); Myron P. Gutmann, *War and Rural Life in the Early Modern Low Countries* (Princeton, 1980); G. J. Ashworth, *War and the City* (London, 1991); and Stephen Porter, *Destruction in the English Civil Wars* (Stroud, 1994). Herbert Langer assesses the cultural, intellectual and social impact of *The Thirty Years War* (London, 1980).

The causes of war are considered in Jeremy Black ed., *The Origins of War in Early Modern Europe* (Edinburgh, 1987). Martin van Creveld, *Supplying War: Logistics from Wallenstein to Patton* (Cambridge, 1977) and John A. Lynn ed., *Feeding Mars: Logistics from the Middle Ages to the Present Day* (Boulder, CO, 1993) differ in their understanding of logistics. Military technology is dealt with by Bert S. Hall, *Weapons and Warfare in Renaissance Europe* (Baltimore, MD, 1997) and B. P. Hughes, *Firepower: Weapons Effectiveness on the Battlefield, 1630 to 1850* (New York, 1974). Christopher Duffy's *Siege Warfare: the Fortress in the Early Modern World, 1494–1660* (London, 1979) and *The Fortress in the Age of Vauban and Frederick the Great* (London, 1985) form an admirable introduction to fortification and siege warfare. Battlefield tactics are covered by Brent Nosworthy, *The Anatomy of Victory: Battle Tactics, 1688–1763* (New York, 1992); David G. Chandler, *The Art of War in the Age of Marlborough* (London, 1976); and John A. Lynn, 'Tactical Evolution in the French Army, 1560–1660', *French Historical Studies*, xiv. (1985). Charles Carlton, *Going to the Wars: the Experience of the British Civil Wars, 1638–1651* (London, 1992) provides a worm's-eye impression of the realities of campaigning and combat. Manpower and mercenaries are covered by Fritz Redlich, *The German Military Enterpriser and his Work Force: a Study in European Economic and Social History* (Wiesbaden, 1964–5), 2 vols.; J. E. Thompson, *Mercenaries, Pirates, and Sovereigns: State-Building and Extra-Territorial Violence in Early Modern Europe* (Princeton, 1994); and Peter H. Wilson, 'The German "Soldier-Trade" of the Seventeenth and Eighteenth Centuries: A Reassessment', *International History Review*, xvii. (1996).

The standing army and associated governmental changes are best studied through works on the military and institutional history of individual states, most of which also provide information on the wars in which those countries participated. On the Austrian Army, consult Thomas M. Barker, *Army, Aristocracy, Monarchy: Essays on War, Society and Government in Austria, 1618–1780* (New York, 1982), and for France, see John A. Lynn, *Giant of the Grand Siècle: the French Army, 1610–1715* (New York, 1997). Peter H. Wilson, *German Armies: War and German Politics, 1648–1806* (London, 1998) is invaluable on all military institutions within German lands and he also pursues an interesting angle in 'German Women and War, 1500–1800', *War in History*, iii. (1996). On Great Britain, see Mark Charles Fissel ed., *War and Government in Britain,*

1598–1650 (Manchester, 1991); J. P. Kenyon ed., *The Civil Wars: A Military History of England, Scotland, and Ireland, 1638–1660* (Oxford, 1998); Ian Gentles, *The New Model Army* (Oxford, 1992); and John Childs, *The Army of Charles II* (London, 1976); *The Army, James II, and the Glorious Revolution* (Manchester, 1980); *The British Army of William III, 1689–1702* (Manchester, 1987). For Ireland, see T. Bartlett and K. Jeffery eds., *A Military History of Ireland* (Cambridge, 1996). Geoffrey Hanlon, *The Twilight of a Military Tradition: Italian Aristocrats and European Conflicts, 1560–1800* (London, 1998) deals generally with Italy whilst Christopher Storrs, *War, Diplomacy and the Rise of Savoy, 1690–1720* (Cambridge, 1999) is a mine of information on the Savoyard Army. The Dutch Republic and the Eighty Years War is discussed in Marco van der Hoeven ed., *Exercise of Arms: Warfare in the Netherlands, 1568–1648* (The Brill, 1998). W. C. Fuller, *Strategy and Power in Russia, 1600–1914* (New York, 1992) and John L. Keep, *Soldiers of the Tsar: Army and Society in Russia, 1462–1874* (Oxford, 1985), give adequate attention to the seventeenth century. There is a useful chapter in Lindsey Hughes, *Russia in the Age of Peter the Great* (New Haven, 1998). In *The Army of Flanders and the Spanish Road, 1567–1659* (Cambridge, 1972), Geoffrey Parker studies both logistics and the Spanish Army in the Netherlands, whilst I. A. A. Thomson, *War and Government in Habsburg Spain, 1560–1620* (London, 1976) looks at the impact of war on government. Christopher Storrs studies the Spanish army in Italy during the second half of the century in 'The Army of Lombardy and the Resilience of Spanish Power in Italy during the Reign of Carlos II (1665–1700)', *War in History*, ix. (1997). Swedish military history up to 1632 is expertly covered by Michael Roberts in *The Early Vasas: A History of Sweden, 1523–1611* (Cambridge, 1968); *Gustavus Adolphus: A History of Sweden, 1611–1632* (London, 1953–8), 2 vols.; and *Gustavus Adolphus* (London, 1992). A. F. Upton, *Charles XI and Swedish Absolutism* (Cambridge, 1998) looks closely at the military reforms whilst Alf Åberg, 'The Swedish Army from Lützen to Narva', in *Sweden's Age of Greatness, 1632–1718*, ed. Michael Roberts (London, 1973), and Stewart P. Oakley, *War and Peace in the Baltic, 1560–1790* (London, 1992) provide more general coverage. Essays on Poland and Eastern Europe can be found in *War and Society in East Central Europe*, ed. B. K. Király & G. E. Rothenberg (New York, 1979), vol. 1.

Ronald G. Asch, *The Thirty Years War* (London, 1997) and Geoffrey Parker, *The Thirty Years War* (London, 1987, revised ed.) are the most recent histories of the eponymous conflict. John A. Lynn, *The Wars of Louis XIV, 1667–1714* (London, 1999) is an excellent general survey. In *The Nine Years War and the British Army, 1688–1697: The Operations in the Low Countries* (Manchester, 1991) and 'Secondary Operations of the British Army during the Nine Years War, 1688–1697', *Journal of the Society for Army Historical Research*, lxxiii. (1995), John Childs looks at the operational history of the Nine Years War. Thomas M. Barker, *Double Eagle and Crescent* (Vienna, 1983) and Derek Mackay, *Prince Eugene of Savoy* (London, 1977) cover the Austro-Turkish War.

Diplomacy, peacemaking, and the implementation of treaties can be followed in Derek Croxton, *Peacemaking in Early Modern Europe: Cardinal Mazarin and the Congress of Westphalia, 1643–1648* (London, 1999); J. A. H. Bots ed., *The Peace of Nijmegen, 1676–1678/79* (Amsterdam, 1980); and John Stoye, *Marsigli's Europe: the Life and Times of Luigi Ferdinando Marsigli* (New Haven, 1994). The jurists are reconsidered by Richard Tuck, *The Rights of War and Peace: Political Thought and the International Order from Grotius to Kant* (Oxford, 1999) whilst J. J. Johnson, in *Ideology, Reason, and the Limitation of War: Religious and Secular Concepts, 1200–1740* (Princeton, 1975), and *Just War Tradition and the Restraint of War* (Princeton, 1981), investigates the theories governing the limitation of war. The practical aspects of restraint are investigated by Barbara Donagan, 'Codes and Conduct in the English Civil War', *Past & Present*, cxviii. (1988). Theorists of war are investigated by G. E. Rothenberg, 'Maurice of Nassau, Gustavus Adolphus, Raimondo Montecuccoli, and the "Military Revolution" of the Seventeenth Century', *Makers of Modern Strategy from Machiavelli to the Nuclear Age*, ed. Peter Paret (Oxford, 1986) and Thomas M. Barker, *The Military Intellectual and Battle: Raimondo Montecuccoli and the Thirty Years War* (New York, 1975).

INDEX

PICTURE CREDITS

ENDPAPER: *At the battle of the Kahlenberg, 12 September 1683, an Imperial–Austrian–Polish army under King John III Sobieski of Poland and the Duke of Lorraine routed the Turks to lift the siege of Vienna. Sobieski rides, sword in hand, in the left foreground and in the centre is Elector Maximilian II Emmanuel of Bavaria.*

die Belägerung

16